LAW AND SOCIAL ACTION

SELECTED ESSAYS

Law and Social Action

SELECTED ESSAYS
OF
ALEXANDER H. PEKELIS

EDITED BY MILTON R. KONVITZ

A Publication of the New School for Social Research

CORNELL UNIVERSITY PRESS

ITHACA AND NEW YORK, 1950

PRINTED IN THE UNITED STATES OF AMERICA BY THE
VAIL-BALLOU PRESS, INC., BINGHAMTON, NEW YORK

Introduction

PROFESSOR ALEXANDER H. PEKELIS was one of the few persons in this country who made a conscious effort to bridge the gaps between, on the one hand, the law and, on the other hand, economics, politics, and sociology. He had mastered these disciplines, as well as others, and was equally at home among them. To his way of thinking, interdisciplinary co-operation was an urgent personal and social need. Because his knowledge was not compartmentalized, he could not limit his view of the world to looking down a single street. Ever adventuresome, ever ready to push on to new frontiers, ever ready to meet a new philosophical or personal challenge, his was one of the freshest minds.

His mind was as critical as it was keen—a mind that did not permit him to take any of his own conclusions in other than a tentative way; for he knew that what he might affirm as the truth now might be proved to be only a half-truth or a falsity later. If at times he seemed overpositive, it was only because the heat of an argument compelled him to express his thoughts as sharply as possible; but at the same time he was quite ready to acknowledge that he had not grasped the cosmos by the tail.

Those who were privileged to hear him read some of the papers included in this volume before the General Seminar of the Graduate Faculty of the New School for Social Research (the University in Exile), of which he was a distinguished member, will never forget his brilliant performances. Were our society to consider intellectual performance with the same regard with which we consider musical performance, Pekelis on those occasions would have addressed an audience at Carnegie Hall rather than at the New School. The consummate skill with which he analyzed issues and presented his arguments brought to mind a Menuhin playing Handel or Bach. Here was no priest speaking *ex cathedra*, but a great artist, a keenly sensitive and searching mind.

At the end of his first essay in this volume, he states that the central problem that he had set out to explore still remains. "Jurisprudence of welfare," he said, "is no answer to the problems of our time. In fact, it is no answer at all, but rather a mode of inquiry. It is an invitation to learn, a suggestion as to how questions should be asked. . . ." This withdrawal from ultimates was typical of his mind. It is a quality of spirit hardly ever found among European thinkers. It was an American, William James, who shouted across to Josiah Royce: "Damn the Absolute!" Pekelis, in flight from the criminal madness of Stalin, Hitler, and Mussolini, found himself at home in the philosophic atmosphere created by Jefferson, Emerson, Holmes, William James, Brandeis, John Dewey, Horace Kallen, and Alvin Johnson. The mind of Pekelis was ever on a quest; his death in flight was the kind of death one would have expected if one had ever thought of Alex Pekelis dying at the age of forty-four. Although he believed in no final answers, Pekelis was no cynic; he was neither a nay-sayer nor a yea-sayer. To use his own words of great beauty: he was a man with a "will to enlarge the tiny segment of the world we know, the will to learn and to do better, the firm and deep-seated conviction that men may, again and again, in everyone's lifetime, see

> . . . thin with distance, thin but dead ahead,
> The line of unimaginable coasts."

His mind's eye was very keen. More frequently and more clearly than is given to most of us, his was the gift to see in the distance the line of unimaginable coasts.

Friends of Alex Pekelis, with Max Ascoli in the forefront, want this volume of writings published as a memorial to his great genius. But let it be said: the readers of this volume who have not known

Pekelis will not see him here face to face; they will, however, be afforded an intimation of his immortality.

Pekelis was born in Odessa, Russia, in 1902. After graduation from the Odessa Gymnasium in 1919, he studied at the University of Leipzig and at the University of Vienna for two years; then he studied law for four years at the University of Florence and the University of Rome. In 1928 he was awarded the law degree by the University of Florence. In 1929 he studied at the London School of Economics and Political Science on a fellowship awarded by the Ministry of Education of Italy. He then returned to Italy and was licensed by the Ministry of Education to teach law at Italian universities. In 1931 he was admitted to the Italian bar; for several years he lectured on jurisprudence at the University of Florence, and in 1932 was declared eligible for a full professorship, but the Fascist Party of Florence prevented him from teaching at the University of Florence. In 1935 the University of Rome appointed him full professor of jurisprudence, and he taught there for several years. In 1938 he founded and edited a review, *Il Massimario della Corte Toscana*. The Fascists made his life quite uncomfortable, so he went to Paris and practiced law there in 1939 and 1940. In 1941 he came to the United States and was appointed Professor on the Graduate Faculty of the New School for Social Research, and he maintained this position until the time of his death. In 1942 he began to study law at the Columbia University Law School; in 1943 he was named Editor-in-Chief of the *Columbia Law Review*. Upon his graduation from the Columbia Law School, a new editorial office was created for him, namely, Graduate Editor-in-Chief. In 1945 he became Chief Consultant to the Commission on Law and Social Action, American Jewish Congress. At the time of his death in an airplane accident in Ireland he was on his way home from Switzerland, where he had attended a Zionist conference as a delegate of American Labor Zionists. His death occurred on December 27, 1946.

M. R. K.

ACKNOWLEDGMENTS

THE kindness of the following publishers and periodicals in granting permission to reprint in this volume some of the writings of Alexander H. Pekelis is gratefully acknowledged: *New Republic*; American Society for Public Administration, publisher of *Public Administration Review*; New School for Social Research, publisher of *Social Research*; *Jewish Frontier*; *Michigan Law Review*; American Jewish Congress and its Commission on Law and Social Action. Grateful acknowledgment is also made of the courtesies of Will Maslow and Herbert Prashker.

Foreword

ALEXANDER H. PEKELIS

(1902-1946)

ON DECEMBER 27, 1946, an airplane accident in Shannon, Ireland, ended the life of Alexander Pekelis. As the one member of the Graduate Faculty of the New School for Social Research who was a close and intimate friend of his in the two countries where he spent most of his life—Italy and America—it is my sad privilege to pay to his memory the tribute of his colleagues.

I remember the first day I saw him. It was in 1929 in Florence, in the house of an Italian scholar who wanted to bring us together. I cannot say that Pekelis came into the room; he burst into it. It was shortly after the Vatican and fascist Italy, having made their peace, had started their controversy on the interpretation of it. The Pope, a doughty, sharp-tongued mountaineer, had just stated his point in an encyclical: the Concordat and the Treaty stand together or fall together. That key sentence in the encyclical had particularly struck Pekelis. *Simul stabunt aut simul cadent.* He was repeating it at the top of his lungs, with the characteristic lisp in his pronunciation, talking too fast and at too high a pitch, in a metallic, high-powered Italian, perfect in logical and grammatical structure, utterly alien in accent and intonation.

Yet, there was nothing foreign in the way he stated lucidly, in controvertibly, as in an ironclad legal case, all the reasons for the irrepressible conflict that was bound to result from any attempt to bring the Church and the State too close together. This was the opinion of the leading Italian liberals, an opinion seasoned and flavored with the century-old tradition of Italian anticlericalism. It was almost shocking to see how thoroughly and how articulately this foreigner had grasped all the richness of a school of thinking that stems straight from Dante. But there was not a doubt; he had made the grade and was among the best.

It was like that all his life. He had an amazingly disturbing power to assimilate the culture of any country, to make himself into a citizen of every community. He never limited himself to absorbing and reformulating the principles of a culture he had adopted. All his life he was a student, and he gave back to every school, with compound interest, everything he had received from it. If the capacity of absorbing and dramatizing cultures is, as I think, a Jewish trait, then I have never met in my life a man who was so thoroughly a Jew. He was the unblended Jew.

Wholehearted perhaps is the best word for him. He was wholeheartedly an Italian, wholeheartedly a liberal, a European, a Jew, an American. He identified himself with each one of these cultures and traditions, always keeping his powerful will and powerful intelligence under the control of his big, loyal heart. A Russian student, an Italian scholar and lawyer, a French and European intellectual, an American scholar and lawyer, a businessman, a father, a son, a husband, and a friend—the miracle is that Alexander Pekelis could be many of these things at various periods of his life and, to a large extent, all of them throughout his life, unstintingly and unreservedly. It was not the result of facile mimetic cleverness, but of thorough dedication and hard work. The miracle is that this man, who was uprooted three or four times in his life and who, because of the vigor of his intellect, was primarily an intellectual, had nothing in him of the uprooted dilettantish intellectual.

Pekelis' philosophy of life and his rule of action in life stemmed precisely from the multiplicity and the thoroughness of his personality. Pekelis the teacher, the thinker, and the man of action was the uninterrupted projection and unfolding of Pekelis the man. He believed that his hard, loyal work gave him the right to be whatever he wanted in all his various fields of activity. He believed that the limit of man's power should be his willingness to pay a fair price for the attainment of his ambitions. For the fairness of prices, Pekelis fought all his life.

Max Ascoli

Contents

LAW AND SOCIAL ACTION

SELECTED ESSAYS

The Case for

a Jurisprudence of Welfare

POSSIBILITIES AND LIMITATIONS [1]

> Now take the map. The map is what we know
> And it means nothing. I've seen many maps,
> Talked to a thousand seamen, in my time,
> And, in the end, there is but this to say,
> One ventures as one ventures.
> STEPHEN VINCENT BENÉT, *Western Star*

I

DECENT RESPECT for the patience of readers would seem to bar new dissertations dealing with the relation between law and the social sciences. The period between the two wars saw such a flourishing of schools of "sociological" or "experimental" jurisprudence, "legal realism," "social law," legal "fact-finding," "juristic functionalism," "institutionalism," and "pragmatism" that one may wonder whether any further exploration of the subject matter is needed. There is, however, a trend in the present attitude of American judges which is worth investigating. In one sense this attitude is the outcome of the modern schools. In another sense it represents, curiously enough, a reversal of their position.

The American Twenties and Legal Realism

It is impossible to do justice in a few paragraphs to the theories and the effects of these schools. It seems safe to say, however, that they have at least three main characteristics in common. These are:

---

[1] The author is greatly indebted to Jerome Frank, Paul R. Hays, George Jaffin, Alvin Johnson, Adolph Lowe, Edwin W. Patterson, Herbert Prashker, and Hessel

mentalistic preferences of Francis Bacon, philosopher and attorney-general, whose contribution to the shape of Anglo-American legal institutions is generally underestimated. In reading the pleas for a free law (*freie Rechtsfindung*) or the good judge (*le bon juge*), which sounded utopian in Germany and France, some common lawyers must have felt like Molière's Monsieur Jourdain, who in his first philosophy lesson learned that he had always been speaking in prose; and they began to be less apologetic about their uncodified laws and their unsystematic legal science. Doctrines of judicial freedom were at any rate a fitting rationalization of the position in which judges and administrators found themselves by virtue of the American constitutional and legislative technique.

It must be remembered, indeed, that in a sense the United States has no written constitution. The great clauses of the Constitution, just as the more important provisions of our fundamental statutes, contain no more than an appeal to the decency and wisdom of those with whom the responsibility for their enforcement rests. To say that compensation must be "just," the protection of the laws "equal," punishments neither "cruel" nor "unusual," bails or fines not "excessive," searches and seizures not "unreasonable," and deprivation of life, liberty, or property not "without due process" is but to give a foundation to the lawmaking, nay, constitution-making, activity of judges, left free to define what is cruel, reasonable, excessive, due, or, for that matter, equal.

In their turn, Congress and state legislatures have long adopted the same technique in many a strategic spot. Rates were required to be "just and reasonable," consolidations of carriers in the "public interest," regulation of radio stations inspired by "public interest, convenience or necessity," methods of competition not "unfair," allocation of marketing areas among states and producers made with due consideration of economic factors, and intraindustry classifications based on a number of named and unnamed "relevant factors." Nor is it sure that the majority-getting mechanics of the modern legislature permits any less ambiguous drafting.

I do not contend that all constitutional or statutory provisions leave the determination of their content to judges. The Seventh

Amendment, for instance, prescribes that "in suits at common law, where the value in controversy shall exceed twenty dollars, the right of trial by jury shall be preserved"—and I concede that it would be difficult to interpret twenty dollars to mean fifteen or twenty-five, although, in an inflationary situation, it could easily be construed to mean two thousand. But when is a suit a "suit at common law" rather than in equity? When is a trial a "trial by jury" rather than a trial by the judge, who directs a verdict or enters judgment *nonobstante veredicto?* An analysis of our statutes and constitutions may reveal a great many precise and important provisions. The only trouble is that the precise ones, such as the twenty dollars provision, are rarely important, and the important ones, such as the due process clause, are rarely precise.

Judicial Freedom for What?

It would be wrong, however, to conclude that the rise of legal realism only revealed a peculiarity of the American institutions without changing them. The revelation itself was bound to operate a transformation. The king in the fable had long been naked and—although Andersen does not say it—a few sages, like Bacon, Bishop Hoadley, and Holmes, had always known it. But it certainly made a lot of difference when that lovely boy shouted it out in the street. True enough, the lawmaking freedom of judges and administrators was only a feature of the "common law tradition." But now, as the Bible has it, their eyes were opened and they were as gods knowing that they were free.

The consequences of this consciousness were bound to be considerable. To begin with, when realists became judges or administrators they found less gusto in the emphasis upon the discrepancy between books and reality. Somehow, first-person realism—"law is what we judges do in fact, not what we say"—sounded far less appealing. It was hardly helpful to persist in defining law as the prediction of judicial behavior, since no judge could regulate his own behavior by trying to predict it. If it is true that the mere presence of an observer influences the reality being observed, the nature of the judicial process had to change when judges began to philos-

[5]

ophize about it or when philosophers, searching the reality of judicial law, became themselves the reality they were looking for.

The resulting transformation of the judicial process is not everywhere equally apparent or deep. But, on the whole, leading legal opinion knows today that policy making only begins with the adoption of a constitutional amendment or of a statute. Leading judges in their turn avow that they cannot be expected to be more certain about the course of their action or more infallible than other men, including legislators.

It is against this background of skepticism and freedom that a quest for a new framework of references develops. Realists in the law schools have sought to borrow the methods of the social sciences in the investigation of what the living law is. Today realists in positions of responsibility turn to the social sciences for guidance not in the description but in the shaping of legal reality.

A great many contemporary judicial decisions show this threefold leitmotiv—awareness of freedom, confession of fallibility, and quest for extralegal guidance. A recent opinion of a federal district court has it that judges are now willing "to modify their procedures so that there may be a more realistic trial of the complex issues of economic fact and industrial policy" and "to accept economic testimony appropriate for laying down a broad rule of industrial government." The attitude is more pronounced in the appellate courts, and particularly in the federal judiciary. In *Wickard* v. *Filburn*,[2] decided on the first day of its 1942–1943 term, the Supreme Court of the United States said that "questions of the power of Congress are not to be decided by reference to any formula," and that the "economics of the wheat industry" rather than the "mechanical application of the legal formulae" should determine the constitutionality of a certain application of the Agricultural Adjustment Act. On the last day of that term, taking an analogous stand in the field of political liberties, the Court asserted that the Constitution was not meant to be a "political straitjacket for the generations to come" (*Schneiderman* v. *United States*[3]). During the same term the

[2] 317 U.S. 111 (1942).
[3] 320 U.S. 118 (1942).

Supreme Court Justices refused on many occasions to bow to the consequences "that would flow from [a] legalistic notion" (*Williams v. North Carolina* [4]); to "extract from episodes in isolation abstract questions of evidence and procedure" (*Johnson* v. *United States* [5]); to be "confined to so mechanical a test" (*Parker* v. *Brown* [6]); or to treat a constitutional dictate "as though it were a mathematical abstraction, an absolute having no relation to the lives of men" (*Martin* v. *City of Struthers* [7]).

They know how difficult it is to draw the line even between a "purely commercial activity and a religious one" (*Murdock* v. *Pennsylvania* [8]), and do not assert "pretenses of exactitude" or "scientific validity" (*Group of Investors* v. *R. R.*[9]). Judges "frequently reach different conclusions despite the fullest and most careful examination of all available data, including the difference of opinion on the part of their associates" (*De Zon* v. *American President Lines* [10]). They are not faced with "a question in algebra as to which there is a demonstrably right or wrong answer" (*Altvater* v. *Freeman* [11]), and—as the Court said this year—in some situations "doubts will remain whichever way the case [is] decided" (*Davies* v. *Bowles* [12]). Again, "words are inexact tools at best" (*Harrison* v. *Trust Co.*[13]) and their "uncritical use bedevils the law" (*Tiller* v. *R. R.*[14]). "Nor is the matter aided by "substituting one general formula for another" (*Galloway* v. *United States* [15]). The Court is aware of the fact that "this does not satisfy those who seek for mathematical or rigid formulae," but emphatically warns that "such formulae are not provided by the great concepts of the Constitution."

---

[4] 317 U.S. 287 (1942).
[5] 318 U.S. 189 (1942).
[6] 317 U.S. 341 (1942).
[7] 319 U.S. 141 (1942).
[8] 319 U.S. 105 (1942).
[9] 318 U.S. 523 (1942).
[10] 318 U.S. 660 (1942).
[11] 319 U.S. 359 (1942).
[12] 321 U.S. 144 (1943).
[13] 317 U.S. 476 (1942).
[14] 318 U.S. 54 (1942).
[15] 319 U.S. 372 (1942).

II

Welfare Approach in Private Law

One need not take these statements at their face value to admit that they indicate the existence of a situation which is big with hopes and dangers. To speak first of hopes, it may be the dawn of a new judicial approach, the beginnings of what I should like to call a jurisprudence of welfare. In other words, our judges, who have long been asking themselves a series of inadequate questions about canons of construction, intents of the legislators, or lines of judicial authority, may be about to ask themselves, with increasing frequency, the only question that really matters: "Which course of my action—which rule of law—is going to serve best the general welfare of the society I am sworn to serve?" And they may be inclined to ask this question openly and explicitly, and attempt to answer it intelligently, with the help of all available data that the social sciences can offer.

A responsible judicial approach based on the utilization of such data could build upon foundations already laid by legal writers in many fields of public and private law. Thus, for instance, the recognition of the risk-spreading function of the law of torts hinged the intrinsic validity of that law on the degree to which society's welfare is served by the adopted patterns of distribution of risk. The recent exposition of the importance of "constructive conditions" read by judges into contracts of private parties has further weakened the notion that a contract is the creature of the contracting parties only, and has called the attention of lawyers to the degree of influence exercised by community conceptions of propriety and usefulness. Studies of the "unexpressed major premise" in mental incompetency, undue influence, and fraud cases have shown how their results depend on the evaluation of the social desirability of enforcing the particular contracts being litigated, rather than on the objective appraisal of the existence of the pleaded vices of consent. A more general view has led to the identification of a wide category, of daily increasing importance, designated as "compulsory contracts" and dominated by the social notion of expediency and fairness rather than by that of individual consent.

[8]

The importance of the welfare question and the necessity of furnishing an intelligent and informed answer to the so-called problems of public policy become increasingly apparent as one moves from the classical fields of contracts or torts to laws governing domestic relations, business organizations, insurance, special commercial transactions, or conflict of laws. A moderately close analysis of the crucial issues with which courts are confronted in these fields shows that they cannot be solved by legal syllogisms only, or without making a more or less conscious choice between alternative social policies. And it hardly seems desirable that this choice be made, as it only too often is, without any real information about the social reality upon which the force of legal measures falls—without any real knowledge about the direction, sharpness, or depth of their incidence.

Welfare Controls of an Economy

The welfare approach to legal questions seems particularly promising in the regulation of economic activity. The machinery of anti-trust statutes could be put to work in a more useful fashion if, for instance, the theories of imperfect or monopolistic competition were permitted to exercise an influence upon the judicial doctrines governing the practices of freight absorption, the adoption of single and multiple basing points, or the protection of marginal producers by trade associations. To give just one specific example, the struggle between mail-order houses and local storekeepers, still spoken of as a struggle between monopoly and competition, would receive a new significance if the attempt were made to determine which of the two exercises a greater degree of monopolistic power over prices.

But the field in which co-operation between lawyers and economists could be particularly fruitful is, I think, that of public utilities. The public service commissions, for instance, have not yet fully realized the nature of their rate-making task. Although it is becoming increasingly clear that in many instances the practical value of an enterprise depends on the rates which it is allowed to charge, the

[9]

commissions are still working on the presupposition that the permissible rate must be derived from the value of the enterprise, the so-called rate base.

Mr. Justice Jackson, dissenting in the recent case of *Federal Power Commission v. Hope Natural Gas Co.*,[16] has forcefully challenged the derivative nature of the price concept. "Is it necessary to a reasonable price for gas that it be anchored to a rate base of any kind?" asked Justice Jackson, and he concluded that "the reason for resort to a roundabout way of rate base price-fixing does not exist in the case of gas in the field." Although Jackson's conclusion was predicated upon the special characteristics of the natural gas industry, I suggest that it is equally true in the field of utilities in general. The circularity of the customary reasoning becomes apparent when, in a reorganization procedure, the Interstate Commerce Commission, in the exercise of the federal bankruptcy power, declares that it will evalue a railroad's property by capitalizing the rate which the carrier will probably be allowed to charge for its service. This rate, however, has to be allowed by the same Interstate Commerce Commission, acting as a regulatory agency, on the basis of the value of the railroad independently arrived at.

The welfare inquiry broadens the task of utility regulation. Commissions and courts may be called upon to go beyond the determination of the proper return based on past, present, or future-trended value of the utility's property. They may be compelled to determine specific prices and rates with more regard to their social function, and thus shift the emphasis from the producer to the product and to its consumer. Hence they may be called upon to decide how the total burden of fixed joint and overhead costs should be distributed among the various groups of consumers. Mr. Justice Jackson asked that the rate order in the *Hope* case be remanded to the Federal Power Commission because it failed to investigate which utilization of natural gas offers the "highest social as well as economic return." Jackson's own opinion was that natural gas has unique advantages for domestic, as distinguished from industrial, consumers, and that the company should be required to discriminate actively in favor of

---

[16] 320 U.S. 591 (1943).

the former. This, to Justice Jackson, is "the true public utility aspect of the enterprise and its preservation should be the first concern of regulation."

I wonder whether the nature of the rate-making process could not be better understood, and the function better performed, if the studies of Frank Knight on risk, uncertainty, and profit, or the more recent writings of Hotelling or Lange on the function of price in socialist and capitalist economies, were properly considered. Such study would probably lead to a recognition that the present extent of governmental price making is not only a profit-limiting device but also an experiment in welfare price making, capable of becoming the legal foundation of an economic democracy. In Mr. Justice Jackson's words, "we should recognize 'price' for what it is—a tool, a means, an expedient," used "to reconcile the private property right society has permitted to vest in an important natural resource with the claims of society upon it—price must draw a balance between wealth and welfare."

The Judge's Dilemma

The case of *Federal Power Commission* v. *Hope Natural Gas Co.*,[17] from which I have been quoting, illustrates the general situation of the courts in the fields where legislation requires implementation by administrative action. For decades liberals have advocated the repudiation of *Smyth* v. *Ames*, which had read into the Constitution the requirement of specific methods of valuation and rate making. In the *Hope* case, decided last January, the Supreme Court has laid that ghost and declared that, from now on, it is not concerned with the theoretical propriety of the valuation and rate-making formulas so long as the results reached are satisfactory.

The victory left many a liberal wondering. Justice Jackson objected that he "had no instinct by which to know the 'reasonable' from the 'unreasonable' in prices and must seek some conscious design for decision." Justice Frankfurter joined in the dissent and remarked that it "will little advance the public interest to substitute

---

[17] *Ibid.*

for the hodge-podge of the rule in Smyth *v*. Ames, an encouragement of conscious obscurity or confusion in reaching a result, on
the assumption that so long as the result appears harmless, its basis
is irrelevant."

This language has been treated as merely additional evidence
for the conventional picture of Justice Frankfurter betraying the
liberal ideas he professed in law school. The truth of the matter is
that it shows an awareness of the new task liberal judges face today.
After having won the war against conceptualism, the realists must,
as the phrase goes, win the peace. To be an antifascist in northern
Italy today is to hold a heroic title. But a man must be more than
just an antifascist in the south, where you have to make up your
mind on a number of annoying issues, such as Badoglio, Stalin, or
the way you are going to pay workers, run railways, or just feed
people. This is, I think, what Justice Jackson meant when he said,
"If we are to bring judgment of our own to the task, we should
for the guidance of the regulators and the regulated reveal something of the philosophy, be it legal or economic or social, which
guides us."

Strange as it may be to find the foundation of a welfare jurisprudence in the opinions of the author of *The Struggle for Judicial Supremacy*, the quoted language supports the contention.
Justice Jackson makes his new attitude explicit when he adds, "If,
on the other hand, the court is to hold that a given rate is reasonable just because the Commission has said it was reasonable, a
review becomes a costly, time-consuming pageant of no practical
value to anyone."

The plea for a jurisprudence of welfare has thus definite political
meaning. As in every society, the struggle for lawmaking supremacy
is going on in America as well. The distribution of powers among
lawmaking institutions has always been, in fact, a matter of compromise determined by political or even partisan reasons, sometimes cloaked in philosophical solemnities. The position of the
Roman praetor, Montesquieu's separation of powers, and the doctrine of judicial review in *Marbury v. Madison* are but instances
of such political compromises. Institutions, however, have a weight

of their own, and are one of the pulls of the social parallelogram of forces. Today the position of the administrative agencies is in the center of attention. They have conquered advanced positions and are threatening to reduce the courts to an uncomfortably inferior position. This worries those who happen to believe not only that effective legislative or administrative action and intelligent judicial review thereof are compatible, but that their balanced coexistence is the essence of constitutional government—without which, I should add, federalism itself would shrink to mere administrative decentralization. The political equilibrium is threatened today because administrative agencies have seized the weapons offered by social science technology and outdistanced the courts, shackled by their innocence of the methods of modern economics or psychology.

Justice Jackson remarked in the *Hope* case that regulation of the natural gas industry must be treated "as the performance of economic functions, not as the performance of legalistic rituals," and it is obvious that if this viewpoint is accepted, courts will have to get the necessary equipment or be driven off the field of regulation. In another recent case a dissent, written by Mr. Justice Roberts to attack the constitutionality of the Emergency Price Administration Act, has thrown incidental light upon the plight of the judiciary. "No court is competent," Justice Roberts complained,

on a mass of economic opinion consisting of studies by subordinates of the Administrator, charts and graphs prepared in support of the studies, and economic essays gathered hither and yon, to demonstrate, beyond doubt, that the considerations or conclusions of the Administrator from such material cannot support the Administrator's judgment that what he has done by way of regulation or price schedule tends to prevent post-war collapse of values, or to prevent dissipation of defense appropriations through excessive prices, or to prevent impairment of the standard of living of persons dependent on life insurance, or to prevent hardship to schools—to enumerate but a few of the stated purposes of the Act.

Mr. Justice Roberts concluded that the Court should strike down the statute because its standards, when considered in the light of the limited competence of the courts, were too indefinite. But is it true that the courts are left with the choice of being a rubber stamp or a bottleneck?

I submit that the judge's dilemma can be avoided if courts acquire that minimum knowledge of social science which would enable them to exercise a common-sense control over the charts and economic essays which looked so wild to Mr. Justice Roberts. Unless we are resigned to a government by technicians, and ready to submit to a totemistic symbolism evolved by the social sciences, we must be ready to learn their language and, as it were, to see through their charts and graphs. Unless social scientists learn the language and techniques of the law, or lawyers learn their language and techniques, we are bound to see the rise of absentee ownership of the governmental apparatus and witness a new divorce between real and nominal power.

An Educational Challenge

Jurisprudence of welfare is thus fundamentally an educational problem. One of the tasks that educators face today is to narrow the appalling chasm between those who, in schools and research centers, study our community and those who, in legislative committees and courts, shape its life. The clear-cut separation of law schools from schools of politics, economics, and sociology has led to a corresponding separation of the scientific activity of the two groups. Quite naturally, within each of them, a trend away from the slippery borders has developed. The combined effect of these trends has created a scientific no man's land which has become covered by dense conceptual and semantic hedges. A common effort is needed to cut them back.

This situation has placed a great responsibility upon the social scientists. Whether they like it or not, they won't be able to escape it. I do not underestimate the need for investigation free from non-scientific pressures, or the value of social studies developing beyond the concepts of good and bad. There is no question, however, but that the coming decade will exercise increasing pressure upon social scientists. Nor is it sure that this "social commission to scholars," as the early Soviets called it, will exercise a detrimental influence upon the social sciences. It is true that scholars and artists have always longed for freedom from patrons, but the record is somewhat ambiguous as to the justification of their desire. Even the strictness of the "social commission" of the Renaissance popes does not seem to have killed Renaissance art.

It is also a matter of record that, in fact, the social sciences have never been totally *wertfrei*. A book of Myrdal, the Swedish economist, on *The Political Element in the Formation of Economic Doctrines* seems written by a legal realist. Some of its passages, showing how much policy objectives have influenced economic theory, sound pretty much the same note as does Frank's *Law and the Modern Mind* in its analysis of the motivations of legal theory. A participation of the social sciences in the development of a welfare jurisprudence may bring the normative elements in social science into the light of consciousness and thus contribute to a healthy development of social theory. In short, welfare jurisprudence may offer an opportunity to answer not only the question "How do and how should legal institutions shape social reality?" but also the question "How important for the life of a society are social sciences?" If compelled to present the results of their laboratory investigations to an audience of intelligent laymen charged with social responsibilities, social scientists may discover that they and their disciplines are undergoing a severe test conducive to real progress. Welfare jurisprudence may thus become a testing ground of the incidence of legal institutions and of the relevance of social studies.

III

A Summary of Objections

To the contention that judges should openly ask and discuss the welfare question, and attempt to answer it with the help of available social science data, a number of forceful objections may be formulated. They are likely to center on some variation or combination of three main groups of ideas, which may be summarized as follows.

[15]

In the first place it will be said, of course, that the welfare question should be asked, and the available social data should be considered, not by judges but by legislators. And this proposition, in turn, will be justified by various considerations or presented from various points of view. (a) If ours be a government of laws and not of men, we must be ruled by general and impersonal propositions formulated without regard to individual litigants, applying with the same rigor to all of them. (b) If courts are left with the power to ask the welfare question they will be tempted to change their answers with every blow of wind or mood of fashion and their decisions will come "into the same class as the restricted railroad ticket, good for this day and train only"; this would gravely impair the stability of the legal system. (c) There is a particular injustice and hardship in "judicial legislation" because, unlike a new statute which is binding only for the future, the decision of the courts purports to be only declaratory of the law, and thus applies retroactively. (d) If the welfare of the people requires a change in the law it must be made by the people themselves, through their duly elected representatives, composing their legislative assemblies.

The second group of objections may center on the notion that the pursuer's full awareness of his goal does not necessarily promote the success of his pursuit. It may be maintained, indeed, that most lawmakers have asked the welfare question, at least unconsciously or secretly, and that judges too must have done so, to the extent that they were lawgivers. Against the background of these contentions several more specific objections may be stressed. (a) The awareness of his lawmaking function and a conscious pursuit of welfare do not necessarily make a man, or a judge, a good or better lawgiver. (b) Even if judges should be perfectly conscious of what they are doing, people, for their own good, should not be told of the degree of judicial freedom—and, least of all, in judicial opinions.

Finally, objectors may challenge the usefulness of injecting the welfare concept into the judicial process. (a) To begin with, the agreement that laws, judge-made and others, should be good (or serve the general welfare) is as general as the disagreement on what serves the common good. (b) The difficulty is not solved by reference to the social sciences, for there is no agreement among social scientists in general, or even among the students of a single branch of social studies, on what is welfare, on what are the means of furthering it, on whether or not it is proper or possible for the social studies to give guidance for the solution of social problems. (c) If, on the other hand, some social scientists—not necessarily the better ones—should prove willing to provide such guidance, the result might be intolerable paternalism, a tyrannic government by experts.

It may be said at the outset that some, if not all, of these objections have considerable philosophic validity and that, however great my inclination to disagree with them ultimately, I shall not attempt, in this writing, to demonstrate their theoretical fallacy. It willl be sufficient, for present purposes, to point out that the alternatives these objections tender—implicitly, since their explicit formulation is extremely rare, and this for reasons to be stated— are at such variance with the fundamentals of American society that an attempt to effectuate them would encounter far greater difficulties, and lead to consequences more upsetting and revolutionary, than may be apprehended from the development of a wel fare jurisprudence.

IV

Government by Law and the Unfinished Statutes

The argument that the welfare question should be asked in the legislatures and there answered, with the help of pertinent data in the form of impersonal propositions, free from any regard to individual litigants, was forcefully stated by Beccaria:

The disorder which arises from a rigorous compliance with the letter of a criminal statute cannot be compared with the disorders which arise from interpretation. . . . When a fixed code of laws . . . leaves to the judge no other task than to examine the acts of a citizen and to adjudge whether or not they conform to the written law; when the norm of right and wrong, which must lead the actions of the ignorant citizens as much as of the citizen-philosopher, is a matter not of controversy but of fact; then subjects are not exposed to the little tyrannies of the many, so much more cruel as the distance between the one who suffers and the one who makes him suffer is the smaller.

I do not underestimate the weight of this argument, which has had among its advocates the noblest minds of many a century. For the purposes of this inquiry it is not necessary, however, to reopen the ancient question, not confined to the realm of political philosophy, on the relative weight and value of general rules and individual variations. Nor need we discuss whether the ideal of a Benthamian code—which would deprive the judges of their power to interpret the law, do away with the uncertainties of the jury room, the chancellor's chambers, and the administrator's office, and strike at the root of legal esotericism by suppressing the legal professions—can be approximated anyplace where men are human.

I shall remark presently on the essential relation between laws and welfare. At this point it seems sufficient to say that whether or not a type of legislation which would eliminate the need for judicial lawmaking is desirable or possible, precious little of such legislation is to be found on the books today. On the contrary, the weight of the traditional common-law ideology and the techniques of American political and legislative machinery have joined forces to multiply the instances wherein legislators give judges no better guidance than adjectives such as "just," "reasonable," "fair," "convenient," "adequate," or "proper." And the greater the strategic value of a given provision, the greater the likelihood that the legislative majority for its adoption will be gathered through the use of "neutral" words which do not prejudge the issue. When this is the case it is flatly impossible for judges to proceed in the manner advocated by Montesquieu, Beccaria, or Bentham.

The admissibility of "judicial legislation" is a legitimate and burning issue in countries that have made at least an earnest attempt to heed the call for codification launched by the philosophers of illuminism. My argument would obviously be inadequate if I were confronted with a serious revival of the Benthamian advocacy of welfare by unambiguous legislation. So long, however, as Bentham remains no prophet in his common-law homeland, the real question is not whether judges should finish the job left unfinished by constitutional conventions and legislatures, but whether they should do it in full awareness of their lawmaking functions and with the avowed aim of serving the welfare of their community.

It is true that there are many fields, and fields of vital importance, where the unfinished job is left to administrative agencies. There, of course, the courts could refuse to give any intelligent contribution to welfare problems, by either supinely approving or blindly obstructing all experiments, innovations, or extravagancies of the bureaus. Either course would mean the end, in one or another form, of judicial review. And if the judiciary chose to be bottleneck rather than rubber stamp, this could not long postpone the inevitable. But whether judicial review perishes from atrophy or from overexertion, the opponents of "judicial legislation" will hardly be pleased with the result. Nor can I imagine any meaningful judicial control of administrative activity which would not follow, in substance, the methods and the criteria of a welfare jurisprudence.

Law as the Foundation of Welfare

A further investigation of the objection I have been discussing should make clear another point, which is quite independent of the impossibility of practicing judicial aloofness in a country where no corresponding ground has been laid by legislators. This point is that the ideal of a jurisprudence of welfare is in no way inconsistent with that of government by law.

The notion that government by law presupposes and requires a legislative lawmaking monopoly may have been justified in a given historical and political setting, but, considered in itself, it is totally unwarranted. Such a monopoly is neither sufficient nor necessary for the preservation of the ideal of government by law: on the one hand, statutes, and indeed constitutions, may and sometimes do contain *ad personam* provisions which fly in the face of that ideal; on the other, the ideal has often celebrated its highest expression in catholic rules of purely judicial origin.

The real test is not by whom an order is given, or whether it is given in a general and impersonal form or on the occasion of particular litigation. The test is whether or not the order is predicated upon a maxim capable of acquiring that universality which characterizes law in its higher sense. Welfare jurisprudence should never attempt to escape this fundamental requirement. It would misconceive the essential relation between law and welfare if it neglected the truth that law is an element in and, indeed, the foundation of welfare itself. The question "What is good for our society?" is crucial, and must be asked by all those—be they legislators, judges, or administrators—who are in fact entrusted with lawmaking functions. And it must be answered with the help of all pertinent nonlegal data, originating in the social studies or elsewhere. The answer itself, however, must be a *law*making one.

Jurisprudence of welfare must not be corrupted into a jurisprudence of expediency. It must remain faithful to Goethe's admonition that "man where he appears significant behaves as a lawmaker." The expediencies of specific situations must be valued from a general viewpoint and shaped into an intelligible pattern. It is not enough that specific actions of governmental agencies be wholesome and serve the expediency of the moment and the needs of an individual situation. In the words of the *Nicomachean Ethics,* "to be just, they must be done and distributed in a certain manner. And this is a more difficult task than knowing what things are wholesome." A true jurist, mindful of the general welfare, instead of merely investigating what specific judicial action or administrative measure would best serve the public welfare in individual situations, will ask himself what canon of action can best serve that purpose, upon what maxim, capable of becoming a universal law, the specific measure can be predicated.

Concrete cases cannot be decided by general propositions—nor without them. Even in the most narrow sense welfare is measured not only by the absolute amount of goods and services enjoyed by men but by their relative distribution as well. In this sense, welfare and law both come under Dante's definition of law as proportion of man to man, the *hominis ad hominem proportio*. It may be possible to psychoanalyze away the father complex and the quest for security. But the quest for a conformity to rules, for a recognizable pattern of action, for an *ordo voluntatis* is nothing else than a quest for harmony and beauty. It is a trait of mankind; even more, it is the mysterious prime force of our universe, which gives a rhythm to the crooning of savages and the games of children and a geometrical form to the crystallization of salt.

The economic and social facts of life, which legal realism has taught us, have banished the belief that judicial decisions are brought ready-made by constitutional storks. This discovery should not, however, lead to a cynicism as silly, in its own way, as the stork tale. To follow the metaphor, one should not forget that mere lust could not have made man into what he is now; that, in other words, love is a biological fact without which the present state of the human race would be inconceivable. Similarly, society cannot be built upon judicial whim or expediency alone. Human craving for regularity and legality is the foundation of society, and its satisfaction a condition of welfare. The framers of the greatest codification undertaken among the western peoples, the Corpus Juris Justinianensis, were aware of the nature of this quest—and of the metaphor I have traced—when they dedicated their work to the "youth longing for laws," *legum cupidae juventuti*.

Legal Stability and Legal Change

The foregoing discussion of the first and fundamental objection to welfare jurisprudence is a sufficiently clear indication of the answers to the other objections of the same group. It may be useful, however, to dwell a little on them, in order to make even more explicit what welfare jurisprudence is not intended to be.

To begin with, the principle that courts should always ask the welfare question does not mean that their decisions would be like "tickets good for this day only." Having determined that a new rule of law will serve the welfare of the community better than the old one did, courts must ask themselves whether welfare will be served by the change at the time their decision is being made. Stability has an obvious social, political, and moral value, which it would be foolhardy to deny. Builders would build in vain if the material they use did not embody the great force of this universe, inertia. Political and legal institutions of every people testify to the recognition of this force. Statutes of limitations, acquisition by prescription, the principle of *res judicata*, other forms of finality of judgments, references to custom, the fiction of "lost title"—all show that society recognizes what Jellinek called, in another connection, the normative force of facts, and what could also be called the moral power of time.

Inertia, however, is a good servant and a bad master. Skyscrapers cannot be built without inertia—or by it alone. If evidence were needed of the political wisdom of the common law it could be found in its attitude toward the problem of legal stability and legal change. On the one hand, the common law evolved—to be sure, in chancery, where, paradoxically enough, the common law found its most distinctive features—the concept of laches, which bars an equitable suit and freezes the factual situation even before the period of limitation has completed its course. On the other hand, the inexhaustible arsenal of chancery furnishes the courts with weapons, hardly known in civil law countries, for overcoming the rigidity of *res judicata*, thus divesting it of the sacrosanct character it possesses elsewhere. On the one hand, there is a suggestion that the United States Constitution itself requires that judicial decisions possess a certain degree of finality, without which there could be no exercise of the judicial function. On the other hand, it is held that the Constitution forbids the attribution of an excessive degree of finality to judgments, which must always remain open to challenge on certain grounds.

American courts have accepted the principle of *stare decisis*. But they have never treated it as a master. It is too late in the day to advance the claim that no precedent should ever be overruled. As the Chief Justice of the United States has recently put it, "to give blind adherence to a rule of policy that no decision of this court is to be overruled would be itself to overrule many decisions of the court which do not accept that view." The real problem is not whether, but when, precedents should be overruled.

A court is faced with the problem of *stare decisis* only when it is reasonably satisfied that the old decision is wrong, or that the issue would have been decided differently if it were presented in a case of first impression. Since no court believes that precedents should never be upset, judges who think that a "decision cannot be determined by results which may flow from it" may be tempted to overrule every obviously "wrong" decision. Only judges who have the courage to ask themselves, "Right or wrong, would the change serve the people's welfare?" will have any criterion on which to base a distinction between precedents to be disregarded and those to be honored. Welfare jurisprudence may thus prove an element of stability as much as an inducement to change.

A recent and already famous case, decided by the United States Supreme Court, affords a vivid illustration.[18] When that court was asked to reverse the long-established persuasion that insurance is not interstate commerce, it was the minority, arguing against reversal, that approached the problem from a welfare angle. After having recognized the limitations of the doctrine of *stare decisis* —I have just quoted his words—the Chief Justice went on to argue that right or wrong is not the ultimate test which should govern the overruling of precedents: ". . . the rule of *stare decisis* embodies a wise policy because it is often more important that a rule of policy be settled than that it be settled right." The practical effects of the decision should guide the Court's choice. "And before overruling a precedent in any case it is the duty of the court to make certain that more harm will not be done in rejecting than in retaining a rule of even dubious validity." When the Court finds that this would be the case, this finding "might well stay a reversal of long established doctrine which promises so little of advantage and so much of harm. For me these considerations are controlling."

Mr. Justice Jackson made it equally clear that his refusal to over-

---

[18] United States v. South-Eastern Underwriters Assn., 322 U.S. 533 (1942).

rule the insurance precedent was predicated on welfare considerations. "Abstract logic," he said,

may support [the majority], but the common sense and wisdom of the situation seem opposed. It may be said that practical consequences are no concern of a court, that it should confine itself to legal theory. . . . I think we not only are free, but are duty bound, to consider practical consequences of such a revision of constitutional theory. This court only recently recognized that certain former decisions as to the dividing line between state and federal power were illogical and theoretically wrong, but at the same time it announced that it would adhere to them because both governments had accommodated the structure of their laws to the error.

The problem of relation between stability and change cuts right across the dogmas of separation of powers, and has little, if any, relation to the problem whether judges should have the power to make law. Legislatures and courts may both err in the timing of changes, and may be either behind their time or before it. Nor does the simple asking of the welfare question guarantee that a correct answer will be given. But no matter how fallible legislators or judges may be in administering the test, it seems obvious that only considerations of the wholesomeness of a given change, at a given time, in a given society, and not abstract logical theories on the limits of *stare decisis*, can furnish intelligent guidance. And the test would seem particularly appropriate in a country whose foremost tradition has been the tradition of change.

Retroactivity, a Welfare Problem

There remains, however, the argument that a different test should govern the changes in judge-made law because, unlike new statutes, new judicial doctrines apply immediately and retroactively, thus causing "confusion, surprise and injustice."

There is no doubt that a certain amount of nonretroactivity of the law is a condition of its wholesomeness. It is equally true that all new laws, like all human disturbances of the existing order of things, cannot help being retroactive in some sense. The uncertain line between permissible and nonpermissible retroactivity has been variously drawn in respect to statutes, but no consistent attempt to limit undue retroactivity has been made in respect to judicial decisions. The criticism with which we are dealing now is thus only too well founded. And it is not hard to discover the reason for the neglect of the problem and for the unhesitatingly retroactive application of judge-made law. The reason obviously lies in the legal fiction of the law-finding nature of judicial activity. Since judges are not supposed to make law, either old or new, the newly discovered law is presumed always to have been that way, whatever the prior and "erroneous" cases may have said. Hence there is no injustice in applying the law to legal relationships originated before it was revealed.

It was against this fiction that the realistic attack was directed, and today hardly anybody believes the old notion. But, once again, the necessary consequences were not drawn from the realists' victory and, once again, it may be the task of welfare jurisprudence to do so. In full awareness of the true nature of the judicial process, courts should be able to escape the dilemma either of operating retroactive harshness or of eternalizing harmful rules. The Roman praetor made judicial law prospective to some extent, by yearly framing his *judicium dabo*, I *shall* give judgment, and there is good modern authority, domestic and foreign, for the adoption of a similar course of action in the American courts. Judges should be able to set aside a precedent for the future only, while still applying the old law to the case at hand. The explicit and informed positing of the welfare question will necessarily lead to a more responsible approach to the problem of judicial retroactivity. Instead of proceeding on the obsolete fiction of judicial law finding, courts may be induced to take a realistic view of the true incidence of their decisions.

Judicial Legislation and Popular Sovereignty

There is, finally, the objection that in a democracy law should be made not only for the people but also by the people. Congress and state legislatures, it is held, are the expression of the will of the majority, and all judicial legislation amounts to usurpation of

[25]

popular sovereignty. This argument has recently been presented with particular forcefulness on Jeffersonian authority, in connection with the problem of judicial review of the constitutionality of statutes.

For the purposes of this study it may be sufficient to answer this objection by pointing out again that, whatever the desirability and possibility of exhaustive legislation, under the present American constitutional and legislative techniques, the only alternative to a welfare jurisprudence is lawmaking by judges who do not know, or do not let people know, that they are making law. The desirability of this alternative will be discussed in the next section, but I should like to note here that welfare jurisprudence in no way attempts to deprive the legislatures of their chance to gain or retain the monopoly of lawmaking and of responsibility for the welfare of the country. If the legislators really resent the judge's lawmaking they may be induced to put into practice their often voiced belief in government by law, to restrict the use of "legislation by default," and to take responsibility for the drafting of more precise statutes. All that welfare jurisprudence calls for is that where, and to the extent to which, the lawmaking process has not been exhausted by the legislature, and is being in fact completed by the courts, the latter act according to their true role and not according to a fable which would give us, instead of a real government by law, an irresponsible government in disguise.

Moreover, I doubt the basic soundness of this objection. I doubt whether the notion that the legislative monopoly of lawmaking is the basis of popular self-government is tenable in countries and in times which do not witness the struggle for power in which the notion originated. And it certainly remains to be seen whether, and in what sense, it could be said that American legislators, rather than American judges, are necessarily more "truly representative" of the American people and of their "general will," that is to say, of their basic trends, as distinguished from their transient attitudes.

V

The Lost Paradise

It may very well be doubted whether there is more wisdom in a man's rational activity or in his uncalculated performance, and whether "planned" composition or unconscious growth of patterns offers a greater probability of final harmony and vitality. This problem has appeared, in one form or another, in almost every field of human endeavor. There have been thinkers who viewed even language, family, and society as the result of purposive, planned creation, of an explicit social contract; and others who asserted to the contrary that common economic welfare can be, nay, inevitably is, achieved by individual and un-co-ordinated activities, inspired by motives totally unrelated, to put it mildly, to such an aim. Lawmaking itself, even in its legislative manifestation, has not always been conceived as a purposive act.

Indeed, courts are not the only class of lawgivers who conceal their lawgiving function under the disguise of law finding or law disclosing. Nor is it always the judges who claim to confine themselves to the mere interpretation of the legislator's will; sometimes the opposite is true. Scores of codifications, governmental and private, have been presented as mere interpretation of judicial decisions, and it does not take a realist's zeal to discover how much outright legislation these codifications contain. An even greater number of laws—some of them wholesome and necessary indeed —have been predicated on divine revelation, magic lore, absolute reason, or manifest geopolitical destiny. Romantic influences led jurists to deplore the increase of lawmaking by legislation on the ground that its willful purposiveness impaired the spontaneity of the growth of legal institutions nourished by unconscious folkways and the *Volksgeist*. Their arguments have not been heeded by a century which has seen legislation run riot in all countries of western civilization. But this does not necessarily mean that the arguments were untenable, nor does this essay purport to prove it. I am not discussing here whether or not it is desirable to have judges who believe themselves to be either the mere voice of the law or the expression of the popular genius for unconscious achievement of justice and welfare. My point is simply that the overwhelming majority of the leading judges of today's America do not believe it. Whether or not a judge who knows that he is a lawgiver makes better law than one who does not know it, the short answer is that today's most influential judges do know, and can hardly be persuaded of the contrary in our lifetime.

This essay began with a discussion of the fundamental tenets of legal realism and of the influence they have exercised upon the judicial mind. To put it briefly, realism gave the judges a bad conscience. After having taught, or absorbed in the classroom, a belief in the creative nature of the judicial function, the new generation of judges could hardly be expected to have forgotten, once on the bench, the canon they had taught or learned. Whether or not it is wise for the king, discovered to be naked, to continue to act as if he were wearing rich and embroidered garments, he certainly can be relied upon to possess no longer the magic virtues credited to virgin innocence. The simple fact is that, to paraphrase an already quoted dictum of Justice Jackson, leading modern judges, upon whom judicial lawmaking ultimately depends, "have no *instinct* by which to know the 'just' from the 'unjust' and *must* seek some *conscious* design for decision." It may be that mankind was happier in a state of nature, but no panegyric of its glories has ever succeeded in bringing back the lost paradise.

Pursuit of Welfare

I shall discuss presently the possible advantages of a situation in which judges would just "pretend" to be mere law finders, while consciously acting as lawmakers. But I should not like to leave the present subject without registering some doubts about the supposed virtues of unconscious lawmaking.

In the first place, it may be remembered that the reluctance to assume the responsibility for a conscious pursuit of welfare has inhibited, for many generations and among many peoples, the adequate development of the main, the legislative, branch of the lawmaking activity. It has prevented legislation from seeking openly "the greatest happiness of the greatest number," that is to say, from becoming a welfare legislation. It is enough to think of the deep and beneficent changes which were brought about in the field of criminal justice when the emphasis was shifted from an algebra of proportionate retribution to the search for a penal code which would deter repetition of crimes, and reform or incapacitate criminals. This shift from an etiological (punishment as a consequence) to a teleological (punishment as a means) criminal law has been accomplished largely by the legislatures, and represents one of the major victories of legal illuminism. But, of course, its fruits could not have been reaped if Benthamian legislation had not been supplemented by judges quite dissimilar from those whom Bentham considered ideal. A tremendous amount of judicial and administrative ingenuity, flexibility, humanity, and, not least important, awareness of purpose was and still is needed for the modernization of criminal law. But considerable progress has been made, and it is significant that this most ancient form of law has been the first to draw heavily upon the teachings of nonlegal sciences—psychology, medicine, sociology—and thus approximate the ideal of a jurisprudence of welfare.

In the second place, judges have not always, even unconsciously, asked themselves the welfare question. Judges, no less than other men, dislike facing responsibilities. Lawmaking, or at least conscious and responsible lawmaking, is a painful, brain- and heartbreaking process. It is even more so when it is judicial lawmaking, lawmaking on the spot, lawgiving in the field, where you solve a legal problem by hanging a man, a mother's son. It is human, only too human, to fall back upon the alleged inevitability of results dictated by statute or precedent. Even in so-called cases of first impression, the responsibility for relating the litigated question to criteria of welfare, or for that matter to any other teleological criterion, can often be escaped through the invocation of legal symmetry or through the adaptation of the new decision to the prevailing legal climate. But actually, of course, the judges are still left with a wide latitude of choice. Thus, with the lawfinding alibi firmly established, opportunities for real judicial arbitrariness have been offered to them by the ambiguously drawn statutes and precedents, in which a shift of emphasis could bring out a new distinction from the inextricable maze of holdings and dicta.

Some judges may have used their freedom consciously, for good or bad purposes. But I suspect that the majority, escaping the light and responsibility of full awareness, have succumbed to the temptation of dwelling in the penumbra of intellectual laziness, and of following habitual patterns of superstition and prejudice. Even when these patterns are a projection of well-defined sectional interests, dear to the judge's heart, he need not proceed in bad faith. He can act in defense of these interests honestly, his words faithfully reflecting his thoughts. The adjustment operates at an earlier stage: it is his thoughts which are shaped according to his interests. And it is in this surreptitious adjustment, in the bona fide betrayal of justice and welfare, that lies the main danger of unconscious lawmaking. It seems to me fortunate that its possibilities and extent have been impaired by the new attitude of the modern judiciary, grown aware of its role in society.

Judicial Law and Public Opinion

To proceed now to the next and somewhat analogous objection —even if judges know, should they tell the story? Should they, as the federal courts do with increasing frequency, openly and explicitly discuss the real problems involved in the cases? After all, lawgivers may know what they are doing, may pursue what they conceive to be welfare, without professing that they are lawmakers. Augurs exchanging smiles among themselves have been seen, or could have been seen, by attentive observers in many an ancient or modern temple. Even if new law has to be made today, why should judges directly predicate the changes upon welfare, instead of using, as the old wise men used to do, the persuasive symbols of judicial astrology? Is it not true that in many situations people would fare better if they were convinced that mediocre decisions reached by judges are the inevitable result of the dictates of The Law, produced *jure ac necessitate dictantibus*, than if they were faced with excellent decisions, avowedly grounded in the judges' freely chosen conception of welfare?

Similar objections have been advanced in other societies, with an explicitness and frequency unlikely to be encountered "in a country of free speech," to quote Holmes, "that affects to regard education and knowledge as desirable." But it should be noted that the exclusion of public opinion from the judicial lawmaking process is implicitly accepted by those who think that judicial activity, no matter how lawmaking in nature, should not be inspired by a conscious pursuit of welfare ideals. While the lack of public discussion does not necessarily exclude the conscious pursuit of welfare on the part of the judges, the converse is not true; and those who advocate unconscious judicial lawmaking necessarily bar the possibility of a continuous and intelligent participation of public opinion in that important phase of lawmaking.

I shall not attempt to prove here the fundamental fallacy of this conception by taking an absolutist, Fourth-of-July view of free speech and government by discussion. I shall not even make the claim that as long as, and to the extent to which, lawmaking functions are in fact left to the judges, a welfare jurisprudence is, everywhere and at all times, necessary to assure the democratic nature of the judicial process, the people's enlightened participation in the lawmaking process. I acknowledge that social reality is more complex than constitutional absolutes could make us believe. One of the manifestations of this complexity is that, throughout the history of mankind, even disinterested, unafraid, and humanitarian philosophers have felt the necessity of imposing certain limitations upon their own freedom of speech. The "clear and present danger" that a full and precise manifestation of their thought would lead to its deplorable misunderstanding by the many has often induced them to express themselves indirectly, incompletely, or even with self-contradicting ambiguity.

Therefore I do not deny that there are cases in which a man, a philosopher, a general, or a judge is under a moral, political, and, if you please, constitutional duty not to say all that he thinks of the case before him. Where to draw the line between the right and duty to speak and the right and duty to remain silent is obviously a historical problem; as Leo Strauss has it, "the line of demarcation between timidity and responsibility is drawn differently in different ages." And it may very well be that open pursuit of common welfare by judges or, for that matter, by legislators may prove pernicious in some societies. But, unless I am deeply mistaken, at this time, in this country, history has drawn the line of demarcation—and, I cannot help adding, fortunately so—in such a way that the free discussion of welfare elements involved in the adjudication of litigated issues is unquestionably within the "philosophical limits" of freedom of speech to which I have been referring. Whatever the doubts about the desirability of letting people know that judges are lawmakers, the historical fact is that today not only the judges know it, but also that part of public opinion which is seriously concerned with the administration of justice.

And what is more, today's leading judges are unwilling to conceal that knowledge from the people. Some of them may hesitate to go on telling a discredited tale and to behave as if no one knew their priestly secrets. Others would refuse to act as depositories of a divine revelation even if their oracular wisdom were not doubted. On the one hand, realistic analysis of the judicial function has informed public opinion, or at least legal public opinion, and thus has exercised a pressure upon the judges. On the other hand, the force of public opinion is being called into play by the judges themselves; vacancies in the federal and state judiciaries have been increasingly filled by exoteric believers in direct and outspoken discussion of the real issues presented by the cases, rather than by men with more diplomatic background or temperament. Whether or not such a close relation between the bench and public opinion is desirable, historical forces have brought it about. The failure of a comparatively recent attempt to force a summary change in the personnel of a court shows that the composition of the judiciary possesses a considerable degree of stability in this country. It seems futile to attempt a return to the esoteric solemnities of the past.

The responsibility of our time with respect to the judiciary is similar to that accepted and fulfilled by the Century of Enlightenment with respect to the executive and legislative powers. We know already that judges do not sit *par grâce de Dieu*. But a far more enlightened and informed mutual action between people and judges is necessary to make them really sit *par volonté de la nation*. The result cannot be brought about by the courts alone. Jurisprudence of welfare is in no sense an exclusively judicial affair. It requires action on the part of lawyers, philosophers, social scientists, and educators, who must expound the courts to the public and guide public opinion's influence upon the courts.

VI

Welfare, an Ambiguous Concept

Most men are against sin, and it may be doubted whether the difficulties of the judicial process would be eased if all judges joined in the maxim "If it isn't welfare, I am against it." In other words, does not the case for a welfare jurisprudence beg the main and perhaps the only real issue, by failing to define welfare? Even more, does it not proceed on the unwarranted assumption that there is such a thing as common welfare, the welfare of the community as a whole? Does not the reality of our political and social processes consist in a struggle among the irreconcilably conflicting interests of various groups?

What is more, these interests, it is often contended, are as incommensurable in theory as they are conflicting in practice. Pareto has already remarked that interests of different groups or individuals cannot be "weighed" or "balanced" with any degree of objectivity, and more recently F. C. Benham and L. Robbins have led the attack against the welfare economists by insisting that there is no way of comparing the satisfactions of different people and no means of testing their relative magnitude. In a very recent case Judge Learned Hand has sounded the same skeptical note, and also has given, with his usual incisiveness, the general reason for the reluctance of some courts to adopt the welfare approach, or at least to do so openly. "It always gives an appearance of stronger authority to a conclusion," he said, "to deduce it dialectically from conceded premises than to

parisons of utility" shrink to utter insignificance for the purposes of immediate and practical action.

There may be some who will question whether the outlined issues, on which a widespread agreement was assumed, are such that normal judicial activity will have many occasions to deal with them. This doubt will probably disappear, however, if it is taken into account that modern legal institutions tend to affect an increasingly great number of people. After having digested the niceties of estates "fee tail male" or the statute *De Praerogativa Regis*, one may feel disappointed to learn that they affected a numerically negligible segment of the population while the overwhelming majority lived under servile tenure, of which so little is heard in the classroom. But modern statutes—ranging from regulation of competitive and labor standards to price, rate, and wage fixing, from taxation to distribution of risks—directly affect great masses of the population, shape the very price and wage structure of the country, and influence the working and living conditions of everybody. A considerable share of judicial work centers on these statutes.

It must be noted, furthermore, that the present state of articulated public opinion in the United States is such that a considerable degree of unanimity may be found on a number of issues going much beyond the recognition of elementary needs. For instance, class or race supremacy is openly advocated only exceptionally, and hardly ever from or before the bench. There is also an equally considerable consensus, so far as manifested opinion is concerned, in regard to a minimum degree of protection due to unwary consumers and minor workers, or the rights and duties of labor. Things have changed from the days in which child labor laws or the criminal responsibility for unionization was frankly in issue.

In this sense the task of welfare jurisprudence is much less difficult than that of welfare economics. Pigou's theories, for instance, have been criticized by his fellow economists on the ground that he treated propositions based upon the assumption of equality of human beings as essentially part of economic science, while in fact such assumptions were more ethical than scientific. Lawmakers scarcely need fear a similar attack. No lawyer conceives of law as a science having the dignity or the logical aloofness of Positive Economics. Unlike its economic companion, welfare jurisprudence is on comparatively safe ground when it assumes as its end the ethical and political ideals professed by our society and attempts to find in the arsenals of judicial doctrine and social science the means for their realization.

Vice's Tribute to Virtue

It must be recognized, of course, that to a very considerable extent the agreement to which I have been referring is only skin-deep. Sometimes it does not go beyond lip service. Even more often, the sincerity of the theoretical agreement is not matched by a willingness to make the personal sacrifices involved in the execution of measures necessary to remedy the deplored situation. But we must not forget that knowledge of the real conditions under which people live is only now beginning to be spread on a large scale. It has already been pointed out that jurisprudence of welfare represents a means of achieving closer co-operation between law and public opinion. The spread of this knowledge cannot fail, as time goes on, to influence the real attitude of a great many people.

In the words of a report published by the League of Nations on the eve of World War II,

to know what is necessary for the mere survival of the many should make it intolerable for the few with a relatively high standard of living to contemplate a state of affairs in which the minimum is not attained. In the absence of any higher motives the mere instinct of self preservation should oblige them to strive to make good contemporary deficiencies.

The whole problem of the degree of sincerity of the agreement reigning in a society on such or analogous issues must be dealt with realistically. It would be dangerous, indeed, to build a policy on popular lip service, treating it as solid rock. But it would be equally unrealistic to neglect its immense social value. The French say that hypocrisy is a tribute that vice pays to virtue, and it may be added that it is often a rather heavy tribute. Social progress would be frustrated if we were not able to utilize people's reluctance to appear in

[37]

their worst light. Nor is it sure that the real personality of a man, a group, or a people is better revealed by their secret thoughts than by the discipline that their own words impose upon them to a greater or lesser degree. More often than it is repudiated, moral responsibility is avoided by disguising the real issues involved. The educational and civic function of a welfare jurisprudence consists precisely in its presenting issues squarely, and at points which the drafting technique of our statutes and the judicentric structure of our legal system have made crucial.

The Tyranny of Experts

Finally there is, thank goodness, an area of disagreement, genuine and frank disagreement—disagreement on ends, and disagreement on means. Far from being the field to which welfare jurisprudence does not apply, the area is one in which its endeavors are particularly needed. No matter how much we may hate to admit it, a court faced with an issue on which society frankly disagrees, and on which the legislature has given no unambiguous guidance, cannot but side with one of the contending factions. The only question is whether it will do so by commission or by omission—that is, whether or not judges will discuss in their opinions the arguments in favor of and against the real issues which underlie the litigation and on which society has split. They may do it, or they may avoid it by several means. Thus they may discuss canons of legislative construction; or deny their own jurisdiction, this being "the easiest way to impress the disappointed litigant with the fact that it is the law, not the judge that refuses to hear him"; or leave the solution of the question to an administrative agency.

An enlightened welfare jurisprudence providing the judge with intelligible findings reached by the social studies, and keeping him in contact with an informed public opinion, would enable the courts to weigh the conflict before them intelligently, to state their reasons, and to *adjudge* the conflict, thus truly performing the function entrusted to them. I have already discussed the advantages of conscious and articulate judicial lawmaking. It suffices here to make the point that such lawmaking is in no way confined to the area in which society has already reached an agreement on welfare. On the contrary, jurisprudence of welfare is itself one of the most powerful means for the research, refinement, and development of the welfare concept.

Apprehensions may be voiced, however, as to the role of social scientists in this development. It may be feared that their growing intimacy with and influence upon the judicial process will result in a managerial paternalism, or in an outright dictatorship of technicians. Whatever the real degree of this danger, it is enough to say here that, if it exists, it has not originated with the beginnings of a welfare jurisprudence, and that it would find in the development of an informed judicial review its most powerful antidote.

The drafting of economists, sociologists, and psychologists to the national and state capitals did not start with the war, and will not end with it. We cannot turn back the clock. Social scientists are with us for good, and are going to remain in the very midst of government. It is true that some experts, or some specialized agencies or even a specialized court, may develop a new father complex, beaming the eternal human quest for objective certainty on the power of technicians. To prevent this result is one of the main tasks of an intelligent judicial review. Judges may and should become acquainted with the various nonlegal disciplines. But because of the variety of these disciplines, and of the variety of their judicial tasks, they will always remain intelligent *laymen*, as far as these disciplines are concerned. And intelligent lay control of technical administrative activity seems the best defense against the tyranny of experts.

A judge should know more about social studies precisely in order to acquire the conviction that they can furnish no more certainty than constitutions, statutes, or precedents. In their quest for unerring guidance men have tried many *ductores errantium*, but never successfully. It would be unreasonable and unfair to their authors to expect that doctrines of imperfect competition or social change or the learning theory will succeed where Aristotle, the Roman law, and Karl Marx have failed. A better knowledge of social sciences will enable judges to use their findings without abdicating the responsibility of the final choice of policy, which must rest with lay society represented by its lawmakers.

Jurisprudence of welfare is thus no lawyer's farewell to arms. It is one thing to recognize that law is too serious a business to be left to lawyers, and that even if there are legal problems there are no strictly legal answers to them. It is quite another to pretend to solve problems by saying, "It's simple; it is somebody else's business." Economists, for instance, are tempted at times to pass on their own questions to sociologists, psychologists, physicians, moral philosophers, and even lawyers. The passing of responsibility from lawyers to economists may easily degenerate into a vicious circle. What is more, a lawyer's unconditional surrender to social sciences would betray the essential relation between law and welfare, which I tried to show in discussing law as welfare's foundation.

Without giving any kind of scientific certainty, welfare jurisprudence cannot fail to infuse a greater degree of precision in the answers to legal problems than we possess now. "How far short this degree of perfection may be of the conceivable point of perfection?" was Bentham's question, quoted in Wesley Mitchell's discussion of the felicific calculus. And Bentham's answer, given to defend a welfare legislation, seems equally to support a welfare jurisprudence he had opposed: ". . . at any rate, in every rational and candid eye, unspeakable will be the advantage it will have, over every form of argumentation in which every idea is afloat, no degree of precision being ever attained, because none is ever so much as aimed at."

Jurisprudence of welfare is no answer to the problems of our time. In fact, it is no answer at all, but rather a mode of inquiry. It is an invitation to learn, a suggestion as to how questions should be asked, a call for the growth of a systematic participation of the judiciary—burdened with responsibility and stripped of its pontifical robes—in the travail of society. Jurisprudence of welfare is no easy solution of legal and social problems. It is the assignment of a grave task, whose very formulation would have been impossible without the encouragement flowing from the new attitude of our present courts. To be sure, it is the rejection of an issueless life and of an issueless jurisprudence. But it is not an attempt to impose a given concept of life or to present a given answer to the issues before us. We know too well that no new world can be discovered by mapping it in advance or proving its existence beforehand. What is more, one may not even suspect its existence, and having discovered the continent of new welfare, may die believing that it was only the old continent of wealth, the fabulous Indies.

Purposiveness is not advance planning of the results to be reached. It is the will to discover, the will to enlarge the tiny segment of the world we know, the will to learn and to do better, the firm and deep-seated conviction that men may, again and again, in everyone's life-time, see

> . . . thin with distance, thin but dead ahead,
> The line of unimaginable coasts.

Legal Techniques
and Political Ideologies:

A COMPARATIVE STUDY

THE PROBLEM with which we are going to deal is one of comparative law, a discipline probably even more illusory than legal science itself. A body of laws represents in itself neither a social reality nor a social ideal. One of the difficulties that every historian faces in trying to reconstruct a period of the past with the help of legal monuments is due to the great variety of relations existing between legal rules and social reality.[1] So, e.g., legal monuments generally contain in an inextricable confusion at least two contradictory types of rules: rules which are a simple restatement of an existing custom, and rules which are enacted with the very purpose of reversing existing customs and which, in terms of social reality, should be read as we read the negative of a snapshot: white for black and black for white.

The science of comparative law suffers from the same difficulties, and can acquire a meaning only if it faces them in full and becomes a part of the history of civilization. But in this endeavor, comparative law runs the risk of losing its character of legal science. Once engaged on the sociological path, the temptation to drop the technique of strictly legal approach altogether is great. The difficult task before the comparative lawyer is that of reading the technical results

---

[1] See, particularly with regard to studies of foreign law, Justice Holmes in Diaz v. Gonzales, 261 U.S. 102, 43 S. Ct. 286 (1923). See also 2 Jhering, *Geist des roemischen Rechts*, 2d ed., 133 (1866).

against the light of a more general political, social, and historical experience.[2]

We shall attempt the comparison between some typical principles of the common law at large with those which prevailed—prior to the advent of totalitarian regimes—in what we may call Latin countries. We are conscious of all the methodological qualifications involved in the idea of comparison between *types*, based necessarily on a somewhat arbitrary classification. On the other hand, only *typical* characteristics are the proper subject matter of comparative research. The first condition for the solution of this methodological difficulty is to be found, as is usually the case with many "preliminary problems," in the completion of one or more concrete pieces of work.

In justifying, however, the classification adopted for the present investigation, we might say why we centered it upon some aspects of the law of the Latin type instead of engaging in the more familiar comparison between common law and civil law at large. Such comparative studies have often treated, on the civilian side, institutions of German law to an extent unwarranted by the importance, however great, of the systems of that type on the Continent. Europe is by no means coextensive with Germany, and it might add to the completeness of the picture to put the emphasis on a different group of countries, for a change. We thought, furthermore, that such an approach was bound to yield results somewhat different from those of studies of the dominant type, since the countries of the German type, although strongly influenced both by the political ideologies and the legal techniques which originated from the so-called Latin countries of Europe, still retain too many old Teutonic institutions and attitudes to present a sufficiently striking contrast with the common-law system. Finally, the expression "civil law" is generally associated with the countries of the European Continent, while we are trying to emphasize the fact that the contrast between the two

---

[2] See Yntema, "Roman Law as the Basis of Comparative Law," 2 *Law, A Century of Progress* 346 at 373 (1937); Lepaulle, "The Function of Comparative Law," 35 *Harv. L. Rev.* 838 at 853 (1922); Rheinstein, "Teaching Comparative Law," 5 *Univ. Chi. L. Rev.* 615 (1938).

systems we are studying means, today, practically a contrast between North and South America, between English and Latin America.

Among the most frequent general statements concerning the typical features of the common law we find the assertion of its individualistic character, for which it is sometimes praised and sometimes condemned; and, of course, even more often we find the general statement asserting the individualistic character of the American way of life.[3] It may therefore be interesting to see whether and to what extent a strictly technical legal test would lead to the substantiation or the refutation of that general assertion.

We do not attempt to give an exact definition of individualism. It is safe, however, if not trite, to say that under individualism we all understand a particular type of relationship between individuals and society, and precisely a type of relation in which the interests of the individual and those of society are balanced at a point relatively favorable to the individual. It is, of course, a relative or comparative statement and therefore the existence of individualistic features in a given society can best be ascertained only by comparing it with other existing societies rather than with ideal standards. And in this study the aggregate of the means and devices used by a given society in order to enforce upon the individual the laws of that society, the amount of social pressure used for this purpose, may be fairly indicative of the degree of individualism existing in that society. It seems to us, in other words, that a comparison between the different techniques of enforcement used in the common-law countries and in other types of legal systems may be significant in our investigation.

We shall start our investigation at the very point at which the literature of comparative law generally stops: we shall ask ourselves what happens *after* the judicial decision has been rendered. A good

---

[3] See Pound, "Puritanism and the Common Law," 27 *Kan. Bar Assn. Proc.* 45 at 48 (1910); Bohlen, "The Moral Duty to Aid Others As a Basis of Tort Liability," 56 *Univ. Pa. L. Rev.* 217 at 220 (1908), reprinted in Bohlen, *Studies in the Law of Torts* 291 at 294 (1926); Bryce, "The Influence of National Character and Historical Environment on the Development of the Common Law," 28 *Can. Law Times* 89 (1908); Ancel, *La 'Common Law' d'Angleterre* 206 (1927); Eliot, *The Conflict between Individualism and Collectivism in a Democracy* 5 (1910); Turner, *The Frontier in American History* 30 *et seq.* (1920).

romantic novel ends with a marriage. But sometimes the tragedy starts just afterward. One of our finest scholars of comparative law concludes a recent article of his by stating that "The problems which courts have to decide are essentially the same on both sides of the Atlantic and, I venture to say, eighty per cent or even more of the solutions are the same." [4] We think that a far greater degree of dissimilarity between the two systems would have been discovered had the problem of enforcement been given more thorough consideration.

We are going to start with a very simple, even naïve remark: the common law knows an institution, called *contempt of court*, which to our mind is most important for the working of the whole legal system. Legal writers do not indulge too often in rationalizing on this institution, probably because it belongs to the self-evident presuppositions of the legal method. It is, in a certain sense, not surprising that a striking contrast between the two legal systems we are considering may be found just in connection with this institution. The existence of such a contrast becomes certain when we give full weight to the fact that the self-evident common-law principle of responsibility for contempt is, as principle, simply unknown in the civil-law countries, at least to the extent to which it represents a sanction for nonperformance of substantive duties.

It may be said that in the Latin countries the relation between the courts and the parties is in general far less close, I should say less intimate, than here. The Anglo-American idea of responsibility for contempt means, indeed, that the party who does not abide by certain specific decrees emanating from a judicial body is a contumacious person and may, as a rule, be held in contempt of court, in the king's mercy, so to say, and consequently fined and jailed. And although the institution is not utilized to the same extent in all areas of enforcement, it is still a highly characteristic illustration of the philosophy underlying the whole mechanism of the Anglo-American legal machinery.

Now, this very concept of contempt simply does not belong to the

[4] Rheinstein, "Common Law and Civil Law—A Comparison," 12 *Pa. Bar Assn. Q.* 7 at 19 (1940).

[45]

world of ideas of a Latin lawyer. It just does not occur to him that the refusal of the defendant to deliver to the plaintiff a painting sold to the latter, a purely *private* matter between plaintiff and defendant, may, as soon as a judicial order is issued, become a matter to a certain extent *personal to the court*, and that the court may feel hurt, insulted, "contemned," because its order has been neglected or willfully disobeyed.

The Latin conception of the means of enforcement is of a far more mechanical or formalistic character: it is a play with certain rules, traps, catches, and loopholes; and the court itself is one of the cogs of the mechanism, a party to the play. It does not occur to the actors that you have to bow to the judge's will, or that you may be punished by him, or, even more absurd, *blamed* for not having complied with his orders. The court says that the painting belongs to the plaintiff? Very well, let him try to get it! He may send the sheriff, and the defendant certainly will not prevent him from coming into his house and looking for the painting; if he is lucky enough to find it *there*, not elsewhere, well, he has won. Neither the sheriff nor the court can ask where the defendant put the painting. Once, in Italy, a simple-minded creditor who, by special leave, assisted at the futile attempt to attach a painting in the debtor's house, requested the sheriff to inquire of the defendant where the painting had been put. A general chorus of laughs and chuckles, in which even the plaintiff's attorney joined, was the answer. The Anglo-American solution of this situation, namely, to send the debtor to jail until he chooses to deliver the painting—theoretically for life—simply does not occur to the Latin lawyer. His first reaction to this common-law practice is generally: "Don't you think that this kind of punishment is a little too severe for a simple refusal to deliver?" The answer of the common lawyer—which only adds to the astonishment of the civil lawyer—is that of course we are faced here with so-called *civil* contempt; there is no punishment involved; the proceeding is not a criminal one. He just disobeyed—a term that for a Latin lawyer's ear is likely to suggest a parent-child relation, rather than a court-party relation—he has disobeyed the court, he has been a bad boy, and he has to stand in the corner until he changes his mind. Nothing mysterious about it!

The enforcement device known to the civil law of the Latin countries, which is compared frequently to the contempt sanction,[5] is the French "astreinte." This is a pecuniary sanction imposed by the court for every single future act or single period of violation of a judicial decision. This sanction can either consist in the simple means of liquidation of damages *in futuro* or have a comminatory or coercive character. The line between the two forms is not always easily drawn, but it is obvious that only to the extent to which the astreinte has the latter character is it an enforcement device at all, and only to that extent does it fall within the scope of our investigations.

It is true that some apparently impressive instances of strong pressure exerted by astreintes assessed in amounts obviously beyond any possible liquidation of damages can be found and are often quoted in support of the analogy. We believe, however, that a closer analysis of the astreinte not only shows that its role is altogether incomparable, in terms of legal reality, with that of the sanction for contempt but also illuminates the deep contrast in the political approach to the problems of enforcement.

First of all, the decision of a tribunal granting an astreinte never operates in personam. That is to say, the debtor can never be imprisoned for nonperformance of the order. This evidently takes away the usefulness of astreinte in cases where the inadequacy of damages is due to the difficulty of collecting them. Second, and this is their most surprising feature, astreintes do not operate in rem either. Strange as it seems, *creditors cannot collect the astreinte* that has been assessed by the court. No process by execution or otherwise assists them. The decision remains on a merely platonic plane. If, despite the judicial threat, the debtor persists in his refusal to comply, the only thing the creditor can do is to go back to the tri-

---

[5] See Amos, "Specific Performance in French Law," 17 L. Q. Rev. 372 at 373 (1901); Brodeur, "The Injunction in French Jurisprudence," 14 *Tulane L. Rev.* 211 (1940).

bunal in order to make the provisional decision final.[6] But this making the decision final is a somewhat euphemistic description of what really happens to the first decision through the process of "finalization." In it, the astreinte judgment is, and has to be, *deprived* of every comminatory element and reduced to a simple liquidation of damages. Planiol and Ripert describe in the following way the dilemma confronting the French judges:

Now the amount actually collected by the creditor must be measured by the damage suffered by him and serves only to repair it. Indeed, either the judges intended from the beginning to render a final decision, and they had to confine themselves to the allowance of damages calculated in the usual way; or they intended to render a comminatory judgment whose amount they could fix arbitrarily but which cannot be enforced as it is and is subject to revision in order to be reduced to an assessment of damages. This is to say, the penal element which it may be appeared at the beginning, will vanish at this moment and will not materialize.[7]

As the French Supreme Court puts it, an astreinte is *either* comminatory *or* final.[8]

In other words, the French judge finds himself in the somewhat peculiar position of one who may threaten but who may not carry out his threat. Strictly speaking, astreinte becomes nothing more than strong language intended to impress the recalcitrant loser of a law suit. If, however, the latter is not impressed to the point of performance, so much the worse for the winner. The court has done for him all it possibly could do: it used strong language against his opponent. It is an open secret that before giving the winner title for execution the court *must* reduce the amount of the astreinte to the size of the damage suffered. True enough, there is every reason to expect that in assessing such damages the court will solve many if not all doubts about the actual amount of the damage in favor of the

[6] E.g. Coquelin v. Société des Comédiens Français, (Ct. App. Paris, April 21, 1896) Dalloz 1897.2.177, 182; Consorts Lantzenberg v. Veuve Dreyfus, (Ct. App. Dijon, April 28, 1910) Dalloz 1912.2.36; Fouché v. Consorts Chancerelle, (S. Ct., Jan. 20, 1913) Sirey 1913.1.388; Société hôtelière de Marseille et de la Riviera v. Comte de Beauregard, (Ct. App. Aix, Feb. 15, 1937) Dalloz Hebdo. 1937.211.

[7] 7 Planiol and Ripert, *Traité pratique de droit civil français* 95 (1931).

[8] Galbrum v. Durand, (S. Ct., March 14, 1927) Sirey 1927.1.232.

winner. But this judicial discretion is strictly limited by the court's duty to explain in its opinion the way in which the damage has been appraised (duty to motivate). It is safe to say, therefore, that there is nothing in the powers of a French tribunal in this respect that might exceed the powers inherent in the Anglo-American system of assessment of damages by unmotivated jury verdict.

One cannot help wondering why the French tribunals use astreinte at all if it is just an unrealizable threat. The answer is probably twofold. First of all it must be remembered—and astreinte is a revealing institution from this viewpoint—that shadows and ghosts and words and powerless threats have a reality of their own. They might and in fact do impress people, laymen and lawyers, to an extent far greater than that justified by rational expectation. In the second place, the somewhat futile comminatory astreinte is still the first step toward the "final astreinte" which consists in the anticipatory liquidation of damages generously measured and payable from period to period. The efficacy of the periodical form given to the compensatory sanction increases, of course, its secondary deterring effect. But this is, by and large, all that can be said to explain the existence of astreinte. In investigating the psychology of a game one may discover that bluffing is an important weapon and maintain, if in the mood for paradoxes, that to have or not have cards in one's hands does not make much difference. But we should not be misled by elegant contemplations on the marginal effects of an institution lest we lose sight of its main lines. Astreinte is an institution substantially different from contempt of court. It is a bluffing threat by naked words and does not really add to the dignity of the courts, at least as understood in the common-law countries. The truth of the matter is that the French—judges, lawyers, and laymen—do not believe in what constitutes the essence of the Anglo-American legal system, i.e., the existence of an inherent contempt power of judges as a fundamental attribute of their being judges. Characteristically enough, a scholar of the standing of Professor Esmein felt the necessity of writing a learned article in which, with the help of historical and political arguments, he attempted to prove that French judges do have contempt powers, and tried to give a foundation to astreinte

[49]

in its comminatory character.[9] But his has been and is a *vox clamans in deserto*. His main contention, that judges have imperium—a self-evident truth to every common lawyer—presents itself to the French public as a heterodox doctrine militating against the general consensus of jurists and politicians. The work of Esmein has been largely admired, widely quoted, unanimously rejected. In the field of astreinte the French judges could never get rid of a certain timidity, an unequivocal symptom of their "bad conscience." Esmein tried in vain to tranquilize them (and in so doing he was abandoning his basis of inherent-imperium doctrine) by pointing to some secondary provisions of the French Code. But the provisions were actually saying the contrary of what Esmein attempted to read into them, and every lawyer knew it. One of the highest courts of France, the Conseil d'Etat, speaking of the astreinte, considered it a useful and necessary contrivance but without any juridical foundation and a *"procédé antijuridique."* [10] Instead of a self-evident, primary, and fundamental attribute that judges possess as a matter of principle, we find in France an arrangement confined to the back yard of legal principles, created timidly on the margin of, and perhaps against, the Code, this sacred and dominating body of law, an enforcement device surprisingly enough not enforceable itself.

It must be added that in Latin countries other than France even this timid "astreinte," this shadow of contempt proceedings, has been considered a tyrannical device opening the door to the worst evils of judicial arbitrariness.[11] Indeed, despite the wide influence exercised by the French civil code in almost all countries of the romance language group of Europe and America, in none of them, with the exception of one Swiss canton, Geneva, has astreinte been received. A few unsuccessful attempts to introduce it have been

---

[9] Esmein, "L'Origine et la logique en matière d'astreintes," 2 *Revue trimestrielle de droit civil* 5 (1903).

[10] Le Noir, (Council of State, Jan. 27, 1933) Dalloz 1934.3.68.

[11] Belgium: Commune d'Engis v. Compagnie d'Electricité de Seraing, (S. Ct., Jan. 24, 1924) Pasicrisie Belge 1924.1.151; Italy: 2 Giorgi, *Teoria delle obligazioni nel diritto moderno italiano*, 7th rev. ed., 238 (1930); Argentina: 3 Machado, *Exposición y comentario del codigo civil argentina* 349 (1932); Colombia: 6 Velez, *Derecho civile colombiano* 229 (1926).

made in Europe and in America. The lack of such attempts in the majority of the countries, and their failure where they were made, seem equally revealing of a certain historical tradition, if not of a deep-rooted conception of legal relations at large.

This conception is clearly distinguishable, to say the least, from that prevailing in the common-law countries. While Anglo-American equity bluntly confesses to act in personam, the idea which dominates the civil law of the Latin type is still *nemo ad praecise factum cogi potest*.[12] What is meant by this formula is not simply that a man *cannot* be coerced into acting in a certain way. That statement would be of a doubtful philosophical value. Indeed, if no line between coercion and inducement were drawn, the statement would be incorrect: *coactus voluit tamen voluit,* says another handy Latin maxim. If, on the other hand, the line between inducement and coercion were drawn somewhere, the statement would mean simply that an event is not an *act* if it is coerced, and thus shrink to mere tautology. But under a philosophical cloak, the formula offers political content, and mirrors the conviction that courts cannot, that is to say, *should not*, use personal coercion upon a man in order to obtain his acting in a certain way.

The most common form of personal coercion is represented, probably throughout the world, by the sanctions of the penal law, and these obtain, of course, on the European Continent to the same extent as elsewhere. But the uniqueness of the common-law sanction consisting in imprisonment for civil contempt lies in the fact that, unlike the criminal sanctions, it is imposed not so much *quia peccatum est*, not as a *consequence* of a certain act, but *ut agitur*, in order to provoke an act. The legal significance of punishment is in its etiological character, whereas that of the contempt sanction is in its teleological aspect; punishment is mainly a willed *consequence* of human behavior; jail for contempt is mainly a *means* of bringing about certain behavior. Even when the criminal sanctions are explained not on the theory of retribution but on that of deterrence (*ne peccetur* as opposed to the *quia peccatum est*), the intended effect is that of an indirect action upon men generally, not that of

---

[12] See 7 Planiol and Ripert, *Traité pratique de droit civil français* 76 (1931).

directly coercing the punished person into a certain behavior. It is true, of course, that whatever be the theory upon which punishment is predicated, the threat of punishment induces the threatened to behave in a certain way, and that this effect looms large in the intentions of the lawmakers. But the contempt sanction still differs from the punitive one in the exclusiveness of its coercive purpose, in its functional structure well adapted to its aim. The magnitude of the pressure is measured not by what has been done (be it the heinousness of the crime or other elements) but by the resistance to be overcome. Once the will of the person subject to treatment is bent, coercion ceases. The judge jailing the reluctant party engages in an active struggle with the will of the latter, and as soon as he changes his attitude he is freed, even though the injury which caused the proceedings has meanwhile become incapable of reparation. The future behavior of the defendant or of other individuals is incomparably less in the foreground in a criminal case. What happened—the crime—is now beyond the powers of judges and parties. The law imposes certain consequences, and repentance, reparation, good behavior, reformation, and future deterrence are only secondary characters in the play. In every type of society you can jail a man or put him to death *because* he did something. But in many societies the doubt is raised whether it is proper to jail him for a single day *in order* to do violence to his incoercible freedom to do or not to do something. Has society an enforceable claim to his specific behavior? Everywhere that contempt sanction obtains the answer is "yes"; where it is missing, the answer is "no."

The same criterion makes it possible to distinguish the contempt sanction (particularly in its pecuniary form) from the sanction of damages and other noncriminal sanctions. Here again it must be conceded and pointed out, from the outset, that an element of coercion or inducement is obviously present in every sanction. What makes for the uniqueness of the contempt sanction is that it is the only one which, in order to achieve the restoration of the legal order, counts upon and aims to provoke the co-operation of the debtor. All other sanctions rely upon a certain behavior of agents of the government directly aiming at the achievement of certain objective results consisting generally in the transmission to the injured party of certain things and/or values from the possession or ownership of the debtor. The structure and mechanism of the sanctions is shaped in a way to dispense completely with co-operation. As matter of fact, the debtor is not expected to *act*, and not even to *forbear* to act, but only to *suffer* other people's action, to *pati*.

Execution, e.g., is not directed against the debtor, whose person remains free from every compulsion, but only against his goods. He might care to stop the march of execution through voluntary compliance. And in this sense every sanction functions as inducement or coercion of the debtor. But this is a collateral and accidental aspect of sanctions other than those for contempt: they may be brought to ultimate and satisfactory conclusion without having exercised the slightest effect upon the debtor's behavior. Only the contempt sanction is directed against the debtor's person, has its magnitude measured not by that of the wrong committed or the injury inflicted but by the expected resistance and the need of bending the reluctant will. Inducement or coercion is not a secondary, accidental, or implicit aspect of this sanction, but represents its essential and exclusive functions conditioning and shaping its structure. The sanction for civil contempt stands alone as a *pure enforcement device*; its sole and avowed purpose is that, declared impossible by Continental law, of *cogi ad praecise factum*, i.e., to coerce a man into a certain behavior.[13]

It is probable that at this point the question spontaneously arises: what are the remedies upon which the creditor in Latin countries may count? These remedies consist primarily in the award of damages. This is of course a common-law remedy as well, being the typical, if not the only, remedy at law as distinguished from equitable relief.

Let us see, therefore, how this common remedy of damages works in the two legal systems. For if, by any chance, the remedy of damages were stronger in the civil-law countries than in the common-law countries, this could offset the weakness derived from the lack of

---

[13] For an attempt at a general classification of enforcement devices somewhat along the above lines, see Pekelis, *Diritto come volontà costante* 94–104, 121–131 (1931).

specific relief. But on examination of the two systems, it appears that the opposite is true.

Take, for instance, the case of libel or slander: in many cases the issue fought by the lawyer in this country is to find out whether or not special damages have to be shown in order to make the defendant liable. The ruling of the court that the plaintiff must show special damages because the oral defamation did not fall into any of the classes of slander per se is often considered a substantial defeat for the plaintiff. But this is all a plaintiff in a typical Latin country can reasonably hope for in any event; the idea of getting what is called here general damages does not even occur to him. The only recovery he can secure in any case is these meager special damages, and he knows that he has to prove specifically and concretely each and every penny thereof. It is true that you speak sometimes about moral or nonpecuniary damages. But how modest and cautious they are! According to the doctrine prevailing in Italy, they may be awarded only in the case of a criminal offense, and even there some writers contend that the monetary reparation is justified only to the extent to which these moral damages have produced financial loss.[14] The same result obtains substantially in Latin American countries.[15] The rule is even more strict in Germany.[16] In France and in Belgium, things are apparently different, but a student who makes the effort to go beyond the words of the decisions and look into the actual awards of damages will find rather instructive results. Thus, in defamation cases the awards average between 5,000 fr. ($200) and 100 fr. ($4). And these latter cases are by no means six-cent verdicts; they are considered to be genuine compensation for

---

[14] E.g. Ronsini v. Lettieri, (S. Ct., May 21, 1932) Il Foro Italiano (1932) 57.1.1322, and Unione Italiana Tramways Electrici v. Marugo, (S. Ct., May 7, 1934) *Rivista di diritto privato* 1935.2.17. See also Montel, "La Réparation des dommages moraux en droit italien," 64 *Bulletin de la Société de Législation Comparée* 361 (1934).

[15] E.g., for Argentina: Scaramuzzi v. Parma, (Ct. App. Rio de Janeiro, June 18, 1907) Juris. Civil V 187.394. For Brazil, see 5 Clovis Bevilaqua, *Codigo civil, commentado*, 4th ed., 321 (1939).

[16] Bürgerliches Gesetzbuch, (1938) art. 253. See also zu Dohna, "Die Stellung der Busse im reichsrechtlichen System des Immaterialgueterrechts," 1 *Abhandlungen des kriminalistischen Seminars an der Universität Berlin*, N.F., No. 4, esp. 443–444 (1902).

the injury suffered. Malicious and intentional libel by big news-papers results as a rule in verdicts for about 500 fr. ($20), hardly enough to compensate the unfortunate plaintiff for the inconven-ience of prosecution, and certainly by no means a deterrent penalty.[17] In a single case there was a substantial deviation from the average range of recovery. A French nobleman, M. de Brissac, succeeded in collecting 75,000 fr. ($3,000) from an American motion picture company,[18] but even that sum does not appear substantial when compared with the £25,000 ($125,000) awarded in 1934 by an Eng-lish jury in the analogous case of *Princess Youssoupoff* v. *Metro-Goldwyn-Mayer*.[19] That is why a European newspaper would classify under the heading "Things American"—"Americana"—the news that a girl in New York has been awarded $5,000 because the defendant kissed her in the street.

These instances are but an illustration of the general contrast, based, on the one hand, upon the existence of such institutions as exemplary or multiple damages and, on the other, upon the idea—fundamental for the modern civil lawyer—that damages are strictly a compensation for injury suffered. This explains why he does not understand institutions such as nominal, punitive, and multiple damages. The concept that, while judicially ascertaining your dam-ages to amount to $100, the judge may award you $200 or $300 simply does not fit into the structure of a contemporary civil-law system. And the comparative investigation of the law of damages only stresses further the greater energy of the common-law enforce-ment technique.

Thus, considering, among other instances, the "civil" contempt of court involving fine and imprisonment, thinking of punitive and multiple damages, we cannot help feeling that the line separating public law and private law in Europe is far less clear-cut in Anglo-

---

[17] E.g. Callman-Lévy and Psichari (Anatole France) v. X., (Ct. App. Paris, April 24, 1936) Dalloz-Hebdo. 1936.319; and Me. Roche v. Bozon Viallé, (Ct. App. Chambéry, Oct. 22, 1936) Gaz. Pal. 1936.2.780. See also Givord, *La Réparation du préjudice moral* 258 (1938).

[18] De Brissac v. Société Paramount des Films, (Civ. Trib., Dec. 1, 1926) Dalloz-Hebdo. 1927.127.

[19] (Ct. App. 1934) 50 T.L.R. 581, 99 A.L.R. 864.

American countries, and that a certain *penalistic flavor* is a characteristic of the whole common-law system. But it is probably impossible fully to understand the true spirit of the common law without recognizing and frankly admitting its religious and moralistic character. The philosophy of the civil-law countries is that law has to do with the *external* behavior of man in society, and questions of conscience are reserved to the moral forum. The law has to translate its aims in a series of *objective* rules which will be the guide of the individual, who is bound only by what is said, and who is free where loopholes are to be found in the network of the laws. Franz von Liszt, the great German criminologist, used to contend that the criminal code is the Magna Charta of the criminal.[20] No law, and particularly no court, shall meddle with the conscience of the litigants. While this is the secular civil-law approach, we have on the other side, in England, a Court of Chancery, which had its very origin in the aim, to use its own words, to meddle with the "Conscience of the Party." [21] The Court of Chancery was of course not an ecclesiastical court: but it is just its secular structure and its secular functions that make certain aspects of its tradition significant. The fact that until 1529 the Lord Chancellor had always been a high ecclesiastic dignitary, that he exercised civil jurisdiction in his capacity of the Keeper of the King's Conscience, and that his devices were those used widely in ecclesiastic tribunals contribute to the obliteration of a clear-cut line between the techniques of ecclesiastic and secular courts. And we are not surprised to find lay chancellors using a typically ecclesiastical language. For instance, the opinion in the famous case of the Duke of Norfolk, decided as late as 1682, was based in part on the reasoning that certain long-lasting arrangements of property holdings could not be protected by the law because they disclosed a mentality inconsistent with that of a true Christian: "Such do fight," said Lord Nottingham, "against God,

---

[20] Von Liszt, "Die deterministischen Gegner der Zweckstrafe," 13 *Zeitschrift fuer die gesamte Strafrechtswissenschaft* 325 at 357 (1893).

[21] Arguments Proving from Antiquity the Dignity, Power, and Jurisdiction of the Court of Chancery, 1 Chan. Rep. (Appendix) 1 at 47, 21 Eng. Rep. 576 at 587 (1616).

for they pretend to such a stability in human affairs as the nature of them admits not of." [22]

The influence of religious beliefs upon the economic development and the very origin of English capitalism has been the subject of many valuable and famous studies.[23] The influence of religious philosophy and ecclesiastical technique upon the substantive and adjective law was not less important. As a matter of fact, this influence is probably the only factor in the development of Anglo-American legal institutions that can show a continuity of more than a thousand years. Almost two centuries before the Norman invasion, Alfred the Great thought it advisable to begin his Dooms with the re-enactment of a somewhat revised edition of the Ten Commandments. Thus, in section 3 he made legislatively certain that "in six days Christ wrought the Heavens and the Earth, the Seas and All Creatures that are in them and rested on the seventh day and therefore the Lord hallowed it." [24] And the Commandments are still a part of the law of the land. Thus, a few months ago, a judge in Pittsburgh held a witness in contempt of court who, in a divorce suit, said, "My mother is not a lady." "Honor thy father and thy mother, as the Lord thy God hath commanded thee," says the Bible. American tradition backs the Pittsburgh judge. We find, for instance, a paragraph in the Blue Laws of New Haven reciting: "If any child above sixteen years old and of sufficient understanding shall curse or smite his natural father or mother he shall be put to death . . . Exodus Ch. 21, verse 17; Leviticus 20; Exodus 20:15." The same provision is to be found in section 13 of the 1671 version of the Liberties of the Massachusetts Bay Colony. We all know that biblicism was extremely strong in American colonial life; a great number of the laws enacted in New England contained as a usual feature a reference to the biblical passage deemed to be their truest source of authority. To "deny God or His creation or government of

---

[22] Duke of Norfolk's Case, 3 Cas. Ch. 1 at 31, 22 Eng. Rep. 931 (1682).

[23] See, e.g., Max Weber, *The Protestant Ethic and the Spirit of Capitalism*, translated by Parsons (1930); Tawney, *Religion and the Rise of Capitalism* (1926).

[24] Thorpe, *Ancient Law and Institutes of England* 44–45 (1840).

the world" was one of the capital offenses in the Massachusetts Colony, and probably not there alone.

One of the most impressive consequences of the influence exercised by the ecclesiastic procedural technique through the medium of the equity courts upon the administration of justice at large is to be found in the creation of a closer, almost confessional atmosphere in the relation between the court and the party. This somewhat vague atmosphere has materialized in at least two very precise legal relationships, which can be described as the duty of disclosure and its far-reaching complement, the right of investigation. The decisive importance of this duty and this right for our investigation becomes clear when we consider that, under the rules of civil procedure in Latin countries, no person may testify under oath in his own cause, not even if willing to do so. You cannot be a witness in your own case any more than you can be a judge in your own case. In the Anglo-American system, on the contrary, every party has the right today to testify under oath in his own case, and has, as a rule, a strong interest in doing so. It is true that we sometimes see a party take an oath in, say, an Italian or a French court, but never as a *witness*. The party may swear upon a given formula. He cannot be examined, much less cross-examined. The party's oath is not a means of finding the truth; it is rather a means of closing a litigation haphazardly, or a chance taken by a party who feels he is going to lose and tries to put his opponent under pressure by making him swear to his allegations. This, of course, makes the party oath an institution of very limited practical importance, and it is in no way comparable to the cross-examination of the parties under oath which takes place in the common-law countries. Prior to 1933 there were a few exceptions to this rule; the most prominent of these was the Austrian *Parteivernehmung*, shaped expressly on the British pattern,[25] and an outstanding and rare instance of successful reception of a common-law institution on the European Continent.

The situation of the defendant in a criminal proceeding is not less significant. I do not know of a single civil-law country in Europe or

---

[25] See 2 Pollak, System des Oesterreichischen Zivilprozessrechts mit Einschluss des Exekutionsrechtes 2d ed., 687–688 (1932).

America in which the defendant in a criminal suit is allowed to take the stand in order to make declarations under oath. This is, however, the defendant's privilege today in England and in all but one of the American jurisdictions, a situation perfectly in line with one of the most basic chancery traditions. This right of the defendant to testify is, of course, at the same time quite a burden, and the defendant who fails to avail himself of the privilege is liable as a matter of fact to discredit himself in the eyes of his judges. At the International Congress of Criminal Law held in Palermo in 1933, the question of the defendant's oath appeared to be almost the only point of unbridgeable conflict between the common and the civil lawyers.[26] The attitude of the latter was that the defendant has to be given a chance in his struggle against the accusation. After the criminal code, the code of criminal procedure becomes the Magna Charta of the criminal. The argument of the civil lawyers—and it is noteworthy that one of the most violent indictments of the United States's system of criminal proceedings was read by the delegate from Cuba— was that in order to make the common-law guarantees against self-incrimination effective, not only the duty but also the right to testify in their own case must be taken from the parties; otherwise the *prejudice de facto* is an incentive to perjury.

This sweeping duty of disclosure in Anglo-American countries is beyond doubt of ancient origin. The Court of Chancery subpoenaed the defendant to present himself before the court and to file under oath an answer containing the full disclosure of all facts pertaining to the cause. This duty of disclosure reached its climax in the proceedings before the High Commission and its ex officio oath, which invited the thunders of Sir Edward Coke, who argued that judges "ought not examine *partem ream,* upon their oath." To prove the point, he explicitly had recourse to a civil-law principle, and went on to say "for as a civilian said, that this was *inventio diaboli ad destruendas miserorum animas ad infernum."* [27] The High Commission disappeared, King Charles I was beheaded, but

---

[26] Troisième Congrès international de droit pénal, Actes du Congrès 491–533 (1935).

[27] 12 Coke 26, 77 Eng. Rep. 1308 (1607).

it is still the spirit of the chancery, and not that of Lord Coke, which rules common-law procedure.

The importance of the right to investigate and of the duty to disclose goes, in Anglo-American society, far beyond the scope of judicial activity. Even where there is no question of violation of existing laws, an individual may be subpoenaed to appear before an administrative agency or a legislative investigating committee and disclose every detail of his business and his life, and a subpoena *duces tecum* may order him to produce every possible kind of record or document pertinent to the inquiry. We tried to explain elsewhere the reasons for our belief that the power of the American administrative agencies and the scope of their activity are much greater than those of administration in civil-law countries.[28] Here it is enough to stress the fact that the subpoena is the main weapon of administrative and legislative investigating bodies. Without the duty to disclose, their activities are unthinkable, and indeed an investigation as sweeping, for instance, as that described by Judge Pecora in his *Wall Street under Oath* [29] is a phenomenon practically unknown in the civil-law countries. In France, for instance, the powers of the parliamentary committees are uncertain at best, and the success of their investigations practically depends upon the willingness of witnesses to testify.[30] The timid legislative reform of 1914 failed to change the situation substantially, but did not escape the vigilant attention of leading constitutional lawyers and statesmen, who, like Duguit, Barthélemy, and Reynaud, were ready to see in it an obvious violation of the doctrine of separation of powers and a curtailment of the fundamental rights of man and citizen.[31] The ideological strength of this individualistic principle was such that

---

[28] See the next essay.

[29] Pecora, *Wall Street under Oath; the Story of Our Modern Money Changers* (1939).

[30] See Joseph Barthélemy, *Essai sur le travail parlementaire et le système des commissions* 245 (1934) (International Institute of Public Law, Vol. 5).

[31] See 4 Duguit, *Traité de droit constitutionnel*, 2d ed., 398 *et seq.* (1924); Barthélemy, "Les Limites du pouvoir législatif," 125 *Revue politique et parlementaire* 355 *et seq.* (1925); *Le Temps*, Nov. 14, 1925.

even the indignation provoked by events like the Panama scandal
or the Stavisky affair was not sufficient to swing the balance of
public opinion. Not even in Germany, where the Weimar constitution followed the English precedent by introducing the principle of parliamentary investigation, was the situation different. An
early episode is probably sufficient to show the difficulties with
which the reception of the common law on European soil usually
meets. The German right-wing leader Helfferich, while testifying
before a parliamentary committee, declared that he would not
answer any question put to him by Oscar Cohn, one of the members of the committee. The outraged committee, in the climax of
its fury, assessed a fine of no less than 300 semi-inflated marks. The
order was sent for collection to a local court, which apparently upheld certain procedural exceptions of the contumacious witness and
canceled the fine.[32] It is highly probable that an English or American committee would, in a similar case, have kept Mr. Helfferich in
jail "as long as we please." [33]

It is important for the purpose of our investigation to note that
this far-reaching duty of disclosure in common-law countries has
its roots not only in the clerical and moralistic manners of approach
we have spoken about but also in another characteristic of the
common-law tradition. This feature is represented by the importance of the control that the community at large exercises over the
individual. To a certain extent the law represents always and everywhere social custom and public opinion about what is wrong and
what is right. But the common-law countries possess a series of
institutions which succeed in maintaining a constant relationship
between the state of law and the state of public opinion, and particularly the state of opinion of the immediate community to which
a given individual belongs.

The main device through which this constant check is effectuated
is probably the institution of the jury, and, possibly even more, of
the grand jury. Trial by jury is the birthright of every Englishman,

---

[32] See W. Jellinek, "Revolution und Reichsverfassung," 9 *Jahrbuch des oeffentlichen Rechts der Gegenwart* 1 at 91 (1920).

[33] See, e.g., *Cong. Globe*, 42d Cong., 3d sess. (1873), p. 982.

accepted and guaranteed in the Constitution of the United States. It may be worth while to recall some of the ancient English institutions, which may place in relief the true significance of the jury.

One of these institutions is the tithing, or the frankpledge. It is an old Saxon institution that existed in England long before the Norman conquest, and the Norman invaders were only too glad to develop and strengthen it. It is said that each boy, on reaching the age of fourteen, was obliged to find some such pledge or be *committed to prison*,[34] and it is an interesting circumstance that the frankpledge was not unknown to Colonial America, and seems to have been in effect in Pennsylvania.[35]

We do not think there is any need to comment on the significance of such an institution. Its underlying philosophy is obviously that it is the quality of being a good neighbor that makes a man a good citizen, or better, a citizen at all, that gives him his political status and his personal liberty. Other institutions were inspired by the same philosophy. Take, for instance, the compurgation, or wager of law. A defendant in a criminal or civil proceeding could purge himself by his simple oath, provided, of course, he presented himself to the court with a sufficient number of oath-helpers, or compurgators. This means, of course, that good neighborliness not only imposed certain duties but could pay very well indeed in certain contingencies through this institution of the wager of law. The latter was common to all Teutonic tribes, but England is the only country in which, as late as 1833, it required statutory abolition.[36]

Against this background, the origin of the jury takes on a particular meaning. It is to be remembered that this reform was not imposed, as some seem still inclined to think, by humanitarian reformers against a cruel royal tyranny. The jury, a device invented by the royal courts, was sometimes rather cruelly imposed upon litigants or at least upon certain types of litigants. A descendant of Norman conquerors, in his "rugged individualism," probably

[34] Blount, A *Law-Dictionary* (1670), "Frank Pledge" and "View of Frankpledge."
[35] For an urgent recommendation to introduce the frankpledge, see Granville Sharp, A *General Plan for Laying Out Towns and Townships on the New-acquired Land in the East Indies, America or Elsewhere* 13–15 (1794).
[36] 3 & 4 Will. IV, c. 42, § 13 (1833).

would consider as his inalienable birthright the right to a trial by battle, and not a trial by jury, which would expose him to the mercy of his peers. He wanted to fight his opponent sword in hand, and kill him or hear the groveling word "craven" issue from his throat —even at the risk of being killed himself. And even the humble Saxon would sometimes prefer the terrible trial by ordeal, the judgment of God, who in His infinite mercy and justice had so many times miraculously saved innocents from accusation and persecution. Rather a deal with God than with the neighbors, who had been bad neighbors to him or to whom he had been a bad neighbor. Of course, the more peaceful part of the population was only too happy to pronounce the sacramental words that represented the waiver of their birthright to the ancient forms of trial, and say, "I put myself upon the country, for better or for worse." But a few of them would refuse to pronounce these words, and rather than submit to the ersatz of the voice of God—the voice of the people— they would submit to the *peine forte et dure*, being pressed to death.

We think that the jury, not only in its historical origins but also in its practical functioning, particularly in the small and medium-sized communities, represents a principle manifestly contrasting with the more formalistic or legalistic functioning of a Latin court appointed by a central authority. This method of selecting the judiciary, especially since it is coupled with the fact that—at least in civil proceedings—the personal appearance of the parties is a rare occurrence, tends to dehumanize the trial. Not only does the judge not know John or Jack personally, as in some small communities the jurors do, but the considerations of being liked or disliked by his neighbors cannot generally affect the judge's appraisal. He has before him certain facts, or, better still, certain legal facts, and to these facts, *as they appear in the files*, he has to apply the law.

One of the fundamental principles of civil-law procedure is that a fact-finding tribunal cannot use in the trial its private knowledge of the facts in issue.[37] In theory, analogous rules exist in common-

---

[37] See F. Stein, *Das private Wissen des Richters, Untersuchungen zum Beweisrecht beider Prozesse* 138 *et seq.* (1893); 2 (Dalloz) Savatier, *Nouveau Dictionnaire pratique de droit* 224 (1933).

law countries. But it is of course an open question to what extent the personal knowledge of the jurors gathered from newspapers and even from back-fence gossip may influence their decision. The old rule that the jurors *had* to know the facts of their own knowledge has of course long been reversed. Nevertheless, more than one defendant could, even today, make the old objection: "These men have their hearts big against me and hate me because of this ill report which is surmised against me," and therefore refuse to put himself upon "the good folk of this Vill." [38] It is often said that the institution of the jury is declining in America and England.[39] However, the reliance upon the judgment of the community and particularly the small community is still extremely strong. The mobilization of millions of soldiers in a nation at war through the selection system operated by local draft boards is certainly a new triumph for the law of the neighbors, and a feature unthinkable on the European Continent.[40]

Let us see how the institution of the jury works in those civil-law countries in which this institution is known. Once again the picture is easily drawn, the differences being of macroscopic dimensions. To begin with, there the jury *never* intervenes in private litigations, nor does it deal with misdemeanors, except possibly those committed by the press. Thus, in effect trial by jury is limited to felonies—or better—certain exceptional classes of felonies, numerically an insignificant fraction of the total judicial life. Of particular interest is the fate of the jury in Latin America. Many of the South American constitutions, following the example of the United States, explicitly declared the jury to be the birthright of every citizen, a guarantee of democracy. Actually, however, the jury system has never assumed great importance in the South American countries.[41] In some nations, in spite of the constitutional re-

---

[38] *The Court Baron*, Maitland and Baildon, ed., 4 *Publications of the Selden Society* 63 (1891).

[39] See, e.g., Howard, *Criminal Justice in England* 308–310 (1931); Emery, "Government by Jury," 24 *Yale L. J.* 265 (1915).

[40] Compare also the functioning of local rationing boards described by R. Oppenheimer in a forthcoming article in 43 *Col. L. Rev.* (1943).

[41] See 3 Garcia, *Juicio oral*, esp. pp. 520–566 (1938); M. Costa, *O Jury* (1938),

ception of the jury, no statutes were ever passed providing for trial by jury. Other countries, while passing such statutes, limited them commonly to criminal cases, and even there the jury was not favorably received and was applied to a very limited number of cases. In several recent revisions of codes of criminal procedure, trial by jury has been almost completely eliminated because, to use a characteristic expression of a Mexican writer, the jury is "contrary to the rhythm of judicial life in Mexico." [42]

The German experience is strikingly similar. The jury, which had been introduced in the German legal world under the influence of the French Revolution, was abolished by simple governmental decree in 1924. With the exception of a few experts, this act was met with almost complete indifference in the country.[43] One can imagine how different would have been the reaction of the people of the United States had a president tried to abolish trial by jury by executive order—even in the midst of an emergency as grave as the one Germany was facing in 1924.

In civil-law countries the jury plays almost no political role whatsoever, and does not have that social significance which it has in England and the United States. A study by Dr. Alvin Johnson has shown the educational importance of the jury in a small New England community.[44] Alexis de Tocqueville remarked, more than a century ago, that if trial by jury is not always the best possible way to accomplish justice for the parties, it is of the greatest moral benefit to the jurors. But the jury is not only the object of education—it is also an educator.[45] In amplifying this, we have to consider that in civil-law countries the jury—if it intervenes at all—can render only a decision analogous to the common-law "special verdict," that is, the jury has to answer specific interrogatories limited

---

passim, and Bergé, "Etude sur le jury en droit comparé," 6 *Revue de l'Institut de Droit Comparé* 1 at 7–14, 86 *et seq.* (1913).

[42] Gonzales Bustamante, *Principios de derecho procesal penal mexicano* 189 (1941).

[43] See Mannheim, "Trial by Jury in Modern Continental Criminal Law," 53 *L. Q. Rev.* 388 at 404 (1937).

[44] Johnson, "The Substance of American Democracy," *Political and Economic Democracy*, ed. Ascoli and Lehmann, 318 at 320–321 (1937).

[45] 2 De Tocqueville, *Democracy in America*, translated by Reeve, 2d ed., 195–200 (1836).

as far as possible strictly to questions of fact. In this country, on the contrary, it is the duty of the trial court to expound the law to the jury. The jurors are not only going to ascertain the facts; it is equally their function to apply to those facts the law which the trial court has had to explain or translate to them. This job of translating law into plain, popular language, or of reviewing the translation made by the court below, to which the most influential class of common lawyers—I mean the judges—are daily compelled, is a kind of job that a European jurist faces perhaps once in his life, when, rather reluctantly, he has to deliver a paper on legal problems at what is called over there a people's university. The everyday link between judge and jury, between law and plain English, makes again for the popular, neighborly character of the common-law institutions. This may also be one of the many reasons why the common-law writers indulge less in efforts at generalization and systematization than do the civil-law writers. The need to expound the law to a lay jury would break down every ambitious excursion into the higher spheres of jurisprudence.

If we try now to give an answer to the question we formulated at the beginning, we must say that the aspects of legal life in England and America which we have just examined do not substantiate the contention of the individualistic character of the common-law technique. On the contrary, the strength of the enforcement devices, the clerical and moralistic character of legal approach at large, the duty of disclosure, the close control exercised by the community upon the individual and upon the law, if compared with the analogous legal institutions of the Latin countries, seem to disclose rather a more collectivistic than a more individualistic character of the common-law system. Does this mean, however, that the contention of the individualistic character of the common law and of the American social structure is only and simply a commonplace? And were it but a commonplace, would not we still have to account for its rise and appeal?

We ask leave to submit an explanation and to a certain extent a reconciliation of our preceding remarks with the prevailing individualistic thesis. It seems to us that what is generally considered as and taken for the individualistic aspect of American life is simply the existence and coexistence of a plurality of communities and— let's not be afraid of this quantitative element—of an extremely great number of communities of various types. Through a kind of optical error this phenomenon of decentralization of collectivistic pressure, which by its very decentralization only *increases* in power, has sometimes been taken for individualism. "Things are so well arranged in America that the strict allegiance to collective behaviour is called individualism," remarked Max Ascoli many years ago, and added, "The highways are filled with cars running towards the solitude of the country." [46] When, for instance, such students of the structure of American society as F. J. Turner or C. W. Eliot emphasize the individualistic and antisocial character of the early American colonists, stressing at the same time the importance of the family, the group, the town, and the section, in American life,[47] they identify individualism with intolerance of a *central* authority. As a matter of fact, what they called individualism seems to be in reality collectivism within a smaller group, and what they called the antisocial tendency may be simply an antigovernmental one.

Now is this only a question of words? Is what we would call collectivism or pluricollectivism just what is usually classified as individualism? We think that, to say the least, the use of the term individualism greatly beclouds the true issue. Should it be admitted that what is typical for the English and American way of life is not the lack of social control but its decentralized character, then, e.g., the popular issue individualism and free enterprise versus collectivism and social control appears as a phantom issue that neglects the third and decisive element, the factual prevalence of a strong social control in its decentralized pluralistic form.

We could speak of an essential federalism of America and we would not, of course, have in mind just forty-eight or forty-nine American jurisdictions. We think of a wider and deeper network

---

[46] Ascoli, *Intelligence in Politics* 199 (1936).

[47] See Turner, *The Frontier in American History*, esp. 125, 258–268 (1920); Eliot, *The Conflict between Individualism and Collectivism in a Democracy*, esp. 7, 8, 31, 91 (1910).

composed of a plurality of legal systems enjoying an extremely great amount of autonomy. Not only the forty-eight states but the smaller territorial communities, the unions, the churches, the trade associations, the exclusive groups, the fraternities, the various klans, the vigilantes, the pressure groups—all these cellular organisms have their own written and unwritten laws, their own enforcement devices, their own forms of social control, their own framework of pressure. When we see the individual challenging the power of the central authority he does not, as a rule, act as an individual. He acts as a member of one of these communities. He is one of the tithing. He presents himself with his neighbors or with others with whom he has common interests. He leans upon the power that even the smallest community has.

Before the rise of the modern state, the existence of a plurality of legal orders was probably too obvious to be remarked on. But even after the claim of the state for the monopoly of lawmaking had made itself felt, the existence of nonofficial systems of law was recognized. As early as 1878, the German jurist August Thon affirmed the existence of a plurality of legal orders, some of which were even illegal, as the Roman Church under the Roman Emperors.[48] Benedetto Croce published in Italy in 1906 a clear exposition of the pluralistic theory.[49] The names of the modern English pluralists are well known.[50] But an investigation into the real structure of these legal systems, representing, so to speak, as many states within the state, is almost completely neglected. To give only a single instance, in spite of the enormous development of commercial arbitration in this country, not a single systematic report on the content of the arbitration awards has been published here. The fact would be amazing if one did not suspect that at certain stages of development lack of publicity and systematization is probably

[48] See Thon, *Rechtsnorm und subjectives Recht; Untersuchungen zur allgemeinen Rechtslehre*, esp. XI–XII, 7–8 (1878).

[49] See Croce, *Riduzione della filosofia del diritto alla filosofia dell' economia* (1907), reprinted 1926.

[50] See, among many, Figgis, *Churches in the Modern State* (1913); George D. H. Cole, *Guild Socialism Re-stated* (1920); Laski, *The State in Theory and Practice* (1935) and *Studies in the Problem of Sovereignty* (1937); Barker, *Political Thought in England from Herbert Spencer to the Present Day*, esp. 175–183 (1915).

the condition of growth, and if one did not recall the reluctance of early equity to keep records, publish reports, and become aware of its compliance with precedents.

At least to a certain extent this lack of legal data on the various minor and less formal legal organisms existing in society at large, such as the constitutions of trade unions and trade associations, etc., is probably responsible for certain formalistic limitations to the investigations of the school of institutional economics. It appears to us that studies of the forms of social or collectivistic controls of economic activity have the tendency to confine the research to the regulation exercised by legislature and court, by the legal agencies in their most narrow sense. Even when outstanding scholars go to work on topics such as monopolistic competition or the economics of imperfect competition, questions in which the consideration of the extent and ways of functioning of group behavior and group control would seem inevitable, they either maintain themselves "in an atmosphere rarefied by the adoption of very severe simplifying assumptions" [51] or limit their study mainly to the problems of state controls.[52]

We find, to be sure, that some economists discuss controlling social factors other than state control.[53] But their statements are usually either overgeneralized statements of principles or investigations on too specific topics. There appears to be as well a lack of any developed techniques or methodology for dealing with the factors of nonofficial controls, and we are probably still far from a systematic treatment of the problem of pluralism in the economic field.

It is certain that much more must be done in the field of law and in the field of economics before public opinion is to realize that the historical development of the American economy cannot

---

[51] Robinson, *Economics of Imperfect Competition* 327 (1938). See also Chamberlin, *The Theory of Monopolistic Competition* (1936).

[52] See, e.g., Burns, *The Decline of Competition* 522 (1936).

[53] See, e.g., John M. Clark, *Social Control of Business* (1939); Commons, *Legal Foundations of Capitalism* (1932); Veblen, *The Theory of Business Enterprise* (1940) and *Absentee Ownership and Business Enterprise in Recent Times: The Case of America* (1923).

be interpreted as a phenomenon of the growth of individual enterprise, and that the real choice is not, and never has been, between freedom of enterprise and state control. This historical development can be viewed only in terms of the relationship between various types of social controls and their relative checks and balances in the total economy. The complete insight into these social controls, which could be outlawed but not destroyed by these antitrust laws, is probably the prerequisite for every type of efficient economic legislation.

We cannot fully understand the political significance of the pluralistic structure unless we are aware of the fact that centralization of power and individualism are far from being contradictory and inconsistent. They may sometimes appear as concurrent and complementary concepts. A historical concurrence of this kind probably explains the tyranny of Renaissance Italy, and why France has been at the same time a typically centralized and a typically individualistic country. The distant boss, the stranger-judge, and other features of centralized government may be more favorable to the development of individualism than the pressure of government by neighbors in a decentralized state. The formalistic and legalistic approach which the very fact of centralization develops by necessity brings about a form of individualism which sees its Magna Charta even in the most severe code. It can be said, furthermore, that the connection between centralized despotism and individualistic tendencies of a country is probably a two-way proposition, and that the strong individualistic attitude of the population may be the source of a decline of political interests and communal solidarities, and become the ideal ground for the rise of antidemocratic institutions.

The strong collectivistic pressure typical for the common-law countries is, on the other hand, outweighed by the fact that the closely controlling communities are here so numerous that, as a practical matter, the great majority of individuals can find a community that suits them more or less perfectly, and to which they may adjust themselves more or less painlessly. Only the "rugged individualists," the eternal dissenters, the true outsiders will have a much harder time in the common-law countries than in what used to be in the past a typical European democracy.

The historical tradition of the pluralistic approach in England and America is very strong. We shall mention here only an example which, although on a different plane, is nonetheless an extremely significant manifestation of this way of thinking. We refer to the known episodes of the struggle among the English courts that constitute in our opinion an absolutely unique feature. The history of the European Continent knows of struggles and conflicts between barons and states, towns and empires, state and church, feudalism and central power. But it does not present us with a struggle between two courts both emanating from the same authority, fighting each other in a period in which that very authority exercised a very strong *central* power. And that is what happened during the Tudor and Stuart periods in England. The King's Bench would, for instance, render a judgment in favor of a plaintiff, but the Court of Chancery, on the prayer of the defendant, would enjoin the winning party from exercising his rights recognized by the King's Bench, and would jail him for contempt if he tried to enforce the mandate of the King's Bench. The latter would then issue a writ of habeas corpus and free him. Sir Edward Coke, Chief Justice of the King's Bench, tried even to indict the Master in Chancery under the Statute of Praemunire for having interfered with the judgment of the King's Bench, and, as Bacon said, "make the Chancellor sit under a hatchet, instead of the King's arms." [54] James I intervened in this conflict between his two courts and decided it, upon the advice of Bacon, in favor of the Chancellor, thus maintaining the plurality of independent courts in his kingdom. He fully appreciated the advantages of a legal polytheism and would not deprive the Olympus of the common law of one of its most industrious gods, the court of equity.

In a way, this royal decision, restated in England by statute in 1872,[55] is also a methodological justification of this paper. It must be conceded, indeed, that most of its conclusions rely on rules and

---

[54] 6 Bacon, *Letters and Life*, Spedding, ed., 91 (1872).
[55] The Supreme Court of Judicature Act, 1873, 36 & 37 Vic., c. 66.

practices of equity rather than on those of common law proper. If we thought this to be a proper approach, it is because equity appeared to be the ultima ratio of the Anglo-American law, prevailing wherever it came in conflict with the common law proper. We must also be conceded that the latter, considered in itself, appears rather similar to the civil law at large. But the very idea of considering common law proper *in itself* implies a disregard for the functional unity of the institutions studied. We are inclined to explain the conclusions reached by the prevailing doctrine of comparative law by a certain neglect of equitable institutions. To us the main distinguishing feature of the common-law countries is in the fact that not common law but equity prevails there. If someone were compelled to explain the essence of civil law to a common lawyer in one sentence, he could perhaps say that civil law is what common law would have been if it had never known a court of chancery. It is true that the answer would hardly be helpful, the picture suggested being probably beyond the imagination of a common lawyer.

The picture of conflicting and coexisting jurisdictions is equally inconceivable to a Latin or even a German lawyer, who believes in the *Einheit der Rechtsordnung*, the uncompromising and sometimes cruel unity of the legal order. Our late colleague, Nino Levi, had long ago noted in his special field this contrast of approach between the English and the Italian type of regulation.[56] The former left the findings of the civil and criminal courts completely independent of one another; the latter declared that the civil judge is strictly bound by the findings of the criminal court, and thus reaffirmed the irretractability of the judicial decision upon the same set of facts, and the fundamental unity of the legal order.

This need for unity probably reached one of its climaxes during the French Revolution. In 1790 two significant events took place in Paris. In that year the first steps leading to the establishment of the metric system were taken in France in order to supersede the medieval complexity of weights and measures. It is true that the French influence strongly felt in the United States in that period manifested itself also in this field through Jefferson's proposals to

---

[56] Levi, *La Parte civile nel processo penale italiano*, 2d ed., 3 (1936).

introduce a decimal division of the various units. But this project, adopted in France, was, except in the matter of the currency, rejected in this country; symmetry, legal or arithmetical, has evidently never been a decisive argument in the common-law countries.

The second event that took place in France in that very year of 1790 was the enactment of the famous *Décret sur l'Organisation Judiciaire,* directing judges to *refrain from the interpretation of laws* and to consult the central legislative authority whenever need for such interpretation should arise.[57] And we certainly do not have to point out that the adoption of a principle depriving judges of their power to interpret statutes would be inconceivable in a common-law country, even during the excitement of a revolution. Not even the *dissenting* opinions of the judges are here considered seditious or subversive. In Europe, with the significant exception of Switzerland, a judge who would dare to reveal publicly or in private conversation that he disagreed with his brethren on the bench would be guilty of grave misconduct, liable to impeachment and removal. The court is considered a unity, its voice is the *viva vox juris,* and it must be assumed that the judges can speak but in a unisonal chorus. The contrapuntal conception of law in common-law countries is shown by the importance that dissenting opinions have in the process of legal change.

We do not forget, on the other hand, that the exigency of unity and of geometric perfection of the legal world has deep roots in human nature. Ptolemy was the first man to give scientific foundation to the hypothesis that the world is a sphere. It is said that the origin of his conception was not a strictly mathematical reasoning, but rather an aesthetic intuition. Since the world could not have been created, he felt, but beautiful and perfect, and since the sphere is the most beautiful and perfect form human mind can conceive, our earth must necessarily be a sphere. I personally have always admired the pathos of abstractness which inspired such a thought. Here was a man who did not have sufficient affection and love for what makes for mortal beings the beauty of the world in which they live—the unevenness of the landscape, the shape of

---

[57] Décret sur l'Organisation Judiciare, August 16–24, 1790, Tit. II, art. 1, no. 12.

mountains, the fanciful ribbon of rivers. To him beauty was something else: an abstract and cool geometric perfection. This Egyptian certainly had in his soul the spirit of the race of Semitic shepherds who, in sleepless dreams under the nocturnal sky at the borders of the desert, conceived the dogma of monotheism.

I must add, on the other hand, that my admiration for Ptolemy is equaled only by my admiration for the man who first had the extraordinary daring to conceive the idea that while singing or playing two or more themes simultaneously you could bring about, not a terrible musical cacophony or political anarchy, but a newer, better, more perfect union and beauty. The strong fabric of the common law, the social structure of the common-law countries, building a unity of their very variety, represent one of the most astonishing achievements of legal and political contrapuntal harmony.

Civil law and common law represent, therefore, not only the two main legal systems of western civilization but also two fundamental trends of human nature. It would be childish to try to find out which one is better. It is only unfortunate that their mutual contact has so far been rather limited. A greater reciprocal influence of the ideas inspiring the two systems is probably one of the prerequisites for a real understanding between English America and Latin America and, through it, of the unity and survival of the western civilization at large. Their deeper interpenetration could eventually become an important factor in the development of less imperfect forms of human coexistence.

Administrative Discretion
and the Rule of Law

I

CURRENT DISCUSSIONS of the characteristics of the common-law countries as contrasted with those of the so-called civil-law countries emphasize the individualistic character of the former. I have undertaken elsewhere [1] a comparison between typical common-law devices of investigation and enforcement and those commonly used in civil-law countries of the Latin type. This comparison did not substantiate the current opinion. The pivotal importance for the very functioning of the Anglo-American legal system of such institutions and principles as contempt of court, duty of disclosure, and the jury system, and the lack of commensurate institutions in the civil-law systems, indicate, in fact, that the common law has a more collectivist character and that there is a pronounced individualism in legal institutions of the Latin type.

But the pressure of the community—the characteristic that I have tried to emphasize—is much more the pressure of the small community than that of the state, say, or of the nation as a whole. The pluricellular structure of American society, with its wide variety of types of communities, fraternities, unions, and churches, and its decentralization of social pressure not only make for greater specific strength but also represent, or at least until recently represented, a safety valve for the system as a whole.

---

[1] See the preceding essay.

The present paper is concerned not so much with the centrifugal forces of social structure as with certain typical manifestations of centripetal forces—more precisely, with the ever-widening activity of administrative agencies operated by the central government.

Until recently all leading writers seemed to agree that the growth of administrative agencies is a phenomenon alien to the spirit and practice of the English-speaking countries. In 1886, on the very eve of the expansion of administrative agencies, two men on opposite sides of the Atlantic were writing on the problem—Albert Venn Dicey, in England, and Woodrow Wilson in this country. The former was an already famous English constitutional lawyer, with a rather Tory background; the latter, a young American liberal. They wrote independently of each other, treated the problem differently, and reached different conclusions. But there was one point of agreement between them. The one speaking of the science of administration, the other speaking of administrative law, they declared: "It is a foreign science speaking very little of the language of English or American principle. It employs only foreign tongues; it utters none but what are to our minds alien ideas." "The absence from our language of any satisfactory equivalent for the expression *droit administratif* is significant: the want of a name arises at bottom from our non-recognition of the thing itself." This seems to be a single passage, written in the same spirit. But actually they are two, the first written by a man who strongly advocated, and the second by a man who vehemently opposed, the growth of administration. And even today many authoritative legal writers in this country and England still maintain that the rise of administrative agencies is a phenomenon repugnant to the spirit of the Anglo-American law. Thus we read in one of Dean Pound's writings:

Throughout the world there has been a revival of absolutism. Administrative absolutism in the United States is but one phase of a type of thought that has infected all the social sciences, has put its mark on international relations, on politics, on legislation and even on judicial decision. But are we, who have inherited a great tradition of justice, prepared to throw it over in order to fall in line with this post-war fashion of absolutism?

And his words are substantially in agreement with the outcry of Lord Chief Justice Hewart, whose book *The New Despotism* appeared in England twelve years ago.

It is safe to say that the essential objection to the activity of administrative agencies is directed against the extremely great amount of discretion with which they are entrusted. The administrative agency does not apply any fixed rule of law: it acts according to considerations of policy—of reason, of public convenience, of economic expediency, of national efficiency, of business fairness, of social progress. The fate of individuals subject to its jurisdiction depends largely on the discretion of the men who run the agency; and the individual is faced with a government by men and not with that government by law—say the critics—which is deemed to represent the very essence of the common-law tradition.

But is there indeed a violation of this particular tradition? In regard to concrete legal institutions, what is the actual role of discretion in the common-law system, as compared with its role in the systems prevailing on the European continent? Is it true that in common law countries the administration of justice—because bound by precise and specific precedents or because closely watched by public opinion, or for other legal or political reasons—is less influenced than in the civil-law countries by "administrative expediency"? To what extent is government by law a specific common-law tradition inconsistent with the growth of administrative agencies?

These questions cannot be answered categorically, and studies that may furnish a basis for judgment have not yet been completed. But even at the present stage of analysis it is possible to say that in common-law countries needs of public policy, exigencies of morality and efficiency, are taken into account in the ordinary administration of justice to an extent undreamed of on the European continent, and that the corresponding amount of discretion inherent in the system of Anglo-American law makes of its enforcement an activity much closer to what in civil-law countries has been considered administrative adjudication than to what has con-

[77]

stituted administration of justice by the ordinary continental courts. It is not possible to present here the material which appears to substantiate this somewhat sweeping statement. But it may be at least illustrated by two typical situations: one concerning the field of contracts, the other that of crime.

II

In regard to contracts it should be remembered how far a court in common-law countries may go by invoking equity doctrines in certain cases to enforce compliance, and in comparison how powerless is the civil-law judge, who does not suspect the existence of contempt powers for the enforcement of substantive law duties.[2] But the exercise of such power is always a matter of judicial discretion, never a matter of course: the social pressure is not applied in all cases, but only in some. This we might call the "selectivity principle of enforcement," its result being, among other things, that not all contractual rights are protected through the sanctions of injunction and contempt of court, but only those of litigants who live up to certain moral and social standards. Injunction is granted by the court of equity, and equitable relief is never a matter of right. Strictly speaking, in a court of equity you have no *rights* at all. Theoretically it is a matter of grace, of judicial boon. Substantially, of course, there is a fair degree of predictability as to what the court of equity will do. But the theory is kept alive, in order to maintain in a state of flux the tests that the court applies—business fairness, social desirability, public policy, perhaps even personal decency.

The situation in the court of equity has two characteristic features unknown to a European court. First, the court is not limited to the choice between granting or not granting the relief sought. It may grant a so-called conditional relief, practically rewriting the contract for the parties, saying perhaps that it will give you relief if you pay in gold instead of in greenbacks; "he who seeks equity must do equity." In the second place, a plaintiff thrown out of a court of equity is not necessarily deprived of his so-called legal remedy. His contract is bad *in equity,* he won't get the *equitable*

---

[2] See the preceding essay.

injunction, but he may, however, be entitled to the *remedy at law.*

Thus, instead of the two rigid civil-law categories, according to which contracts are either valid or void, there is an interplay of law and equity which creates a considerably wider range of possibilities. There is a twilight zone of what could be styled contracts *semipleno jure,* to which belong contracts good at law and conditionally good in equity, contracts good at law and bad in equity, contracts bad at law and good in equity. A merely oral land conveyance, for example, undoubtedly and utterly void at law, may in certain cases be enforced through equitable injunction, while the same relief may sometimes be denied to a written, sealed, and notarized contract.

It should not be imagined that the litigant finds himself on more solid ground when he is once out of the court of equity and confined to the remedies of a court of law. The so-called legal remedy simply represents the constitutional right to have determined by the jury, in a court of law, the amount of damages due for breach of contract. And here the ghost of the court of equity, out of which the plaintiff has just been thrown, reappears before him in the dictum that as to the assessment of damages jurors are chancellors, that is, judges of equity, enjoying, in fact though not in theory, wide discretionary powers to fix the amount of damages *ex aequo et bono,* taking into consideration every possible extralegal element that might seem material to them, be it economic, social, political, or moral. Between a six cent verdict and the granting of compensatory or even punitive damages in the full amount claimed by the plaintiff there is a wide range of possibilities in which every element may find its free expression unchecked by the obstacles of a written opinion. Against the discretion of the jurors the party has only one hope: the judge may set aside the verdict as evidently biased or unreasonable. But this again is most certainly an absolutely discretionary power of the court.

Thus we find the plaintiff committed from the equitable discretion of the chancellor to the "equitable" verdict of the jurors, and from that to the discretion of the trial court. He can never get hold of the firm basis of a rigid law. The legal norm is everywhere carefully cushioned by judicial discretion, and as a result the plaintiff

[79]

cannot escape the slippery and uncertain ground of human discretion inspired by motives too subtle and delicate to be translated into fixed legal formulas. Government by law? Obviously not, if by that is meant "government by the certainty of law." At best, government by gentlemen.

An element of discretion is, of course, involved in every possible judicial system, and in no country at any time has justice been administered by machines of logical subsumption, distinguishing right from wrong with the cold precision of a coin-testing appliance. But the European *Rechtsstaat* was planned and organized with the very purpose of reducing the human element in the administration of justice to its imaginable minimum. The remedies for the breach of contracts—or of the single type of contract, such as sales, loans, partnership—are defined by code. The judge may exercise a certain amount of discretion in holding the contract valid or void. But if he holds the contract valid he cannot for any reason deny any of the code remedies, nor can he, if he holds it void, grant any of them. He cannot discriminate between plaintiff and plaintiff, and no middle-of-the-road position can enable him to proceed to a dosage of relief. Furthermore, the judge has no contempt power in the field of substantive law. The typical remedy consists in the award of damages, but there is never a jury in a noncriminal case, and there is nobody to strike the delicate balance between the indefinable incompleteness of right and wrong on the part of the litigants. There are no verdicts which are rendered without a statement of reasons: the judge has to write out his opinion and show the exact amount of the plaintiff's injury in dollars and cents. The less discretion, the more justice. Government by law, at least in the courts, is the ideal upon which continental institutions were carefully patterned. The highest equity was thought to be found in the rigidity and certainty of the law.

The common law, on the contrary, creates a complicated machinery to avert this rigidity. It calls this machinery equity, and sometimes tries to distinguish itself from this less noble relative. There is no chance, though, that it will rid itself of its yokefellow.

[80]

> Thou robèd man of justice, take thy place;
> And thou, his yoke-fellow of equity,
> Bench by his side.

Thus spoke King Lear in the phantasmic trial of his daughters. And his insanity is probably shown only by the fact that by yoking Robèd Justice and Equity on the same bench he somewhat anticipated the English Reform of 1872.

The existence of this double legal order and the possibilities of individualization that it is made to yield strongly suggest that government by the certainty of law is not the reality, and indeed not even the ideal limit, toward which the Anglo-American institutions aim; it is, in a way, the main danger they try to avoid.

The same principles of selectivity, individualization, and pure administrative discretion can be found in the fields of criminal law and procedure. To begin with, under the American system criminal prosecution is simply a right and never a duty of the federal or state attorney. Its exercise is wholly within the discretion of the prosecuting officers and the grand jury. In Italy even the code of 1931 did not abandon the so-called "legality principle" (as opposed to the "opportunity principle"), which makes prosecution a duty of the attorney general; in France and in Germany the prosecuting agency had but a slight degree of discretion, and this pertained to minor offenses and was subject to review by the court. Here a refusal to prosecute is not subject to any kind of judicial review. The prosecuting agency may even abandon an already initiated prosecution, or prosecute for a lesser crime. Furthermore, it may lawfully enter into the most varied kinds of agreements with the defendants, agreements ranging from the acceptance of the defendant's promise to become a witness for the prosecution to the signing of an elaborate consent decree in an antitrust suit.[3]

---

[3] I should like to add that some of these so-called consent decrees, obtained by an obvious "or else" technique, represent the most interesting experiments in modern lawmaking. I am thinking particularly of the consent decree that created the network of arbitration tribunals in the moving-picture industry, and of the Standard Oil consent decree that set a precedent of compulsory free licensing in the field of patents and of licensing for a "reasonable" royalty.

[81]

Although this type of discretion is apparently only a negative one—the prosecuting attorney can forbear prosecution but he cannot himself sentence a defendant—such a procedural situation might exercise a deep influence upon legislative technique. It is quite probable that the generalities, vagueness, or severity of many penal statutes, such as the Mann Act, the Sherman Act, or the laws concerning conspiracy, mail fraud, income disclosure, and the like, could never have survived if prosecution in each case were the affirmative duty of the federal attorney. Thus the practical administration of criminal justice, at least in its negative aspect, becomes an administrative rather than a judicial activity.

In this situation judges can hardly be expected to leave the Attorney General a monopoly of discretion and of considerations of morality and policy. The very tradition of judicial lawmaking opens to them some possibilities unknown to their continental brethren. Every act which in the opinion of the court tends to public mischief —whether or not foreseen by any penal or other law—is a common-law misdemeanor and must be punished as such. This rule may be of limited practical importance today, but it is worth recalling that it was applied in England as late as 1933, to a woman who "caused officers of the Metropolitan Police maintained at public expense . . . to devote their time to the investigation of false allegations, thereby temporarily depriving the public of the services of these public officers and rendering liege subjects of the King liable to suspicion." The decision which affirmed, in the absence of any statute, the conviction for common-law misdemeanor was rendered by Lord Hewart, Chief Justice, author of *The New Despotism*, mentioned above.

Many other instances of the comparative importance of the discretionary element in the field of criminal law might be added. Mention might be made of the distinction between mala in se and mala prohibita in the felony murder rule, of the power of the court —as distinguished from the jury—to gather and consider every kind of evidence without being bound by any rule of evidence. A close comparison of the relative importance of the pardoning power would probably reveal its institutional character in common-law countries. But the most characteristic manifestation of the difference in the two attitudes may be seen in the fate of the so-called positive school of criminal law.

This school, founded by Lombroso, Ferri, and Garofolo, had a large following in all European countries but never succeeded in making any serious headway in the legislation of those countries. The objections of the European liberals, more or less clearly articulated, have been substantially founded on the contention that individualization of criminal justice would affect or undermine the fundamental principles of punishment by law: *nullum crimen et nulla poena sine lege*. It would reduce the business of punishment to a discretionary although scientific activity of a body which would resemble much more an administrative agency than a judicial tribunal. Among the many surprises that this country holds for a European lawyer, not the least striking is that of finding Lombroso, Ferri, and Garofolo widely translated, discussed, and followed by legislature, judiciary, and administration. Such institutions as pardon, probation, parole, and, particularly, the dreaded indeterminate sentence have by now an unchallenged citizenship in the American penal system.

III

In brief, then, comparative investigations thus far seem to reveal that in the administration of justice the common-law countries have traditionally relied upon a wide exercise of discretionary power to an incomparably greater extent than any civil-law country in Europe. If the American scholar thinks that the tremendous growth of administrative agencies in this country is a development of alien origin, inspired by a civilian philosophy, the European lawyer in turn cannot help disclaiming paternity. The network of American administrative agencies created in the last fifty years represents a phenomenon which, to say the least, appears to be much less inconsistent with the actual mechanism of the common law than with the working principles of the European legal systems.

These merely theoretical remarks are substantiated by examination of the factual situation in Europe and in this country. If one were invited to cite the most typical and significant prewar American agencies one would probably name, among others, the Federal Trade Commission, the Securities and Exchange Commission, the National Labor Relations Board, and, in the first line, the various public utilities commissions, from the veteran Interstate Commerce Commission to the Federal Power Commission. But in these fields democratic Europe carried out no administrative activity that could be significantly compared. No initiative-taking agency which could be mentioned as somehow comparable with the Federal Trade Commission, created here nearly three decades ago, or its predecessor, the Bureau of Corporations, organized as early as 1903, ever existed in the European democracies of the Latin type. In continental Europe the enforcement of the laws and of international conventions concerning unfair competition has been left almost entirely to private initiative, which has meant, of course, a nullification of any protection for the nonorganized consumer or the small businessman.

Various bureaus, either independent or integrated in the treasuries or national banks of the various European countries, could be considered a counterpart of the American Securities and Exchange Commission. But none of them ever had the power or the importance of that body. In regard to France, for example, it must be acknowledged that stock speculation and stock frauds have for many decades been responsible for a great number of panics and crises, that *scandales de bourse* became an almost traditional feature of the Stock Exchange of Paris, that the Panama bubble had economic consequences comparable with those of the Black Friday of 1929 and a political and emotional significance at least equal to that of the latter event. But no effective measure to check the situation was ever taken. Whatever the economic and social causes that frustrated every attempt at control in France (and the same forces were fairly active in this country as well), the formalistic political and legal ideologies of the progressive groups in Europe rendered enormously difficult the introduction of efficient regulation. The Securities and Exchange Commission, on the other hand, was preceded by more than twenty years of experimental blue-sky legislation, a typical American device. The early Kansas Statute of 1911, for example, is much more penetrating and rigorous than anything attempted even during the postwar booms and depressions in Europe.

A comparison between the American and the European techniques in dealing with public utilities is especially enlightening. That the system of administrative controls in this field is particularly developed in the United States is generally admitted. But it is held that the European phenomenon of public ownership of such services is the counterpart of public utility control, and it is usually implied that public ownership represents a much stronger and more complete form of public control of business. It may well be, however, that this is true only with very important qualifications. Public ownership of business, while a direct intervention of the state in economic life, is only an indirect form of control of private business. It should be investigated whether the necessity for the state to enter business directly was not, at least in certain cases, due to the administrative difficulty of regulating other people's business. To go into business, to invest money, to run all the risks and difficulties, is from a sociological and psychological viewpoint quite a different matter from compelling the independent and private owners of an enterprise to run it according to public criteria.

It happens sometimes that a weak person must turn to stronger measures than a strong one, and the necessity to expropriate a business instead of regulating it may have its cause in the lack of a strong and efficient administrative machinery, or of a public opinion willing to accept and to back the penetrating public control that this type of regulation involves. Indeed, it takes much more social pressure to determine the business conduct of an entrepreneur who maintains a certain degree of independence than to buy him out and transform him into a salaried employee.

The history of regulation of public utilities in this country is, as everyone knows, a history of economic abuses, political corruption, administrative inefficiency, and judicial blindness. But through all the uncertainties, inconsistencies, and deviations from sound economic policy and simple business fairness and common sense,

[85]

an impressive and unique experiment has been accomplished and an extraordinary stock of experience accumulated. The public service commissions are today doing most interesting work in the field of setting public standards of rate fixing. Theirs is probably the first quantitatively important planning experiment in our type of society, and it represents a unique wealth of case material for the theoretical problem of the price function in a planned economy. The once narrow concept of public utility has in the last decade undergone a deep change and has been merged into a broader concept having practically an all-embracing meaning. The technique of regulation—in contrast to public ownership—has transcended the scope of administrative law and become an alternative to the apparently inescapable choice between competitive waste and state capitalism or state collectivism. One can hardly overestimate the political importance of this technique if it proves itself able to reconcile the profit incentive of individual inventiveness with the furtherance of social aims of larger production and wider distribution. And the most progressive trend in the field of public service commission policies seems to reduce profit to a function of the social performance accomplished by the enterprise.

The greater extension of the scope of administrative activity in the United States, and its deeper regulatory effect, have in my opinion been made possible by what I should call the three main, original, and traditional characteristics of the Anglo-American legal technique. This technique has traditionally relied upon the possibility of acting in personam in order to obtain a certain standard of personal behavior; upon the sweeping, penetrating, and generally felt duty of disclosure; and upon the wise exercise of broad discretionary powers.[4] On the whole, American administration is always ready to cope with the most complicated and intimate aspects of private life, business or personal, and is backed by a strong public opinion in its expectation of substantial disclosure and substantial compliance.

In a difficult or delicate situation a European democratic government, with the help of extremely able legislative drafting commit-

---

[4] The first two aspects are discussed in the preceding essay.

tees, would engage in the pursuit of a perfect statute that would foresee, classify, and properly regulate in advance every possible case. In this country reliance is placed mostly on the common sense, decency, and skill that every magistrate, be he judge or administrator, is expected to evidence in the handling of individual cases, each of which stands upon its own merits.

If we are right in seeing in this expectation the typical attitude of the Anglo-Saxon democracies, the contention that the growth of administrative action is inconsistent with common-law tradition represents no more than one of those false issues that so often becloud the real ones. One of these real issues probably turns around the expansion of official initiative in the enforcement of individual rights. Long before the creation of the National Commission of Railroads, one of the oldest federal agencies, a private party could obtain from the courts protection against the exaction of unjust rates charged in the exercise of a common calling, against deceitful trade practices, against combinations in restraint of trade, against misrepresentations in the sale of shares and bonds, and even perhaps against the violation of certain labor laws. What makes for the peculiarity of the administrative activity is that instead of possessing only a "cause of action" the individual competitor, consumer, investor, or worker has now a *negotiorum gestor*, a public agency that does the court job for him. This probably means that the type of civil litigation which has hitherto been regarded as fundamental is daily losing its importance. We may witness a phenomenon not dissimilar to that experienced by England in the formative period of criminal procedure, when individual criminal prosecution by the so-called personal appeal was gradually superseded by administrative initiative in the punishment of crimes, exercised by the presentment jury and the coroner.

IV

On the other side of the ocean liberal civilian lawyers took the stand for the *Rechtsstaat*, the *stato di diritto*, the supremacy of legal certainty, against the rising discretion of totalitarian administration, making of this doctrine an ideological weapon. We learned, believed, and taught that certainty, clarity, and normativity are the only ideals toward which a legal system can strive. We asked the state to conform with the Kantian categorical imperative and act in such a way that the maxim of each of its actions could become a universal law. In our distrust of government, bureaucracy, and the discretion of judges and administrators we engaged in the pursuit of that legal bluebird, the perfect law in the form of the perfect statute, which would assure the functioning of a justice independent of human whims. We saw the totalitarian parties, first, and then the totalitarian governments destroy little by little the perfect machine of legality we were building, or at least thought we were building. And we defended it stubbornly and were satisfied that we were accomplishing a socially, morally, and politically useful mission.

When we European liberals were first faced with the dispute between the American liberals and the American conservatives concerning the questions of administrative law and administrative discretion, the first impulse of many of us was to tell the American liberals of our European experience, to warn them against the inherent dangers of the rise of administrative discretion, and to tell them that we could vouch for the truth of the stand of the American conservatives. But a more careful consideration of Anglo-American legal history and a little more thorough investigation of the real tradition of these countries should have convinced us that with them the so-called "administrative despotism" is anything but new, that administrative discretion through the government by unwritten law is centuries old among English-speaking peoples. Moreover, candor required us to compare the record of these peoples with our own political and social record. And we could not help finding that notwithstanding the striking amount of discretion—the lack of legal certainty, Cartesian clarity, or Kantian normativity—civil and political liberties have been protected in the English-speaking countries not less but more than in our *Rechtsstaat* countries, and that people on the whole are certainly not less happy there than those on our side of the water.

We began to ask ourselves whether the success of the totalitarian parties in Europe could not be largely explained by our strict belief in the ideal of government by law, with which we kept faith even when we had control of administration; whether the voluntary renunciation of any investigation going beyond legal formulas, the lack of selectivity in enforcement and prosecution, and the reluctance to solve legal problems by moral distinctions did not deprive the European democracies of strength and efficiency; whether in our belief in the overwhelming importance of perfect legislation we did not neglect fundamental social problems, such as the positive political education of individuals and the creation of an efficient system of recruitment and remuneration of judges and administrators; whether, in short, for the sake of preserving certain ideals we did not make their very defense impossible.

On the other hand, should we, for the necessity of defending it, destroy the very object of our defense; should we, for the sake of life, lose the reasons for living—*propter vitam vivendi perdere causas*? Is this the final deadlock of legal philosophy? Today this is much more than the problem of a *Rechtsstaat* lawyer's adjustment to the common-law background. We have seen in the pluricellular structure of American society and government one of the safety valves that compensates the strength of social pressure, of which discretion and administrative power are but a manifestation. This pluralistic structure would probably not have been possible in the English-speaking countries without the British splendid isolation and the American two-ocean security. The isolation and the security are rapidly vanishing. Under a new external pressure the safety valve of loose-knit relations disappears; a more compact, a centralized, a new state looms. What is the new solution going to be?

In the exercise of discretionary powers the American administrative agencies have gathered and are daily building up mountains of case material. The transformation of this into case *law*—and into law *tout court*—requires great constructive imagination. Every discretionary activity yields after a certain period of time a set of more or less intelligible rules. To produce a rather vague equity law England required centuries. Are we going to wait that long before we form intelligible law out of modern administrative activity? The question before us is not whether we should go back to the rules of, say, a Court of Common Pleas in order to escape the new discretion of administrators. The question is how fast and how well we are going to extract from our new fact material a new law; how soon we are going to create new legal standards and ideas that will fit into our changed economic and social system as well as the ideas of contract, property, claims, debt, and the like fitted into the society that created them.

What these new concepts are I do not know. But I do know that, for example, "lease-lend" does not fit within the obligation concept; that "fair return on fair value" does not fit into the enterprise idea; that the category of "needs" is susceptible of no less important legal developments than that of "rights" or "claims" proved to be. The alternative "discretion or rule" means for too many a choice between a new lawlessness and the old rules. A better answer might be: let us go to work and produce from the new facts a new rule, a new law.

After all, the relation between discretion and rules is like that between thoughts and words. Words never express thoughts entirely; moreover, old words often bar the way to new thought. But the solution is not to do away with words, to substitute "pure thought" for expressed thought, "pure equity" for articulated justice. In struggling for new expression the thought itself finds newer and higher levels. The relation between discretion and rule is not static. It is a living and perpetually renewed relation between creator and creature. To bring this relation into the full light of political consciousness is the lawyer's task today.

Private Governments
and the Federal Constitution

IF A REVOLUTION is a violent movement originating in a dissatisfaction with an existing social order and aimed at its radical and immediate improvement, and if, as an encyclopedia article on revolution puts it, "a recasting of the social order is, at least in modern times, a far more important characteristic of revolutions than a change of the political constitution or the use of violence in the attainment of this end . . . ," then the American Revolution of 1776 was hardly a revolution at all. While it enlisted the physical support of a great number of dissatisfied, turbulent, and to a great extent irresponsible elements present in every society, the leaders of the movement had no quarrel with the structure of the society in which they lived and of which they were the leaders and beneficiaries. The Declaration of Independence, itself the most revolutionary of the three basic—and so different, even inconsistent—documents which the swinging pendulum of that period produced (the Declaration, the Constitution, and the Bill of Rights), asserted the existence of inalienable human rights only for the purpose of laying a broad philosophic foundation for the right of the colonies to shake off the British yoke. If people were asked today to quote the most significant statements of the Declaration of Independence, chances are that phrases like "all men are created equal," the "inalienable rights" to "life, liberty and the pursuit of happiness," and "consent of the governed" would comprise the overwhelming bulk of the answers. The truth of the matter seems to be, however, that as far as their historical meaning is concerned, these famous phrases were only obiter dicta, or at best general philosophical observations not strictly related to the Declaration's subject matter.

The Declaration of Independence was not, in fact, a declaration of human rights, nor even a declaration of the rights of man or of citizens. It was a declaration of war. It begins with the statement of the necessity "for one people to dissolve the Political Bonds which have connected them with another," and concludes with acquiescence "in the necessity, which denounces our Separation," and the determination to hold "our British brethren . . . as we hold the rest of mankind, Enemies in War, in Peace, Friends." This is a declaration of a foreign, not of a civil, war—not of the right of a people to be free, but of one people to be free from another. The historic fact that a declaration written to assert the right of "one people" to be free from "another" is now thought of as a declaration of a people's right to be "free" is, in a nutshell, the measure of the change which the political philosophy of the country has undergone.

It is, therefore, hardly surprising that the original constitution did not put any particular emphasis upon the protection of individual rights. The Declaration of Independence stated, it is true, that governments are instituted among men to secure certain inalienable rights, with which all men, being born equal, are endowed by their Creator. But when, freed from the British yoke, the Fathers gathered to write the constitution of their own government, this constitution did not give any overwhelming evidence of a preoccupation with those rights. If the guiding principle of the new government was to be "to secure life, liberty and the pursuit of happiness," the new constitution was content to leave that principle undefined and undeveloped. Of more than one hundred clauses that comprise our original constitution, no more than five guarantee rights to the governed. These clauses are:

1. Article III, Section 2, requiring crimes to be tried by jury in places specified.

2. Article III, Section 3, defining and limiting the crime of treason (the only individual guarantee which was given the dignity of an entire section of the Constitution—the memory of the danger

of hanging separately must have been pretty fresh in the minds of the framers).

3. Article I, Section 9, clause 2, limiting the power of Congress to suspend the writ of habeas corpus to times of rebellion or invasion.

4. Article I, Section 9, clause 3, and Article I, Section 10, clause 1, prohibiting the enactment of bills of attainder and ex post facto laws by the Congress and state legislatures.

It seems characteristic that clauses 2 and 3 of Section 9 of Article I, which we today think so basic, were sandwiched in between clause 1 of Section 9, limiting Congressional power to forbid the importation of slaves, and clause 4, limiting the power of Congress to impose direct taxes without apportionment. That both clause 1, dealing with importation of slaves, and clause 4, on taxes, were deemed of greater importance than those with which we are now concerned is apparent from the Fifth Article of the Constitution, which declared that for a specified period of time "no amendment shall in any manner affect the First and Fourth clauses in the Ninth Section of the First Article."

These four guarantees of individual rights to which reference has been made were guarantees against action by the Federal Government. One of them, the right to trial by jury, certainly did not, in 1789, extend to trials in state courts, and, strictly speaking, does not to this day. Whether the federal writ of habeas corpus contemplated by the Framers afforded the individual, before the Civil War, any protection from state action and whether the section on treason circumscribed all state attempts to define or punish treason are nice constitutional questions of lesser practical importance. Only one of the individual guarantees mentioned was a protection against state action—that against bills of attainder and ex post facto laws—expressly extended to the states by Section 10 of Article I. This last section, in addition, imposed upon the states one more limitation, constituting the fifth guarantee of individual rights contained in the original constitution—that of the sanctity of contract. As a matter of fact, with a firm knowledge—not entirely made of foresight—of some of the modern principles of functional finance

[93]

or pump priming, the Framers took pains to state explicitly that: "No State shall . . . coin money; emit bills of credit; make any thing but gold and silver coin a tender in payment of debts, pass any law . . . impairing the obligation of contracts." As against the populist inventiveness of the legislature of Rhode Island, no clause could be too repetitious or too explicit.

This is as far as the Framers of the Constitution went to secure "life, liberty and the pursuit of happiness." It was fifteen years, five months, and twenty-six days after July the Fourth 1776 before the president could notify the new nation that some of the dicta uttered in the Declaration that had given birth to it were now part of its law.

The adoption of the first ten amendments, constituting our Bill of Rights, was indeed a vindication of the rights of the individual and was at least a partial return to the general philosophy of the Declaration of Independence, which for its time was, as we have said, a declaration of war, but which for history has always been a revolutionist declaration of rights. But the libertarian and revolutionary spirit of the Bill of Rights was at the same time an antifederalist spirit, a states-rights, republican, and agrarian spirit. While the Declaration of Independence begins with the dissolution of political bands between one people and another, and the Constitution begins with the stipulation that "all legislative powers herein granted shall be vested in a Congress of the United States," the Bill of Rights provides their antifederalist counterpart by its opening phrase—"Congress shall make no law." True, it did not stop there, but this was certainly not the fault of the lovers of freedom.

Those who in eighteenth-century America were devoted to the ideals of human dignity and freedom were clearly worried about one form of tyranny only—the tyranny of the Federal Government and of its Federalist friends. Thus, the Bill of Rights contains not a single word of limitation of the power of the state, or a single clause that could be interpreted as the protection of an individual against the possible abuses of state power. The freedom-loving Republicans of 1789 would have been as irritated by a suggestion that the power of their state governments be in some way limited in the Federal Constitution as New Deal liberals usually were by attempts to limit the power of the Federal Government. The Federalists, on the other hand, were not particularly concerned about the protection of the common man from any government. In any case, the Bill of Rights was their opponents' show, and whatever protection for the individuals the Federalists needed was already embodied in the contract clause.

Thus, even after the adoption of the Bill of Rights, the Constitution stood as a compromise—the common man was protected from the encroachments of the national government, and the bondholder and the creditor from those of the state. And neither party had enough imagination to conceive of the possibility that one day creditors would want protection against currency manipulation or impairment of contract rights by the Federal Government, and that human dignity and liberty and freedom of speech and of religion might be threatened by state legislatures and state officers. Imaginative deficiencies of this sort are hardly infrequent and perhaps not entirely deplorable—a great many beneficial reforms in the organization of human society have indeed been due to the conviction of those responsible for them that their reforms could never be invoked against the reformers themselves.

The principle that the Constitution and the Bill of Rights afforded the individual as against the state only the very limited protections we have discussed was clear and unmistakable. A civil war was necessary to write into our law the proposition, logically so simple but historically so complex, that state governments, too, may fail to live up to the purposes for which governments are instituted among men, i.e., to secure the inalienable rights "of life, liberty and the pursuit of happiness," or of "property" (this closest known institutional substitute for happiness). The Civil War and more than a generation of debate were necessary to overcome the great political obstacle of the identification of human liberty with the immunity of the states from federal interference. But when the smoke of the War disappeared, the sovereign freedom of the state to deal as it pleased with individuals within its jurisdiction without federal interference was gone with the wind.

The Fourteenth Amendment was on the books. Its first section

[95]

admonished the states not to "make or enforce any law which shall abridge the privileges or immunities of citizens of the United States," not to "deprive any person of life, liberty or property without due process of law," and not to "deny any person within its jurisdiction the equal protection of the laws." Nor was the Amendment destined to live on paper only. It was to become the main single source of constitutional protection of individual freedom from governmental arbitrariness. Gone with the wind, too, was the exaltation of slavery as a necessary, morally and socially beneficial human institution. But also gone were a great many precious ideas and thoughts, to which I shall later turn with interest, admiration, and regret.

The Fourteenth Amendment did not, however, embody as broad a range of individual rights as against the states as had the Bill of Rights with respect to the Federal Government. It contained, it is true, a provision for the protection of life, liberty, and property, which seems broad enough to protect all that may be precious to men. But the difficulty was that the Bill of Rights contained an identical clause (Fifth Amendment) as only one of a number of provisions for the protection of the freedom of religion, speech, and press; of assembly; of the right to trial by jury, to counsel, and to be confronted by accusing witnesses; of freedom from unreasonable searches and seizures, from double jeopardy, from self-incrimination, from expropriation without indemnity, from excessive bail or cruel punishment. It took many decades and a world war to overcome the argument of restrictive construction, according to which none of these more specific freedoms could be deemed included within the "life, liberty and property" clause of the Fourteenth Amendment as against the states. Otherwise, it was said, the provisions of the Bill of Rights respecting these other freedoms as against the Federal Government would have been repetitious and thus unnecessary, because just as properly to be implied in the identical formula of the Fifth Amendment. But the logic of this argument yielded to the experiences of the First World War and its aftermath.

The vitality of a country, like the youthfulness of an individual, can be revealed by the constructive use it makes of the crises and emergencies through which it lives. *Omnia manda mundis*—all experience, no matter how trying, turns to the advantage of those who are destined to grow. In some sense, indeed, each cornerstone of our normal institutions owes its being to an emergency. The Bill of Rights, the Fourteenth Amendment, and the application of the First Amendment to state action testify to the impact that the Revolution, the Civil War, and the First World War have exercised upon our institutions. What mark, if any, will the Second World War leave on our constitutional law?

American constitutional law gradually expanded constitutional controls that originated on the federal level, and which were at first interpreted in a strictly procedural sense. The trend seems to indicate an increase in a searching and strict engulfment of the smaller, and more immediate, local sovereignties, which precisely because of their smallness, immediacy, and localness were at first thought to be immune from the dangers of arbitrariness, and too spontaneous and sound as institutions to require external checks and constitutional guarantees. These were the friends of the common man—against them, he needed no lawyer and no defense.

But experience has proved that defense is needed, and that, in fact, there is little point in insuring individual freedom from the distant, and thus theoretically more tyrannical, government so long as no protection is given against the tyranny and the arbitrariness of a close—only too close—petty, and merciless state, county, and municipal government. It is for this reason that the due process clause of the Fourteenth Amendment has proved to be a far more important and vital provision than the corresponding clause of the Fifth Amendment.

If this is the trend, where would its extrapolation lead? It may be that we are falling an easy prey to a superficial historic symmetry when we suggest that the Second World War may lead to a simultaneous deepening of our federal system and to a corresponding expansion of our constitutional controls. But it seems to me that there is more than an a priori hypothesis to support the notion that our generation of constitutional lawyers is discovering a new dimension in our federal structure—the dimension of private governments.

[97]

Just as the Civil War added to our lineal Constitution the breadth of the control of state governments, our generation may be not entirely unwilling to take a glimpse into the constitutional depths of private governments and to recognize that our society is in fact a federation not merely of forty-eight states, subdivided into counties and towns, but of a considerably greater number of private sovereignties, governments, and communities as well.

It is hardly necessary to insist upon the great importance that these so-called private sovereignties have for the life, liberty, and pursuit of happiness of all of us. They do suggest at least three general observations which I shall try to develop. The first concerns what can be described as the danger of being a government; the second, the peculiar importance of private groups for the framework of our society; the third, the peculiar color of hypocrisy that the existence of these private sovereignties may lend to the whole American system of equality.

It may be important to call the attention of nonlawyers to the well-known maxim that "the Constitution runs against governments only." This is supposed to mean that to find out whether or not you have been deprived of a constitutional right, it is not enough to examine the nature of your injury and of your right. There is the further necessity of examining by whose action that injury has been inflicted upon you. Only if the action is the action of a government, an official government, can the answer be that your constitutional rights have been infringed. This is why, for example, a Negro who finds no restaurant willing to serve him, or no hotel willing to give him shelter, is not deprived, according to the prevailing interpretation, of the equal protection of the laws. This, it is said, is true as long as the action of which he is victim is strictly private action, not encouraged or compelled by any statute, decision, or regulation, federal, state, or local. The Negro may freeze or starve to death in a community which reserves its hospital beds and overflowing tables to people of a different color; no one would seriously maintain that he has been deprived of life without due process of law, or denied the equal protection of the law.

A gang may kill or imprison us without violating any constitutional right we may have to life or liberty. In order to commit the "constitutional" crime, the gang must be—or at least pretend to be —an agent of the federal or a state government. And, in light of the Constitution, it would have to be a very silly gang to advance such dangerous pretensions. To begin with, the gang, if it were modest enough to maintain the necessary decorum and privacy, could eliminate indiscreet intervention by the United States attorney, the federal court, and the federal jury by limiting its activities to beatings and killings. These activities would be the exclusive concern—or, as they say in international law, would lie in the internal sphere—of the several states. State, county, or town authorities and the local grand jury can sometimes be relied upon better to understand the imponderables of a situation, to appreciate certain neighborly endeavors at their proper value, and to respect the unwritten law of the village-jungle, where the nosy Washington lawyer sees nothing but plain murder.

So long as you resist the temptation of wearing official insignia, you may do openly and lawfully a number of things you could never do as a governmental official. President Truman has pointed out that the Daughters of the American Revolution were not acting quite in keeping with the spirit of the aforesaid Revolution nor with that of the fine arts when they excluded Negro artists from their concert hall. But, he added, as a private organization they were within their private rights. This is only one of the many instances in which greater freedom is the constitutional reward of private modesty. And it points to the danger of being a government official.

If in old England one had to be a baronet to be a man, it was also true that in old Prussianized Europe you had to be somehow connected with what Kafka has, with his felicitous finality, called the Castle. Unless you were part of the mystery of the "service," and had some kind of counselorship, apprenticeship, or clerkship, or could write on some kind of official paper, or could claim some kind of uniform overcoat or at least a uniform cap, you were actually no part of significant society, but lived in an obscure and servile tenure about which little poetry or history, and even less law, could be written. There was—and I suspect there still is—more than one

[99]

European country in which even janitors were officers of the government, and where university professors displayed little buttons evidencing their rank as lieutenants, colonels, and four-star generals in the hierarchy of education. I succeeded recently in impressing my little boy by showing him a picture taken of me at the age of eleven in the uniform, boasting fourteen shiny buttons, of the Russian Imperial Senior Grammar School of Odessa.

This is not our fate in a free democracy. Indeed, how terrible would it be if our janitors had to become members of some official "service." Then they would come under the constitutional obligation not to conceal vacancies of apartments from Negroes or Jews. The delicately patterned structure of our harmonious Manhattan would collapse, and ethnical promiscuity and racial anarchy would drive us straight to a tinted America!

Nobody, thank goodness, has to be a government official in order to be somebody in America. As a matter of fact, no man in his right senses would ever accept an official position to do a job that can be done equally well from a private desk. If you can stop the sale of a book as chairman of the Booksellers Board of Trade Committee, it is senseless to try to become Boston's chief of police. If you can expurgate motion pictures as the private czar in a private office, why on earth attempt an odious censorship and become its hated chief? There is little point in trying to become the head of a regional United States Employment Service or War Manpower Commission to deprive of their jobs the workers belonging to the wrong union. It is easier when the right kind of union manager can do the job just as well. If you wish to keep Jews or Japanese out of your village, you might better do it as director of a realtors' association than as the village Mayor. "Chief Commissioner of State Elections" is a fine-sounding title, but if it is your intention to keep Negroes from voting, a position as member of the Democratic County Committee is certainly a better means. To head an official agency may have its satisfactions, but to control the voting stock of a private news agency may offer the additional one of excluding from membership and service those papers which refuse to understand what is right and what is wrong.

No sooner do you become chief of police, censor, USES director, mayor, election commissioner, or official news agency head than a frightening, demagogic machine is mounted against you: the Constitution, the First Amendment, the Fifth Amendment, the Fourteenth Amendment, the Fifteenth Amendment, freedom of this and freedom of that, due process and equal protection, discrimination on account of race or color, and simple unreasonable classifications are thrown at you by merciless persecutors. But stay where you are—a private individual, behind a door to a private office bearing your own name or that of a private organization—and this demagogic chant will not turn a hair of your head, for constitutions run "against governments only." On the contrary, remain private and your private sovereignty will instead be able to invoke constitutional protections of its own if and when attempts are made to illegalize or regulate it.

Thus, for instance, the constitutional right to property was for decades a successful bar to governmental private centers of monopolistic power which were, without any semblance of due process, depriving great masses of consumers of their property and economic liberty. And the First Amendment has been invoked by a judge as progressive as Mr. Justice Murphy as a bar against the removal of monopolistic restraints on such vital channels of communication as news agencies and radio networks. In short, if a sovereignty succeeds in remaining private enough, the Constitution, instead of menacing it as a sword, may protect it as a shield.

American democracy is proud of the constitutional restraints it imposes upon its governments. No other nation has developed so majestic a body of laws for the protection of those who are ruled and the control of their rulers. America is also proud of the richness and variety of its social forces, in whose complex interplay innumerable natural and free associations and institutions rise, develop, and prosper. No other nation can and does rely so much upon spontaneous social performance in fields in which a heavy, uniformed, and regimented governmental machinery would otherwise be necessary.

Both statements seem entirely true and both claims entirely justified. But is there some kind of fallacy in their simultaneous presentation? On the streets of Athens some twenty-five hundred years ago, a sophist stopped a boasting smith who claimed that his swords and shields were both invincible, and asked him whether his swords pierced his shields or his shields blunted his swords. Nor is ours merely a logical inconsistency. More than once the suspicion arises that the puritan strictness of our constitutional control of governmental arbitrariness is the actual control of people's lives and happiness.

I remember how, some thirty years ago, my mother cried when, having received only four "excellents" of the possible five, I had for all practical purposes flunked my first admission examination to the Imperial Senior Grammar School. I still remember it and I think no other single fact has influenced my behavior or misbehavior more than this experience in the heart of the ghetto. There was a law on the books duly enacted by the Czar of all Russia, with the advice and consent of the People's Elders and the Imperial Counsellors, which established a "healthy proportion" between Christians and Jews in any given class. Today, my children here do not have to grow up under the humiliation of such a law. No matter what the factual situation, laws on the books have a reality of their own, and, believe me, the phrase "all men are created equal" makes better reading and a better rearing for children than the circulars of a Russian or Prussian minister of education.

Nor is education as a whole regimented and governmentalized in this country, and again quite a few of the best educational talents, native or imported, are the beneficiaries of this educational pluralism. I do not doubt that President Butler would have become a four-star general of the army of education even if education were monopolized by government. But what about James Harvey Robinson, Thorstein Veblen, Alvin Johnson, and so many less prominent but useful, talented, and honest educators? Thus everything seems to be for the best in this happy world—laws and governments proclaim equality and justice for all; private organizations assure a flexibility and a freedom that no governmental scheme could ever achieve! Except that my daughter has said to me: "I'd better keep after my

homework because you know they have a quota system in colleges
—they do not call it a Jewish quota but that's what it is."

Could it be that laws are so ready to assure equality before the
government only because things which are really important are
being taken care of by men who are smart enough to operate without the glamour of the public limelight? Is the Constitution a
polished but empty political shell destined to screen and disguise
the most arbitrary private governments, more dangerous than other
tyrannies because totally anonymous, totally irresponsible, and refined to such a point as to deny their own existence? It has been
said of the Devil that he played his neatest trick when he persuaded
western man that the Devil does not exist. Is constitutionalism *plus*
freedom of private associations the latest and most refined trick of
the age-old enemies of justice and liberty who went underground
and persuaded mankind that they cannot possibly be tyrants for the
simple and conclusive reason that they are not governments?

The monistic theory of state and the doctrine of absolute sovereignty pictured individuals united into a single community under a
single government. The autonomous reality and legitimacy of lesser
groups were denied. At first this denial put these groups at the mercy
of the absolute central power. But when this central governmental
power became subject to constitutional restraints, when the doctrine of the rights of man was added to the doctrine of absolute
sovereignty, these private groups found themselves in an unex-
pectedly privileged position. The charters, and even the fraudulent land grants that had been given to them by society,
became irrevocable—by virtue of the sanctity attaching to contracts
between government and individuals. But these charters and grants
did not make these private groups subject in their turn to any governmental or quasi-governmental duties of decency, fairness, or
equal treatment for those in fact subjected to their power.

We are here faced with a major historic dilemma. And if it is true
that in the United States constitutional restraints are particularly
severe, while private groups are particularly powerful, this is indeed,
as Myrdal has put it in a not wholly unrelated connection, an American dilemma.

We have seen that, philosophically speaking, the situation that gives rise to the dilemma is characterized by the narrowness of the definition of "government." This narrow conception may in its turn be rooted in an overly narrow definition of "law." The monistic conception has under various forms proclaimed that there is but one law, the law of the state, and that there is but one government, the government of the state. The Kelsenian identification of law and state was the culmination of a process that was begun by Bodin.

It must be stated, however, that there has been no generation and no country which could not count among its best legal minds one or more opponents to this monistic theory. Rousseau and Bentham, Savigny and Gierke, Durkheim and Duguit, William James and John Dewey, Calhoun and Horace Kallen, Croce and Figgis, Morris R. Cohen and Harold Laski—all approached the problem from different angles: the legal character of rules made by the so-called private groups, the multiplicity of legal orders, the pluralistic structure of the state, guild socialism, vocational representation, concurrent majorities. It must, however, be emphasized that these various "pluralistic"—or, to use a term which may be their common denominator, antimonistic—doctrines were rather ambiguous with respect to the topic we are discussing. On the one hand, while private groups could be *de facto* governments, could be lawmakers, power holders, and sovereigns, as real as the state itself, this did not necessarily mean—and at times necessarily excluded—that they be subjected to any type of restraints of their individual "inalienable rights," and particularly to a restraint derived from a general constitution which would assert the supremacy of a central government and a central constitution, federal or otherwise. In other words, *de facto*, private governments could escape constitutional controls, either because by the doctrines of monistic sovereignty they are not governments, or because by the doctrines of pluralism they are as sovereign as the nation, which has nothing to say about them. Since, however, pluralists are, by and large, less logical than are monists, and since absolute pluralism is in itself as grave a contradiction as absolute relativism, the pluralistic theories can be considered as the forerunners of those which today advocate the limitation on the powers of *de facto* governments.

There have been scholars in other countries who have dealt with this eternal problem of human politics as a philosophical, sociological, or jurisprudential question. What others did with the problem for sociology, legal theory, and political science, Robert Lee Hale did for the theory of constitutional law. In other countries, the question of whether a fraternity or a labor association is or is not a lawmaking group or a government may be a nice philosophical, sociological, or jurisprudential question. But if a distinctive characteristic of America's political organization is what I like to call the justicability of philosophical, sociological, and jurisprudential questions, then it was inevitable that the problem be presented to Americans in constitutional terms, that is, in philosophical terms having an immediate practical, legal, and institutional significance.

Professor Hale, teaching at Columbia Law School, is supposed to teach law as it is. Hence his first concern is to convey to his students the undeniable lawyer's maxim that the Constitution, with the exception of the antislavery article, "runs against governments only." There is in his lectures and articles express denial of this official maxim. But there is no paragraph in these lectures and articles dealing with the maxim which does not say at the same time, at least between the lines: "How odd and how sad, is it not, my friends, that the Constitution should remain blind to the so-called private mischiefs?"

I feel impelled to submit a somewhat different proposition and attest that, within certain limits, the American Constitution is a system of protection of substantive inalienable rights of individuals rather than a mere restriction of the official governmental activities that may impair them. In other words, I maintain that *the protection of individual rights is the primary, direct, and basic content of constitutional guarantees rather than a derivative and indirect result of restraints on governmental power.*

No construction, I believe, which makes the Constitution a system of governmental duties but not of individual rights can quite live up to these great ideals to secure which not only governments but constitutions themselves were instituted among men. Strange as it may seem, I believe what the man in the street has been led to believe for more than one hundred and fifty years—that the first ten amendments to the American Constitution are a bill of rights and not a bill of duties of the Federal Government.

In support of my contention I offer the following considerations:

There is *no logical necessity* that any constitution, or the United States Constitution, be a system of restraints imposed on governmental action only. In some sense all law is a rule of governmental action, because legal rights and duties ultimately rest upon a system of governmental sanctions. But this does not prevent us from asserting that law creates individual rights and individual duties in the fields of domestic relations, property, contracts, or torts. Constitutional law is susceptible of the same construction. There are, indeed, several provisions in our present constitution which concededly run against private individuals as well as against official governments. Anyone is capable of violating the Thirteenth or Antislavery Amendment or the Twenty-First Amendment (transportation of intoxicating liquors). The fact that neither of these amendments is wholly self-executing and that each contains a provision for the enactment of appropriate federal or state legislation is irrelevant. The Fourteenth Amendment also has a provision for the enactment of appropriate Congressional legislation, but such legislation has been held unconstitutional when directed against private violations of the principle of equality.

The cases referred to are generally styled the *Civil Rights* cases,[1] decided in 1883. The United States Supreme Court there held that a Congressional statute which imposed upon intrastate restaurants, hotels, and theaters the duty of serving all citizens without discrimination as to color or race was unconstitutional because the due-process and equal-protection clauses of the Fourteenth Amendment, which that statute sought to enforce, were directed against state action only. That decision has been for a long time the principal authority for all those who maintained that "the Constitution runs against governments only." But the decision of the Supreme

---

[1] 109 U.S. 3.

Court in *Classic* v. *United States*,[2] 1940, greatly limited its scope. Speaking through Chief Justice Stone, one of its most farsighted judges, and over the dissent of Justice Black, the Court there held that interference with the right to vote in a primary is prohibited by the Constitution, regardless of whether or not the interference can be described as state action. This decision is rich in several untapped potentialities, and we shall return to it. At this point it will suffice to say that by distinguishing the problem before it from that of the *Civil Rights* cases, the Court dealt a blow to the much-quoted maxim that "the Constitution runs against governments only," conceived as a general maxim of constitutional law and philosophy.

The decision in the *Classic* case is predicated on provisions of the Constitution which deal in quite general terms with the right to vote. These provisions do not explicitly grant any rights to any individuals, nor do they impose any duties upon other individuals. They simply fix a procedure through which the people "of the several states" shall choose the members of Congress. These provisions were held sufficient to justify the existence of a constitutional duty in any private individual to respect the exercise of the right to vote, and interference with it was held to be an individual private violation of an individual constitutional right. The *Classic* case did not overrule the *Civil Rights* cases, but explained the matter by the specific language of the Fourteenth Amendment: "No state shall . . ."

This means, to begin with, that when the Constitution says nothing as to who shall refrain from a violation of a provision or rule, everyone, official or private government, group or individual, will be under the constitutional duty to refrain from an interference therewith. In other words, *it is first of all no more a question of the inherent nature of constitutional provisions*. It is merely a question of language. And, secondly, the burden of construction is now shifted to those who take the negative of the proposition: Where the language is mute or ambiguous, the provision will run against everyone—government or not. Thus, after 1940 it is not correct to say "the Constitution runs against governments only."

---

[2] 313 U.S. 299.

All that can be said legitimately is that when the language of a constitutional provision expressly restricts its operation to a state government, the provision will serve only against such a government.

In the light of this proposition, let us compare the due process clause of the Fifth Amendment with that of the Fourteenth Amendment. The latter says, "nor shall any state deprive any person of life, liberty or property, without due process of law, nor deny a person the equal protection of the laws." But the Fifth Amendment says, "No person shall be deprived of life, liberty or property, without due process of law." The subject of the Fourteenth Amendment is "state"; the subject of the Fifth Amendment is "person." The language of the Fourteenth Amendment is that of a restriction on the power of government; the language of the Fifth Amendment is that of assertion of an individual right. If language is controlling, then the Fourteenth Amendment creates a state duty, of which individual rights are only a function. But the Fifth Amendment is truly part and parcel of a bill of rights, and creates primarily a right, from which derive as many duties and inabilities of governments and individuals as are necessary for the effectuation of that right.

The objection will be stated that everyone knows that, historically speaking, the Fifth Amendment and the whole of the Bill of Rights were written against the Federal Government only; that the very necessity of fighting a civil war to get the Fourteenth Amendment on the books shows that the due process clause of the Fifth Amendment was not applicable to anyone but the Federal Government. This objection would be insuperable if interpretations based on prevailing notions about the so-called genuine intention of the framers of a document were to be treated as conclusive historic evidence. But fortunately they need not be. And there are several reasons why this so-called historical argument leaves me unimpressed.

No argument is made here that the due process clause of the Fifth Amendment applies to state action. It should be conceded that the historical atmosphere surrounding the introduction and the adoption of the Bill of Rights precludes that its framers intended in any way to weaken, impair, or limit the power of state legislatures or of state governments. But the issue today is not the application of the Fifth Amendment to state governments but its application to private governments. The former issue has been fought out and settled, and the Fourteenth Amendment is now on the books. The latter issue is totally unrelated to the former.

It is a fallacious argument that the conceded inapplicability of the Fifth Amendment to state governments is a kind of a fortiori proof of its inapplicability to private governments. It is perfectly conceivable that certain provisions of the Federal Constitution may be enforceable against the Federal Government or against private usurpers, while their application is denied as against state legislatures, out of rightful regard for their sovereign independence. Nothing in logic or in political theory requires that private intrigues upon people's lives, liberty, or property shall necessarily enjoy an equal or greater immunity than analogous infringements by state governments, and that no limitation on private power is, therefore, thinkable so long as state power goes unrestrained.

Nor has this proposition a greater historical or psychological validity. Let us again concede—because the question is not in issue —that the framers of the Bill of Rights firmly intended that it should not run against the states. Does that mean that they intended with equal firmness that it should not restrain private power? The language is, let us remember, as general as it could be. What historical evidence can be produced to limit it, beyond what has been said about the states? There is, so far as I know, no evidence whatsoever that the Founding Fathers affirmatively expressed their intention to grant private power holders any immunity from respecting individual rights.

It might be contended that the basic notion of a bill of rights was that of a restraint on the power of a particular government, or as a statement of rights specially directed against it, rather than the assertion of rights of individuals against the world and against every earthly power. But this contention would be a clear perversion of historical truth. There is no doubt that the ideological underpinning of the Bill of Rights was in the first place the belief in the existence of natural individual rights "with which men are endowed by their Creator." The limitation of governmental power was only one of the necessary consequences of that self-evident truth. But it has never been the primary purpose or the sole or principal content of its assertion. Hardly any document of the eighteenth, or for that matter of the seventeenth, century speaks in terms of restraint on government without at the same time emphasizing the individual, or, as European lawyers would say, the subjective aspect of the relationship. "The rights of Englishmen" were the rights of the limits of authority. Nor could these rights have been conceived by Coke, Blackstone, Locke, or Jefferson as essentially or exclusively rights against the political authority.

These rights are inherent natural rights which antedate every authority in the world. Their relation to the state is in their inalienability to the state, not in their being essentially rights against the state. George Mason, the author of the Virginia Bill of Rights, expressed the notion in language typical of that period: "All men are created free and independent, and have certain inherent natural rights of which they cannot, by any compact, deprive or divest their posterity, among which are the enjoyment of life and liberty, with means of acquiring and possessing property and pursuing and obtaining happiness and safety." To contend that the letter of the Fifth Amendment said something different from what its authors intended, when it asserted the absolute right of any person not to be deprived of life, liberty, and property, and that what its authors had in mind was a much more modest assertion, that of a limitation on the federal authority only, is not to advance an argument worthy of being called historical. It is in fact the repudiation of the spirit of an entire period of history which could find no words too solemn or sacred to write the absolute, universal, eternal, and unlimited nature of the rights into their declarations and bills. The argument, far from being historical, is simply an unwarranted, legalistic expansion of the fact that the Bill of Rights was not intended, for certain historical reasons, to run against state governments. Hence the fallacious carry-over that it was formulated against one specific government, and not as a general assertion of rights.

It would be much more plausible to contend that the idea of interference by private governments never occurred to the framers of the Bill and that they had, therefore, never envisaged that the broad and impersonal formula of the Fifth Amendment could be invoked against private power holders. This may be perfectly true, but is this a conclusive argument of historical interpretation? In the *Classic* case the Supreme Court did not ask itself whether the authors of the Constitution, while formulating the procedure by which the citizens of the several states would elect their representatives to Congress, actually and psychologically intended to permit federal criminal sanctions against interference with primary ballots. But the Court held nevertheless that the Constitution, by its impersonal language, guaranteed an absolute individual right to have one's vote in a party primary regularly counted. And they held that any individual interference with such a right could be punished by the Federal Government. Was this type of situation actually envisaged by the framers of the Constitution? A party, a primary, a *de facto* control of a general election, a federal criminal statute, an interference by a private party employee—how strange all this would have sounded to the authors of *The Federalist*. Would they really have understood? And having understood, would they not have complained that complicated, overfine, hypothetical questions were being asked of them only in order to discredit the simple political soundness of the Constitution they defended?

Fortunately, proper canons of historical interpretation do not require inquiry into whether or not a given situation was actually contemplated by the authors of a document. The *Classic* case undertook no such inquiry; it examined the logical intent and ideological content of the law, not the psychological intention of its makers. Nor is the *Classic* case an exception. All over the world the interpretation of laws has become clearly distinct from the usually fruitless investigation of the contradictory motives of the multitude of mortal beings who concurred in making the laws. Not unlike Pygmalion's creation, a law once created has a personality, an immortal essence, and an intent, *intentus juris,* of its own. Nor should it ever be forgotten that it is not the lease of an apartment, three rooms and bath, but a Constitution that we are expounding. Article Five of the Constitution, providing for the amending process, is neither the sole nor the principal means through which the youthful freshness of that document can be and is preserved. The Constitution was never intended as a political strait jacket for generations to come. It would become that if its construction were reduced to a process of mind reading of the dead.

The American Constitution has survived so many other charters and has held its own through so many trying experiences not only because its guardians have never followed the narrow and technical standard of historical interpretation of a legalistic variety, but also because they have proved able from time to time to brush aside historical arguments of genuine value and standing. History is made up not only of a nation's past but of its future as well. John C. Calhoun, Francis Lieber, and Alexander H. Stephens knew their constitutional law and their history well. When one compares Calhoun's *Disquisition on Government,* Stephen's *Constitutional Views,* or even William J. Grayson's *The Hireling and the Slave,* with the abolitionists' arguments, with the involvements of Story's *Commentary* or the empty rhetoric of Daniel Webster's Seventh of March speech, one marvels at the wisdom of the nation that chose the right cause rather than the right arguments. When Story or Webster—whichever got the notion first—seized upon the editorial accident of the preamble's "We the People of the United States," and used it to maintain that the "Constitution was not a compact," were they guilty of historical inaccuracy? It depends on what we understand by history. Does history consist only of what people know they are doing? Is it a historical mistake to build a monument to Columbus, discoverer of a continent? As Charles A. Beard said, the Fathers built better than they knew when they wrote "We the People."

I have suggested that when they wrote "No person shall be deprived of life, liberty or property without due process of law" they knew what they wrote: the assertion of an absolute individual right, not a mere limitation on the power of a specific government. But even if I were wrong and they meant only the latter, I say with Beard that they built better than they knew. Their broad and solemn language, "We the People" or "No person shall be deprived," may have been due to editorial accidents, and their historical significance may have been totally unknown to their authors. We are yet waiting for a Story or a Webster to open to our law the third dimension of private governments.

The occasion is not less solemn nor the times less pressing than those which witnessed the struggle over the issue of slavery. As a matter of fact, the very issue is far from settled. Emancipation raised more questions than it answered. It is still, socially, politically, and constitutionally, an unfinished job.

The thesis that the Constitution as it stands today provides ample restraints against the abuse of private power can be substantiated in a number of other ways. Even if the Fifth Amendment were discarded, the result sought by the argument just made could be achieved in other ways. Again, I think the *Classic* case has given us a huge reservoir of new constitutional power and has opened breath-taking constitutional vistas. Let us not forget that it did not deal with the direct exercise of a man's right to vote in a federal election. The vote in question was merely a vote *in a primary*. Nor did the Court hold that the primary elections were so regulated as to become part of the governmental machinery. It assumed— this is why the case is so unlike the subsequent case of *Smith* v. *Alwright* [3]—that there was *no legal connection* whatsoever between the private primaries and the elections provided for in the Constitution. The test established by the Court is the realistic one of factual, actual influence. It is, if you please, a sociological or statistical rather than a legal test. If, said the Court, the outcome of a private primary is in fact determinative of the result in the official elections—if, in other words, what in fact governs the political life of the community is the party poll and not the official election— then the constitutional requirement of fairness in the elections extends further to the private game which really counts.

---

[3] 321 U.S. 649 (1944).

If the principle is fully grasped in its deep meaning and whole-heartedly accepted, its application cannot stop at the counting of primary ballots. These ballots are only an example of factual domination of the political processes of a community. In the light of the unambiguous language of the *Classic* case, the application of constitutional restraints to private-power interference with our main political right, the right to be genuinely, actually, and not colorably free in the choice and selection of our rulers, becomes only a question of evidence. If students of society can prove that certain illegitimate economic pressures or odious restraints on freedom of expression and education do control in fact the political processes of a given society, just as statistics proved the strategic value of Democratic primaries, the philosophy, indeed the holding, of the *Classic* case calls for their outlawry on constitutional grounds. The process involved in this expansion of the principle of the *Classic* case is an application of a method that was used in a familiar constitutional development: that of the inclusion of the substance of various provisions of the Bill of Rights in the due process clause of the Fourteenth Amendment.

Historically, the due process clause was thought of as only one of the many guarantees of freedom, and was conceived, most probably, as merely procedural in nature. It became, through a series of cases, the main formula for restraining state action limiting freedom of speech, religion, et cetera. I submit that the right to keep the political processes free from private interference, the doctrine asserted in the *Classic* case, is a broad formula that must cover, to mean what it says, freedom from vicious private interference with political education and the formation of opinion, and freedom from economic obstacles in its expression.

In this connection, it may be appropriate to recall that the constitutional significance of the Civil War was not limited to the extension of constitutional restraints from the federal to state governments. This was the function of the Fourteenth Amendment. But the Thirteenth Amendment had quite a different meaning. By abolishing slavery, it struck a blow against the most powerful network of private governments of that epoch. Both the Thirteenth and Fourteenth Amendments were written, historically speaking, with the single objective of protecting the Negro in the southern states. Since that time, however, the Fourteenth Amendment has been invoked and applied in the North and in the South on behalf of individuals of all races and of corporations of all persuasions, in circumstances and on issues which have not even the remotest connection with the Negro or the Civil War issues. At the beginning, as in the *Slaughterhouse* cases,[4] this extension was worked with a little bow of apology to history, but that ritual was soon abandoned. The Thirteenth Amendment, however, has not been similarly expanded beyond the original intention of its framers, and I wonder whether it could not be used for wider purposes.

Are "slavery" and "involuntary servitude" simply synonyms, and is the Amendment's express condemnation of both merely repetitious? Or was "involuntary servitude" included to cover peonage only? When from time to time antilabor bills are introduced in Congress, their antistrike provisions are called a violation of the Thirteenth Amendment. Perhaps they are, perhaps not. But, I submit, the Amendment, framed as it concededly is to cover not only governmental but private coercion as well, could find application beyond the conventional master and slave relationship, and could be found to restrain any unreasonable private economic coercion in the labor market. Only if this were done would we have found a complete answer to William J. Grayson's southern pamphlet *The Hireling and the Slave*, which found many aspects of slavery in the wage earner's situation. Economic coercion can come from all types of private governments. I submit that not only some statutory clauses, provisions prohibiting or limiting strikes, but certain provisions of private collective bargaining agreements may be held to be violations of the Thirteenth Amendment.

This suggestion relative to the Thirteenth Amendment must be read in connection with the already discussed principle of the *Classic* case. I submit that the combined right to political (Article One) and economic (Thirteenth Amendment) freedom is applica-

---

[4] 16 Wall. (U.S.) 36 (1873).

ble in both aspects against governments and individuals and that, administered with due regard to factual rather than merely legal power centers, they provide as exhaustive a scheme of constitutional controls of private governments as the direct application of the Fifth Amendment could ever provide.

There is yet another approach to our problem. This approach does not, strictly speaking, deny the orthodox notion that the Constitution runs against governments only. But it may achieve the same results we were looking for in our assertion that the Constitutional rights of political liberty, economic freedom, and due process are rights running against both governments and individuals.

There is the famous dictum of Chief Justice Hughes that the Constitution is what the Supreme Court says it is. I submit that while the Constitution is sometimes more than that, it is often something less: it is often just what the Supreme Court says that decent American legislators or administrators ought to have intended when they passed certain statutes or regulations. In other words, Supreme Court Justices employ only sparingly their power to pronounce what this or that provision of the Constitution means. Frequently they avoid constitutional questions by saying that although a statute is silent on a given point, the legislators, devoted as they are to the constitutional dictates, must have intended a given meaning. This at times creates results of interest to those who believe in historical sequences. Thus, in the *Schneiderman* case,[5] the Court, interpreting a statute adopted in the nineteenth century, said that Congress in passing it must have intended to respect the clear and present danger standard of constitutionality —the standard having first been evolved after the First World War.

Most writers and readers of judicial opinions thus constructed think that they do not decide but avoid constitutional questions. Technically speaking, this may be perfectly true. In fact, however, when a judge, interpreting a statute conceived to be ambiguous, says that he, the judge, cannot suppose that a decent legislator could have intended a certain result because of constitutional devotion,

---

[5] 320 U.S. 118 (1942).

the judge asserts his own constitutional beliefs. Far from being irrelevant to the growth of constitutional law, some of the so-called statutory decisions have considerable constitutional significance.

Among numerous decisions of this kind—so numerous that it has been said that the principal constitutional battleground has shifted from constitutional construction to statutory interpretation—there was the case of *Steele* v. *Louisville & Nashville R.R.,*[6] in which the Supreme Court held that a union which represented all the employees of a craft could not enter into a collective bargaining agreement with a railroad which would establish racial discrimination against the Negro workers in that craft. The Court did not reach—or avoided—the constitutional question. It simply said that when Congress in 1934 amended the Railway Labor Act establishing exclusive bargaining in the railroad industry, it must have intended that the bargaining union should not discriminate in the bargaining process among the employees it represented on account of their race, creed, or color, or any other unreasonable classification. In other words, a union, a private government, must behave in accordance with the same principles of decency which are imposed by the Fifth and Fourteenth Amendments upon a legislature, a public government. Chief Justice Stone, writing for a unanimous court, expressed this notion as follows:

We think that the Railway Labor Act imposes upon the statutory representative of a craft at least as exacting a duty to protect equally the interests of the members of the craft as the Constitution imposes upon a legislature to give equal protection to the interests of those for whom it legislates. Congress has seen fit to clothe the bargaining representative with powers comparable to those possessed by a legislative body both to create and restrict the rights of those whom it represents, . . . but it has also imposed on the representative a corresponding duty. We hold that the language of the Act to which we have referred, read in the light of the purposes of the Act, expresses the aim of Congress to impose on the bargaining representative of a craft or class of employees the duty to exercise fairly the power conferred upon it in behalf of all those for whom it acts, without hostile discrimination against them. . . .

[6] 323 U.S. 192 (1944).

And Justice Murphy, in a separate concurring opinion, said:

The constitutional problem inherent in this instance is clear. Congress, through the Railway Labor Act, has conferred upon the union selected by a majority of a craft or class of railway workers the power to represent the entire craft or class in all collective bargaining matters. While such a union is essentially a private organization, its power to represent and bind all members of a class or craft is derived solely from Congress. The Act contains no language which directs the manner in which the bargaining representative shall perform its duties. But it cannot be assumed that Congress meant to authorize the representative to act so as to ignore rights guaranteed by the Constitution. Otherwise the Act would bear the stigma of unconstitutionality under the Fifth Amendment in this respect. For that reason I am willing to read the statute as not permitting or allowing any action by the bargaining representative in the exercise of its delegated powers which would in effect violate the constitutional rights of individuals. . . .

It would be difficult to overstate the importance of this decision. It opens in the field of public law possibilities similar to those which have been offered in the field of private law through the doctrine of constructive conditions. It is, in fact, nothing else than the doctrine of constructive conditions applied to the field of public law. With his usual directness, Holmes said, "You always can imply a condition in a contract," and it may be permissible to echo his remark by saying, "You always can imply a condition in a statute or in a regulation." Why should a judge imply a condition in a statute, a charter, a regulation? Because this may avoid a constitutional question, or, more realistically, because of his more or less inarticulate conviction that a decent and reasonable legislator operating under the American Constitution ought not and cannot have intended to give exclusive bargaining powers to unions, charters and tax exemptions to universities, franchises to public utilities, licenses to employment agencies, corporate charters to huge business enterprises, or exemptions from antitrust laws to export companies without remembering that they are *de facto* governments, private sovereigns, and without imposing upon them, at least by implication, the duty to act fairly, and with decent respect for the individual rights of those who, as suppliers, investors, workers, or buyers, are subject to their powers.

The doctrine of constructive conditions is a weapon of peaceful reform in every flexible society. It is the vehicle through which judges and administrators are able to pay the highest homage to the intention of those who, once upon a time, had written the constitutions, statutes, charters, or contracts. These documents are proved to be written for the future because they can be adapted to the new times by the insertion of constructive conditions, called for by the new spirit of the community. The only question is whether or not the new spirit calls for the imposition of an equal-protection and due-process constructive condition upon the holders of private power—in other words, whether to treat them as *de facto* governments rather than just as private individuals.

This may be a question of opinion. But before we make up our minds, let me quote two highly respectable exponents of the spirit of the times. One is Beardsley Ruml, the other is the senior senator from Ohio, Robert Taft. The former wrote a book, *Tomorrow's Business*, devoted to a single proposition—the assertion of the truth that business is a private government. The latter introduced a bill in the Senate to combat racial and religious discrimination in private employment. The bill was destined to avoid a more avid, a more aggressive measure proposed by Senator Chavez for the same purpose, and malignant critics say that the Taft bill would be a mere sham. But the point is that in the preamble of his bill Senator Taft states bluntly and unhesitatingly that discrimination by private employers violates the rights guaranteed by the Constitution of the United States. While liberal lawyers are still worrying about the circumvention of the principle asserted in the *Civil Rights* cases that only states, not private individuals, must give equal protection, Senator Taft has long since jumped the gun and is plainly on record that the Constitution is a system of rights rather than a scheme of governmental restraints.

It is, of course, obvious to every lawyer that this constructive-conditions approach can be more easily handled when, as was the case in *Steele* v. *Louisville & Nashville R.R.*, the statute or charter

[119]

to be interpreted is a federal grant. When the document to be construed is a state grant, the position is more complex and I cannot discuss it exhaustively now. I shall only remark that there are cases which have been remanded from the Supreme Court to a state court with the gentle hint that before examining the constitutionality of the state act the federal court would like to know whether, by any chance, the state court can find a constructive condition in it that would make moot the constitutional challenge.

There is a fourth approach to our problem. This approach would consist in the suggestion that the governmental duties asserted in the Fifth and Fourteenth Amendments be construed not only as a duty to refrain from certain action but also as a duty to act in circumstances which clearly call for action. A state can deprive a person of life, liberty, or property by omission as well as by commission. The rigid distinction between malfeasance and nonfeasance has been to a degree discredited in the field of torts. It could be revised in the field of constitutional law as well. After all, the Declaration of Independence called upon the governments "to secure" individual rights, and this verb undoubtedly includes the duty of affirmative action. Chapter 29 of the Magna Charta, made famous by Coke in his advocacy of the higher law that binds governments, included not only pledges of omission but promises of positive assistance as well: "we will not deny or defer to any man, either justice or right."

I believe that this is a fruitful approach for various reasons. First of all, it tends to weaken the unsound distinction between commission and omission. It is a question of constitutional realism and plain legal honesty. When state enforcement machinery breaks down and lynch law takes its place, a state government is in effect depriving, through its inaction, persons within its jurisdiction of their lives without due process of law. It is simple logic to recognize that this deprivation must be "imputed" to the state government as much as its affirmative action would be. The notion that a constitutional duty of a government may call for an affirmative action is made explicit at least in one provision of the Constitution, the one that calls upon the United States "to guarantee to every state a republican form of government." And the quotation is not inappropriate in this connection if one reflects that mob rule and failure to guarantee those rights of life and liberty, to secure which governments are instituted among men, are hardly consistent with the Founding Fathers' conception of a republican form of government.

In some other connections, the duty of the state—and if it fails, the duty of the Federal Government—to act for the protection of individual rights may be less apparent but not less well founded in logic and political philosophy. The cases I have now in mind are those in which an individual is faced with an abuse of power of the very peculiar form of private sovereignty which is the result of the concerted action of several individuals bound together into a conspiracy, a combination, or a monopoly. It must not be forgotten that to the extent to which private governments were neglected and forgotten by the political philosophers who envisioned our present system of government, this was due to a species of political laissez-faire individualism, a counterpart of the economic laissez-faire theories. In other words, political and economic equilibriums could be achieved because independent individuals, each acting for his individual interest, were, in their mutual interaction, guided by an invisible hand to serve the common welfare. But this was possible only if these individuals were numerous enough, weak enough taken singularly and compared to the nation as a whole, and acting independently. Concerted action was interference with the invisible hand, interference with the design of Providence. Hence the highly criminal character of conspiracies, hence the Turgot *coup d'état* against the Guilds and its failure, Du Pont de Nemours' exile to America, his friendship with Jefferson, the final triumph of the antiguild doctrines, and Jefferson's request that a provision against monopolies be included in the Bill of Rights. In modern terms, we may suggest that if a government may not, as the Supreme Court has unanimously held in the *Schechter Poultry* case,[7] delegate its power to a trade guild, it is doubtful whether it has the constitutional right to abdicate in favor of the factual dic-

---

[7] A. L. A. Schechter Poultry Corporation v. United States, 295 U.S. 495 (1935).

tatorship of a trade guild or forego the regulation of a market dominated by a monopoly.

These suggestions will appear less paradoxical if one considers that antitrust laws have been already treated by high federal tribunals as a means of achieving through affirmative governmental action some of our most solemn constitutional dictates, framed, be it remarked, by the way, in a clearly negative fashion. The First Amendment, indeed, if more than any other constitutional provision, was formulated as a restraint on the power of a governmental agency; still, in the *Associated Press* case [8]—and implicitly in the *National Broadcasting Company* case [9]—it has been treated as containing a mandate that can be properly fulfilled not only through mere governmental abstention from interference but also through affirmative governmental antitrust action against combinations of individuals who, despite their private character, were in fact able to threaten the ideals which, if language should control, were to be protected from governments only. The lasting importance of the *Associated Press* case is that the courts have shown themselves inclined to believe that freedom of speech and freedom of the press are not necessarily and exclusively freedoms *from* governmental action, but can become freedoms *through* governmental action as well. Its implication for our purposes is that these constitutional ideals can be conceivably violated not only through governmental commission but through governmental omission as well.

It should be emphasized at this point that this fourth approach to our problem—based on the notion that state action in the constitutional sense may embrace state inaction as well—has a particular advantage because of the federal character of the Constitution we are expounding. Our present suggestion, indeed, does not impair the rightful independence of the states and does not purport to create a federal cause of action for every wrong or injury that an individual could suffer through the action of a private lawful or unlawful group. It preserves that complementary, secondary, interstitial character of the national government which is the essence of our federal system. It gives the state governments a chance. It

---

[8] Associated Press v. United States, 325 U.S. 1, 19 (1944).

[9] National Broadcasting Company v. United States, 319 U.S. 190 (1943).

does not intend to punish every murder in the United States. Only when the state enforcement machinery breaks down should the Federal Government step in.

Ours is, in more than one sense, a federal country. Its federalism is indeed only one aspect of its essential pluralism. These aspects of it must be preserved because they are the very essence of freedom. Our thesis does not envisage a leviathan state, nor even the abolition of private governments. The title of our paper is "Private Governments and the Federal Constitution." What we mean by it is that the private governments should be recognized as the legitimate expression of the pluralistic reality of society; that our society should be conceived as a constitutional federation of an infinite number of *de facto* sovereignties, all united and controlled by certain principles of minimum decency, but free in their wide variety, in their different ways of life, and their interpretation of those minimum standards. That freedom of minor groups, of the *de facto* governments, is indeed the essence of controls called constitutional.

It must be stated emphatically that our doctrine of private government is not premised on the assumption that no private citizen is allowed to do what a government is barred from doing. That assumption is in itself obviously false and very dangerous for the existence of a free society. We believe that certain types of activity by private groups are in fact political activity, indistinguishable, except in scope and degree, from the activities of official governments, and that a realistic conception of the position of an individual in society calls for a constitutional protection of his rights from private as well as from public governments. But we do not maintain, for instance, that an individual should be denied the right to throw a party inviting "practically everybody," but excepting Jews, women, Negroes, Catholics, or just people who do not take to liquor. Nor would we agree that in the enforcement of his exclusionary policy he may not rely on the power of state and that the court may not send a sheriff to help him to keep uninvited persons off the premises because the court could not send a sheriff to enforce a statute embodying the same discriminatory policy.

The notion that no individual can do what a government is

barred from doing ignores one of the main sources of human happiness: the right to be capricious, arbitrary, irrational, irresponsible, even unjust. Let us not try to reduce society to an agglomeration of due process robots or of equal protection automatons. As living individuals we could never breathe in an atmosphere of pure oxygen —nor could we live in an atmosphere of completely rational justice, in which every one of our actions would have to live up to the categorical imperative that Kantian philosophers describe as a maxim capable of universalization, and constitutional lawyers as reasonableness of classification.

As a matter of fact, let us not forget that some of the greatest human values not only escape universalization, classification, and the tests of reason, but, indeed, consist in their being beyond such criteria. While their material or physical expression may indeed be subject to coercion, legal or otherwise, their spiritual essence, their value, can never be captured but only destroyed through such a procedure. To give an extreme example, what we today call love would be destroyed if more than a free "yes" or "no" were required as a justification for an answer. The infinite satisfaction that one derives from real affection is that it is not conditioned on one's being right or clever or handsome or better qualified. This is what distinguishes love from a lawsuit or a civil service examination. Not to discriminate, nay, not to be at least a little bit arbitrary in love, in friendship, in writing a poem, or in forming a club, is almost as bad as to be arbitrary in examining candidates or deciding cases.

These are extreme cases, but their principle finds ample application in the structure of a political society. Plato, who knew how to be consequent, and Socrates, who knew how to choose his interlocutors, clearly saw the links between unity of a society and the total destruction of the element of arbitrariness in all human relations, beginning with the relations between man and wife, parent and child. If we try to match their intellectual courage, we shall concede that unless a certain element of capriciousness and arbitrariness is introduced in the world, unless differences which are in a sense arbitrary, nonrational differences are admitted, preserved, and protected, unless our society is a society of societies, a community of communities, real freedom cannot be achieved. Maybe by say-ing that we side with Aristotle against Plato, we may make entirely clear that we do not intend to settle the question here and now.

The passages from Aristotle are worth rereading: "I am speaking of the premise from which the argument of Socrates proceeds, 'that the greater the unity of the state the better.'" This premise, says Aristotle, is false. "We ought not to attain this greatest unity even if we could," says Aristotle, "for it would be the destruction of the state." "Again, a state is not made up only of so many men, but of different kinds of men, for similars do not constitute a state. It is not like a military alliance . . . ; but the elements out of which a unity is to be formed differ in kind. Wherefore the principle of compen-sation, as I have already remarked in *Ethica,* is the salvation of states. . . ." [10]

The error of Socrates must be attributed to the false notion of unity from which he starts. Unity there should be both of the family and of the state, but in some respects only. For there is a point at which a state may attain such a degree of unity as to be no longer a state, or at which, without actually ceasing to exist, it will become an inferior state, like harmony passing into unison, or rhythm which has been reduced to a single foot.[11]

This is the best defense for a pluralistic conception of society that I can offer. On it I would be content to rest, were it not necessary to reconnect that general position to two peculiarities of American legal and political folklore without which our general position is not fully understandable. These two peculiarities are: (1) constitu-tionalism, and (2) federalism. The more unisonal harmony of which Aristotle speaks is attempted in the American system through the peculiarity of a constitutional control which is not dissimilar to the judge's control of a jury. It leaves ample room for nonrational, intuitional, experimental, and arbitrary elements. It renounces, by definition, the idea of perfection, makes justice a ques-tion of degree, and is satisfied with keeping the juror's whim or dis-cretion and the several governments' discretion or whim within the

---

[10] *Politics,* Bk. II, Ch. 2, 1261a (Jowett trans.).
[11] *Politics,* Bk. II, Ch. V, 1263b.

minimum limits of reason, and thus to reconcile diversity with equality and the rule of law with the freedom of men.

The second and strictly connected principle is that of federalism. We have made throughout our discussion the comparison between the post-Civil War amendments and the now advocated constitutional control of private governments. Let us not forget that not all of the results of the Civil War were favorable. Parrington considered that

the lost cause carried down to defeat much more than slavery, it carried down the old ideal of decentralized democracies of individual liberty; and with the overthrow of the traditional principles in their last refuge, the nation hurried forward along the path of an unquestionable and uncritical consolidation, that was to throw the coercive powers of a centralizing state into the hands of the new industrialism.

To study the main currents, one is almost pushed to the conclusion that the abolition of slavery has impaired the mainsprings of American freedom, a conclusion in which, by the way, both Plato and Aristotle might have concurred. But be that as it may, there is no doubt that constitutional control of *de facto* governments of churches or unions, fraternities or monopolies, trade associations or universities, is big not only with hopes but with dangers as well—the danger of a monistic, centralized, coalescent leviathan state.

There is no doubt that in the last decades we have placed too great a reliance in the Federal Government. There is a curious thing about the alphabetical agencies it creates: a few of them begin with F—FLSA, FEPC, and FTC—and we do not always know at first whether F stands for Federal or Fair; it is sometimes one and sometimes the other, but for many of us it is always both. For this situation the Federal Government is not to be blamed. The trouble is with the local, the state, governments, which permitted the identification of the federal and the liberal causes. But there is no doubt that it would be much better if we could have an LEPC rather than an FEPC, where L would stand for both local and liberal.

I would rather have a country with advanced, progressive local governments and a slightly retarding federal machinery than the inverse situation which this country has had during the Civil War and during the F. D. Roosevelt administration. Again the fault does not lie with Lincoln or with the New Dealers. It is simply a tragedy that a man of the distinction, nay, of the genius, of the author of *A Disquisition on Government*, a man whose masterly translation of a pluralistic, Aristotelian philosophy into the American constitutional language of the eminently sound and liberal doctrine of concurrent majorities should have tied his fate to the cause of slavery. It is a tragedy that a man who had the insight to understand and proclaim that the states are "an aggregate, in fact, of communities, not of individuals," had to assert in the same speech that to regard slavery as a moral and political evil is "folly and delusion" and that on the contrary it is "the most safe and stable basis for free institutions in the world." It is a tragedy that he should have tied his political career with people like Governor McDuffie of South Carolina, who owes his celebrity to the dictum that "the laboring population of no nation on earth are entitled to liberty, or capable of enjoying it." It has been a great American tragedy that the defenders of local liberties, of home rule, of free enterprise, of social and cultural pluralism, of state rights, of *de facto* governments, of social vigilantism have so often been the exponents of social reaction.

The problem of private governments and of their control will and and ought to have its American Gierke and its Durkheim; a new Alexander H. Stephens, a new Francis Lieber, a new John C. Calhoun, possibly nurtured as Calhoun was on Greek books and Greek ideals. May they find new ways for a nonunisonal American harmony; may they find new units, counties or cities, vocational or cultural, which will make up a new federal pattern, a new and more perfect union. But to succeed they will have to be forward-looking liberals, not defenders of slavery, because ours can be only a Greece without slaves.

Private Governments
and the Public Interest

BUSINESS

THIS is a book [1] about business written by one of its most talented lovers. It is a book wide in range and deep in significance. It contains an enlightened philosophical analysis of the idea of freedom and minute suggestions for a fiscal policy. It is sophisticated and impassioned at the same time. It reads easily and contains many passages well worth rereading and meditating. In short, it is a remarkable book. And I hasten to say so at the outset lest what I have to say later, in dissenting from the book, make me seem unfair to its merits.

Beardsley Ruml is fascinated by the way business gets things going and enjoys telling us about it. His story does not begin with production, investment, finance, or management. It begins with the people who use what business produces. Says Ruml:

Final use takes place in the hands of the people—in the hands of Mr. and Mrs. I. M. Consumer, their children and their neighbors. These families use soap and milk, towels and sheets, radios and vacuum cleaners, beds and tables, apartments and houses, fire insurance and the daily newspaper, and a thousand other things besides. . . . In most cases they do not know where, how, or even by whom these things are made. They only know where they can be bought—the rest is generally taken for granted.

---

[1] Beardsley Ruml, *Tomorrow's Business* (New York, 1945).

Who places at their very doorsteps this incredible variety of things Mr. and Mrs. Consumer could not possibly make for themselves? It is business. "The first business of business is to get things ready for use." The second is to "provide people with purposeful activity, with something useful to do." The third is to "give people a place where they can invest their savings."

Getting raw materials, manufacturing and distributing them, and letting the people know that the products and services are available; thinking up things to do and giving people a chance to produce goods which sell at a profit and thus do something that "is not boondoggling, no matter what a philosopher might judge by abstract standards to be the value of the work"; making the pleasurable satisfaction of the universal instinct to save as helpful as possible to the saver and to the community at large—all these, and more, are the activities of business described in loving detail by Beardsley Ruml.

All these and more. In his admiration for business the author sees it as something more important than just a source of goods and services, of jobs and investment opportunities. Business is to him "a source of order and of freedom." Ruml's book is not an exaltation of business as business. Its central theme is business' social responsibility for human freedom. Ruml would not think of claiming for business—as so many of her lesser lovers do—a quiet "private" existence, far from the limelight of public functions, rights, and duties. This book is a book about business; but business is authority and power, direction and decision, and so, says Ruml, "this book about business becomes a book about power." Despite this verbal coincidence, the book does not follow the pattern or the philosophy of Brady's *Business as a System of Power*. But neither is it an apology based on the sacred rights of a privately owned enterprise, which to be free must be free from accountability for the use of its privately owned resources. The adjective "private" rarely occurs in the book except in conjunction with the noun "government." The book has, indeed, enough courage to proclaim that business is not only a producer, but also a rule-maker, a government—one of our most powerful private governments. To do so in America is an act of courage because, by proudly proclaiming that business is a "private govern-ment," one puts business' throne right on top of a powder keg of long-accumulated explosive ideas about the purposes for which all governments are instituted among men.

When Ruml disdainfully repudiates the slogan of the rank and file of business' friends and proclaims that "not freedom for busi-ness, but business for freedom must be the objective," the proud knight jumps into the very midst of our modern, and still romantic, political arena to pick up the heavy glove of a mighty challenge.

Does Ruml's book live up to its initial springboard courage? Does Ruml's business live up to the ideal whose challenge he has ac-cepted? Does Ruml's book establish in fact a concrete plan for business' acceptance of its responsibility for order and freedom? That is the question. The significance and the weakness, the charm and the disappointment of the book lie in the fact that it is a book about the supremacy of freedom over business, written by a man who can't help loving business more than he loves freedom. Ruml is aware of the fact that, to survive, business must be made to fit the end of human freedom and happiness. But he never asks himself— and this is where his acceptance of business as a basic datum of his philosophy comes in—whether freedom and happiness could be better secured by means other than business as we know it today. He writes on the premise that business is a means to an end, but he never fully subordinates the means to the end. His question is, at best, "What is the better way of making business serve freedom?" But it is certainly not, "What is the better way of serving freedom, through business or otherwise?" And the sudden air pockets in his reasoning make the reader sometimes dizzily sus-picious that Ruml is only exploring the minimum concessions busi-ness must make to freedom in order to survive, not the optimum conditions of freedom which present-day reality could afford.

This point can best be seen by examining the central point of the book. Ruml's main thesis is that business is a rule-maker, a pri-vate government. To him this does not mean only that, for instance, a corporation governs itself in a way not dissimilar from that in which any self-governing group performs such a function. Faithful to its initial courage, Ruml's book is outspoken about the fact that business makes rules not only for itself but for society at large. To the question, "If business is a private government, who are the governed?" Ruml gives a complete answer. His answer is, "We are all governed." Not only as stockholders and vendors or suppliers, but also as customers and employees, we are all subject to the rules made by business, rules which "are final and not reviewable by any public body."

The next question would seem to be how well we, the governed, are represented in the body that has the power to make these un-reviewable rules for us. Ruml himself shows eloquently that not even the stockholders and owners (to say nothing of vendors, workers, or consumers) control the rule-making bodies of business, since "the fact is that the stockholders *elect* the directors but they do not *choose* them. They are *chosen* by the Board of Directors itself, which makes the nominations." It is therefore hardly surprising that Ruml expressly recognizes the desirability, if not the neces-sity, that the boards of directors, these central agencies of corpo-rate power, should be transformed so that they may represent "more nearly the interests of those whom business governs." So far so good. But how is such representation to be achieved? At this critical point, we find the logical air pocket. Confronted with a concrete political problem, Ruml seems to take leave of his hard-boiled realism, of his logic, and of his inventiveness and makes a suggestion of breath-taking naïveté: to safeguard the interests of labor, consumers, mi-nority stockholders, and suppliers, governed by but not represented in business, the existing boards of directors—these self-perpetuating bodies practically responsible to nobody—should be asked to ap-point one of their old or newly elected members to act as a "trustee" for one of the group of the governed—for instance, for labor. In other words, to assure freedom, the governors not otherwise respon-sible will choose, appoint, pay, and keep in office as long as they wish "trustees" for the governed!

Is it actually necessary to argue that where there is conflict of interests—and Ruml, once again, is blunt in recognizing that "the

interests of the four groups are in conflict"—the representatives of
one of the interests cannot be appointed by the bearers of the conflicting interest and that, if so appointed, they are not "representatives" at all? Must we prove that the term "trustee" can find no
legitimate application to a person whose appointment, compensation, and continuation in service depend exclusively on the will or
the whim of a party which, by definition, has an interest opposite to
those who must be protected? The ancient query *quis custodiet
ipsos custodes?* would find a solution simple indeed, if the control
of the controllers could be left with the controlled. It is true that
the idea has seduced other lawmakers; for instance, the supervisors
of Italian corporations, the *sindaci*, were appointed and paid by the
directors whom they were supposed to supervise. But is it necessary
to point out that the results were ludicrous? Ruml suggests that
these "trustees" for the interests governed by business be well paid
and seems to think that the "essential point is that the director-
trustee should be paid for his time at a rate that will give the company the services it must have if it is to do more than mere shadow
boxing." But is it not true that, as long as removal is within the un-
controlled discretion of an assembly dominated by the board, a
generous compensation is likely to function as a deterrent rather
than as an encouragement of an energetic defense of interests in
conflict with those who have the power to remove?

Thus the book breaks down badly at its very center, where exercise of power by business was supposed to be checked by the supremacy of freedom. Instead of a plan that would assure a genuine
representation of those governed by business in the councils of their
"private government," we are simply presented with a scheme
aimed at forestalling more drastic reforms. Unless this is done, warns
Ruml, "someone will someday, perhaps at a most inconvenient
time, make it his crusade to turn these interests into rights."

Ruml's administration of the test of "consent" in the field of
business is worth comparing with his application of the same test
in the field of labor. While asserting that the business-appointed
trustees for labor and consumers will be instrumental in "extend-

ing the area of consent in the rule-making of private business," he contends, in speaking of labor, that the first reason why the time for the union shop has not yet come is that "the rule-makers of the labor union do not rule by consent of the employees. . . . The government of labor unions does not truly represent the choice of the governed employees."

Now, it is certainly true that the conditions under which collective bargaining has been established in many companies have involved from time to time the use of "threats, intimidation, misrepresentation, forgery, humiliation, and even physical force." It could be remarked—in fairness—that labor cannot be made solely responsible for the use of these means that have been part of the arsenal of both contending parties. Be that as it may, it is surprising that an author who is willing to recommend the trusteeship system as a means of assuring consent of the governed should assert emphatically, as Ruml does, "This is not government by consent" when confronted with the fact that some union organizers use measures "far stronger than those of example and persuasion."

It must be said that the forms of governmental control upon whose introduction he conditions the wisdom of the union shop seem perfectly reasonable and just to this reviewer. Ruml foresees, and apparently advocates, the public regulation of membership in unions (prohibition of discrimination on ground of race, creed, sex, or politics), of cost of production (prohibition of devices enforcing inefficiency), and of proper forms of fund auditing. As a matter of fact, I can see no reason why such regulation should not be advocated for all unions rather than as "the inevitable concomitant of the general extension of the union shop." Why should the public policy against unfair discrimination, wasteful restraints, and misuses of funds be restricted to labor unions which claim or obtain a union shop?

The reason for Ruml's connecting the demand for governmental controls to the union shop situation is apparently that this situation enables him to distinguish between the position of labor and that of business and to explain away the unfairness of the double moral standard that sets up different tests of consent and control for government by corporations and by unions. The distinction is based on the assertion that the union shop gives the labor leadership monopoly powers that business does not possess or claim. The requirements to which labor organized on the basis of union shops must submit would be applicable to business only, it seems, "if we were asked to give a business or an industry broad monopoly powers." The corresponding "broad monopoly" powers of labor are vividly, and I think correctly, described by Ruml:

These are important rules. They work well as long as the trade-union is open to all workers in its jurisdiction. But many unions are not open to all workers. A number of them keep out Negroes, aliens, and women. Some unions also exclude workers whose political beliefs they do not like. To keep out people because of their race, color, sex, citizenship, or political beliefs, where there is a union shop, means to deprive them of the chance to earn a living at their occupation. This is great power badly used.

In addition, there are "closed unions" which limit the number of full-fledged members. They make it hard for outsiders to join or to gain full membership rights by undue regulation of apprenticeship, by charging initiation fees deliberately designed to keep out members to work on union jobs without giving them new members, and by issuing permit cards to non-membership. Here, again, the union exercises an economic monopoly to the detriment of workers in its jurisdiction.

But does not business have equally great rule-making powers? Why is racial, religious, and political discrimination in employment mentioned by Ruml only in connection with labor? Is it his contention that employers practice it less than unions do? Ruml's answer is to be found in the idea that, while under the closed shop agreement union leaders exercise an economic monopoly, the competitive conditions existing as a rule in the field of business assure workers, stockholders, and consumers a freedom of choice. The stockholder can sell his stock and invest his money in another corporation. "The company he keeps, he keeps by choice." The David customer may be stronger than the Goliath corporation, "if he does not have to buy, or can postpone his buying, or can find something else that will do, or some other place to get it." And, similarly, the strength of the employee "lies in his ability, when he has it, to get another job from another employer or to get along without doing any work." The concluding paragraph of the chapter on "Business as Rule-Maker" reads:

Thus we see that tolerable freedom of the governed under the private rule-making of business, of the stockholders, of the vendors, of the customers, and of the employees of all rank comes from the opportunity to say, "No! I will do my business with another business." When the governed can say "No" they have powers as great as those of the strongest business.

Thus, despite all the appearances of modern sophistication, we are back to the old and long-exploded laissez faire notion that every buyer and seller of commodities or services has the possibility of choosing those with whom he wants to deal. Such opportunity exists in theory—or rather, as the imperfect competition studies have shown, in bad theory. But, in reality, the opportunity to say "No! I will do my business with another business" (a theoretical opportunity a worker has with respect to unions as well) frees stockholders, consumers, and workers from only one business, while the rule-making power is exercised by business as a whole. It is true, as Ruml assures us, that "most forms of collusion in the setting of prices are considered contrary to public interest and are made illegal as 'conspiracy in restraint of trade.'" But did—or can—the outlawing of "most forms of collusion" in fact eliminate concerted rule-making by business, be it in respect to rates, to prices, or to other terms at which business makes its services available? Or does this business power exist—as Ruml seems to suggest at a certain point— only during depression and unemployment? If business is a rule-maker, a private government, this is so only because it is able to act with a certain uniformity. Nor is it important to what extent this uniformity is the product of a conscious conspiracy, is due to "natural leadership" in prices or standards, or is just conformity to "natural" mercantile folkways. What matters is that conspiracy, acceptance of leadership, and compliance with custom are all manifestations of a policy-making, price-making, and rule-making business community.

If business is a government, if all prices are political or, at least,

policy prices, it is essential that the shape of the price structure prevailing in a society be controlled by the objectives of society at
large and not solely by the needs and considerations of a profit-
making government.

Ruml, once more, is outspoken as to the importance of profits as
the main impulse to the action of business as a government.

By all odds the most important energizer of corporate power is profit,
the experience of profit, and the prospect of profit.

Profit is not the only motive which brings corporate power into action.
. . . But . . . the underlying and unifying force, releasing all others and
giving meaning to all else, is profit. It is not merely the spark plug, it is
the spark within the plug.

Why should we give this profit-making government so much
authority and leave to it the regulation of such important aspects of
our lives? Ruml's answer is that the first function of profits is to
assure the compliance of business with the choice of the people.

In the first place, profits are a test of whether the thing that is made is
wanted, and whether enough people want it at the price at which it is
offered more than they want something else at some other price. If they
do not, there will be insufficient sales, and insufficient profits—or none
at all.

At this point, once more, I have the feeling of a logical air pocket.
It seems obvious to me that we are confronted with a totally unwarranted attempt to attribute to profits the function that belongs to
prices. It is true that unless the goods and services put at the disposal
of the public are priced (or otherwise limited, e.g., through a ration
coupon system), production will hardly be able to adjust itself to
the consumer's desire. Money prices (or, for that matter, ration
points) are the meter of the intensity and constancy of the popular
desires and preferences. If we leave aside the question of total purchasing power available to a given individual, economic freedom, as
distinguished from economic totalitarianism, is assured by the possibility of choosing within the limits of his total power (monetary system), or at least within certain relatively broad categories (red and

[136]

blue points), the things and services he prefers. And no choice would be possible if these things and services were not "priced," i.e., marked in the same quantitative symbols (money or coupons) in which the limits of the individual purchasing power are expressed. But why, to perform this function, is it necessary that prices include profits? Prices, not profits, to revise Ruml's sentence quoted above, "are a test of whether the thing that is made is wanted, and whether enough people want it at the price at which it is offered more than they want something else at some other price." As a matter of fact, profits, particularly high profits (and, under fair competitive conditions, Ruml maintains, "the higher the profits the better the interests of all are served" [2]), can and often do prevent people from using a product they would have used if it had been offered at a lower price. That "profits keep the wheels of a business machine turning" may be a correct description of the present state of affairs, but nothing seems to warrant the additional statement that profits keep the wheels turning "in the right direction."

Ruml offers one more "broad social" justification of profits—"they provide a pressure for ingenuity and efficiency"—and three additional reasons why profits serve the safety and welfare of any particular business: "they are a safeguard against errors in pricing; . . . they are the foundation on which additional capital can be raised as it is needed; . . . they are the measuring standard against which the efficiency of the management is tested."

These three additional reasons are not too persuasive. The first, the necessity of an insurance against errors in price-making, justifies margins on individual articles or in individual years, not profits as a permanent and basic feature. The other two reasons assume what they intend to prove. It is true that "the higher the profits have been and the longer and steadier the history of the earnings the lower will be the cost of [new] capital" and that (another way of putting the same thing) the efficiency of management is measured by the profits it makes. But this is so only because high profits are in fact

---

[2] An indication as to how high profits should be can be found in Ruml's remark that, to induce new capital into new business, annual rates of 20 per cent or 25 per cent would be "on the lean side."

the avowed purpose of business management. Since they are the goal toward which it strives, its credit and efficiency are measured by its ability to achieve them. If business management were to set for itself another goal—for instance, the widest possible distribution of goods and services which our generation believes to be essential for the people and a steady minimum return to savers sufficient to encourage saving and to assure industrial expansion—prestige of the management, and consequently the readiness of investors to trust it, would be measured in the light of approximation to these new goals. Confidence produced by somebody's ability to reach a goal is not a justification of the setting of the goal itself.

The same objection applies to profits as a means to stimulate ingenuity and efficiency. Not only may other rewards serve as stimulants of ingenuity and other tests as yardsticks for efficiency, but obviously the profit or compensation motive could produce practically the same results even if its whole scale were reduced in size while its proportions were preserved. What I consider a fallacy in Ruml's conception of the function of profits and compensation is particularly clear in his treatment of compensation. Ruml compares high managerial talents with those of the stars in movie, radio, and literature. He maintains that the method of mass distribution in business and popular arts requires "top talents" everywhere. He is so optimistic as to believe for instance, that today, "with the approval of millions at stake," movies have no more "room for high mediocrity." He concedes that " the difference in profit between great success and good success is out of all proportion to observable differences in the qualities of the offering itself," but argues that astronomic salaries paid "are well-justified on pragmatic grounds" and that any attempt to put a ceiling on them and thus limit the trend toward concentration of the production in the hands of the Big who can afford such salaries is doomed to failure.

Since there would be no competition between companies as to level, high talent would have to be satisfied at the ceiling price, since it would rather work than starve. Yes, but high talent can work part time, and that is exactly what would happen if the rate of pay per month, per year, or per lifetime were to be limited by law. The laws of nature have precedence

[138]

over the laws of man. The production and scarcity of high talent are stubborn facts. The profit of movie and radio companies will be higher with a $200,000 artist half time at $100,000 net compensation than it will with a $100,000 artist full time at $100,000. At the levels where salary limitations would be imposed, the final result would be to deprive the generation of a substantial and irreplaceable portion of the productiveness of its highest genius.

Can the reader imagine the "highest genius of our generation" who works only part time and gives only half of what he would give us otherwise because we don't let him make more than $100,000 a year while he thinks he is entitled—under the divinely decreed laws of our semimonopolistic economy—to twice as much? I confess I cannot. I don't think it does justice to men and I don't think it is good psychology or sound economic theory. I may be all wrong about the relationship between genius and salary, business, and society, but the apologia of profits in the name of freedom does not sound to me more persuasive than Cotton Mather's statement about the "Settled Business wherein a Christian should for the most part spend his time; and this, that he may glorify God," or Richard Baxter's treatment of lesser profits as of a religious delinquency:

If God show you a way in which you may lawfully get more than in another way (without wrong to your soul, or to any other) if you refuse this and choose the less gainful way, you cross one of the ends of your calling, and you refuse to be God's steward, and accept his gifts, and use them for him when he requireth it: you may labour to be rich for God, though not for the flesh and sin.

For once, I prefer the French who say *les affaires sont les affaires* —business is business. And, maybe, nothing is the matter with business or with its ruling us: after all, this base world never had a milder master. Let those who can, make money, and let nobody begrudge it to them. But after we have given to the modern Caesars what is rightfully theirs—the coins with their image on them—could we not stop there instead of going ahead and linking top salaries to genius, money-making to God's service, or business for profit to the promotion of liberty? If we could, quite a few of us would feel a lot better about the whole affair.

RADIO

[Below appears part of the brief prepared by Pekelis on behalf of the American Jewish Congress and filed with the Federal Communications Commission, in the case involving the News Syndicate Company, Inc., publisher of the New York *Daily News*. On April 15, 1947, the FCC issued a tentative decision granting to the *Daily News* an FM permit and striking from the record all evidence introduced by the AJC in opposition to the application. In November 1947 the FCC handed down a final decision denying the permit. This decision was vacated for procedural reasons, but on April 7, 1948, the FCC handed down a new decision denying the permit but for reasons other than those offered by the AJC. At the same time, however, it reversed its prior ruling with regard to the evidence introduced by the AJC and allowed that evidence to remain in the record. This was the end of the litigation. The part of the brief by Pekelis published here has a significance that transcends the specific occasion for its preparation and use.—Ed.]

AJC contends that the consistent bias and hostility displayed by the *Daily News* in its editorial and news columns against Jews and Negroes, its readiness to publish irresponsible and defamatory news items, and the convictions and beliefs disclosed in these proceedings by its executives render the *Daily News* unfit to act as the trustees of a public medium of communication and that accordingly the Commission should not, in preference to more deserving applicants, award it a permit to construct and operate an FM radio station.

FREEDOM OF SPEECH AND FREEDOM OF THE AIR

The AJC and Freedom of Speech

No other aspect of the present controversy is of greater concern to the American Jewish Congress than the question of the consistency between its position in this proceeding and its unwavering attachment to the basic principles of the First Amendment. We wish to state at the outset that we are submitting the evidence we have gathered to the Commission because we are fully satisfied that the acceptance of the theory upon which we have proceeded will result in a fuller protection of the basic aims of free speech and free press.

Our legitimate interest in the elimination of anti-Semitic discrimination and antiminority prejudice has never been conceived by us either as possessing an ideological autonomy or as having a possibility of achievement in a framework other than that of a free society. Our aims are full equality but we know that there can be no genuine equality where there is no freedom. Any short-range "gains" in the protection of minorities would be futile if they undermined the constitutional guarantees upon which the institutions of a free people are built. American minorities have no other weapon and no other hope than American freedom. The American Jewish Congress is no special-interest group and has never sought to achieve any illusory "advantage" for the group it represents at the expense of the general community. Jews, it has been said, are like other people—only more so. Our special interest, if any, in this case lies in the fact that we are twice, as Americans and as Jews, interested in the preservation of our common and basic freedom, freedom of speech, freedom of the press, and freedom of the air.

Free Speech: Competition and Monopoly

There are many mansions in the house of freedom. Freedom of speech from a soapbox and freedom in a courtroom, freedom of fair political comment and freedom of teaching, and freedom on a picket line and freedom before a microphone are not necessarily coextensive in either scope or intensity.

To realize in what form the general principle of freedom of expression can manifest itself concretely as the freedom of the air we must keep in mind the specific origin of at least one of the prevailing conceptions of free speech. This conception is indeed only one of the manifestations of the philosophy of a great century which found another expression in the theory of the free market. Holmes's classic formula, "the ultimate good desired is better reached by free trade in ideas—the best test of truth is the power of the thought to get itself accepted in the competition of the market" (*Abrams* v. *United States* [3]), still bears the clear indication of its connection with the doctrine of *laissez faire* and the underlying assumption that, in a free struggle, the fittest will survive and the best idea triumph. Just as free competition in the economic field will achieve economic equilibrium, social and political equilibrium will be achieved by free trade in ideas.

Once adopted, however, the free market analogy must be fully pursued. No advocate of economic *laissez faire* has ever suggested that the theories of free competition and free play of the laws of supply and demand should be left untrammeled where no free market exists and where such free play is physically impossible. Adam Smith himself emphatically *excepted* natural monopolies from the purview of a doctrine which identified economic freedom with freedom from governmental interference. Where monopolistic power threatens the helpless or unwary consumer, the preservation of ideological symmetry and of a uniform definition of freedom will sacrifice the substance of liberty to its form. Faced with the fact of a natural monopoly and with the dangers of economic or intellectual exploitation, society, jealous of the substance of its liberty, will choose freedom *through*, not freedom *from*, its government. *Laissez faire* means let the market alone, but has never meant let the monopoly alone.

Freedom of the Air

For broadcasting purposes, the air is a *natural monopoly* or at best a natural *oligopoly*. The maxims calling for the "market test of truth," for *laissez faire*, or for "free trade in ideas" sound ironical when applied to a medium of communication whose very existence would be in fact destroyed if the basic condition of free trade —"free access to the market"—were preserved. The competitive test of truth has no meaning in a forum in which not even one thousandth of one per cent of the total population is permitted to own a voice of its own.

[3] 250 U.S. 616 (1919).

[142]

These hard facts of radio life have long been recognized by our courts and commissions. The United States has already experimented with total "freedom" of broadcasting from governmental regulation. "The result was confusion and chaos. With everybody on the air, nobody could be heard" (*National Broadcasting Co.* v. *United States* [4])."The plight into which radio fell prior to 1927 was attributable to certain basic facts about radio as a means of communication. Its facilities are limited; they are not available to all who may wish to use them; the radio spectrum is not large enough to accommodate everyone." "Unless Congress had exercised its power over interstate commerce to bring about allocation of available frequencies the result would have been an impairment of the effective use of these facilities by anyone" (*Commission* v. *Sanders* [5]).

The truth of the matter is that the regulation of broadcasting must be predicated on and related to not only the congressional power over interstate commerce but also its power to protect freedom of speech as well. The freedom to listen is indeed the indispensable counterpart of the freedom to speak (*Martin* v. *Struthers* [6] and *Marsh* v. *State of Alabama* [7]). The freedom to use the air for purposes of communication between those who speak and those who listen would be totally destroyed by unreasonable governmental *inaction* which, under certain circumstances, may become as grave an impairment of constitutional freedoms as affirmative action. "In enacting the Radio Act of 1927, the first comprehensive scheme of control over radio communication, Congress acted upon the knowledge that if the potentialities of radio were not to be wasted, regulation was essential" (*National Broadcasting Company* v. *United States*), which means that if no regulation had taken place, the radio potentialities would have been wasted and freedom of the air denied to the country. A federal statute dealing mainly with economic matters, the Sherman Act, has been construed in at least

---

[4] 319 U.S. 190 (1943).
[5] 309 U.S. 470 (1940).
[6] 319 U.S. 141 (1942).
[7] 326 U.S. 501 (1945).

one occasion as aiming at the protection of "free trade of ideas" as well. A fortiori, the standard of "public interest, convenience or necessity" contained in an Act dealing with communications only must be construed as aiming at the protection of interests "akin to if not identical with those protected by the First Amendment" (Learned Hand, J., in *United States* v. *Associated Press* [8]).

In the field of radio communications, just as in any other field of human interchange of ideas, the basic aims and purposes of the First Amendment must be preserved. On the air, as elsewhere, communication must give the people adequate knowledge of public issues; enable them to make a free, that is to say uncoerced, informed, and enlightened, choice between various opinions and courses of action; elevate their cultural, aesthetic, and moral level; and enable them to exercise their political rights intelligently and to fulfill their political duties and responsibilities. The aims remain the same and the substance of liberty remains identical. But the achievement of those aims in the field of broadcasting can be assured only through and with the help of governmental action and cannot be brought about by the simpler device of governmental abstention. Therein lies the great difficulty with which a government is faced when it is determined neither to usurp the ultimate choice which must rest with the people nor to abdicate its duty to protect that people from a similar, and less warranted, usurpation by monopolistic private licensees and their customers, who have received no popular mandate and bear no political responsibility to anyone.

Private Trustees of a Public Interest

In facing this difficulty, the choice must be made between an affirmative or negative prior control, or censorship, of the specific content of the programs and the grant of a wide discretion to the licensees in the exercise of the public trust with which they have been vested. Congress has chosen the latter alternative and proscribed all censorship of specific programs by the Commission. The

---

[8] 52 F. Supp. 362, affd. 326 U.S. 1 (1945).

primary, the basic, responsibility, the gravamen of the public trust, has been left not with the Commission but with the private licensee. The Commission has consistently recognized this special position of the station owner and has never attempted to substitute its own criteria of operation for those of the broadcaster: "Under the American system of broadcasting, it is clear that responsibility for the conduct of a broadcast station must rest initially with the broadcaster" (*In re Mayflower Broadcasting Co.*[9]). The only form in which public regulation can manifest itself in the United States is the setting up of general criteria of performance and the selection of licensees who can be expected to live up to these criteria and be worthy of the widely discretionary public trust they are seeking from the Commission.

In this sense the Federal Communications Commission has much less power than other administrative regulatory agencies. The Interstate Commerce Commission may, for instance, prescribe not only the rates but the forms of service it expects from the operators. The routes, the schedules, the number of cars, the frequency of the stops, the type of freight, the extension or the abandonment of branch lines, and even the treatment of personnel are under the direct supervision of that agency. The Federal Communications Commission has no comparable powers. Once a license is granted, the licensee remains practically free in his operations. The Federal Communications Commission regulatory requirements and standards are general in form and the Commission has only a very limited power, if any, to issue specific directives to the licensee with respect to his program, be they affirmative in nature or couched in a cease and desist order. *The Commission's only real possibility of assuring broadcasting in the public interest and of enforcing respect for its general standards of operation is to perform its paramount duty and function, that of selection of trustworthy licensees, with utmost care and on the basis of a thoroughgoing inquiry into the ability of the licensee to serve the First Amendment's basic aims of information, discussion, and enlightenment.*

The United States has adopted a unique system of radio regula-

---

[9] 8 F.C.C. 333 (1940).

tions unparalleled in other countries. It is a most daring experiment, substantially based on the belief that a properly selected set of private licensees prompted by the profit motive is capable of performing a delicate public duty and serving public interest, convenience, and necessity in an area as vital for the political and cultural life of a country as that of formation of public opinion and public taste through the medium of mass communications. The success or failure of this experiment based on a great confidence in responsible private enterprise will obviously depend on whether or not the Federal Communications Commission will succeed or fail in establishing minimum ethical and cultural standards of performance and in selecting licensees who can reasonably be expected to live up to such standards and thus serve the public interest. Where there is no genuine competition tending to control standards, the task of creating standards and checking the monopolistic power of the franchise holder falls upon the regulatory agency. To be able to select only those licensees from whom adherence to such standards can be reasonably expected, the Commission must inquire into the specific communications background of the applicants and examine their past performances, particularly in the areas of public information, education of public taste, and enlightenment of public opinion. The evidence introduced by the AJC bearing on the character of newspaper activity of one of the applicants, the *Daily News*, is an illustration of the inquiries which must precede an informed and successful selection.

A "Momentous Issue"

The *Daily News* has objected, however, to the introduction of such evidence and has claimed that it is inconsistent with the provisions of the First Amendment and hence inadmissible.

The objection of the *Daily News* cannot possibly mean that to deny it an FM license is to deprive it of free speech. Whenever there are more applicants than available channels, some of them will inevitably be "deprived of free speech." In the present proceeding, for instance, there are seventeen applicants for the available five channels; hence there must be twelve denials of freedom to broadcast.

Our evidence only tends to show that it is more proper to classify the *Daily News* with the rejected twelve than with the privileged five.

Since the *Daily News* claims no special privileges under the Constitution, its objection must deal not with the purpose for which our evidence has been introduced but with its nature; not with the possibility of denial of a license but with the reasons adduced for it. From the oral argument of its counsel it is apparent that the *Daily News* challenges the power of the Federal Communications Commission (a) to predicate its decision on the content of the broadcasts which may be expected from the applicants; (b) to take into account the applicants' past performances in the communications field and more especially their activities as publishers or owners of newspapers.

This challenge goes, therefore, to what we have shown to be the very heart of the regulatory power of the Federal Communications Commission. By challenging the power to select applicants with a view to their capacity to serve the public need for genuine and unbiased information and debate, the challenge threatens the prime condition on which the American experiment in radio regulation hinges. Therefore, without raising the question as to whether or not the *Daily News* has, as a corporation, the right to invoke the protection of the First Amendment, we shall examine the merits of what the *Daily News* counsel correctly describes as a "momentous issue."

The Choice among Competing Applicants

We believe that the preceding discussion of the nature of the free speech doctrine and of the essential constitutional and political purposes of the Federal Communications Act are sufficient to show the socially dangerous and logically untenable character of the *Daily News* argument. We shall, at this point, add only the proof of their inconsistency with settled constitutional principles.

The United States Supreme Court has expressly stated that the Federal Communications Commission has broad regulatory powers:

While Congress did not give the Commission unfettered discretion to regulate all phases of the radio industry, it did not frustrate the purposes for which the Communications Act of 1934 was brought into being by attempting an itemized catalogue of the specific manifestations of the general problems for the solution of which it was establishing a regulatory agency (*National Broadcasting Company* v. *United States*).

"The touchstone provided by Congress was the 'public interest, convenience, or necessity,' a criterion which 'is as concrete as the complicated factors for judgment in such a field of delegated authority permits'" (*National Broadcasting Company* v. *United States*).

The Supreme Court has also expressly repudiated the fallacious notion that the Commission is permitted to pass on the technological and financial qualifications of the applicants but not on their moral and intellectual competence; or that it may set up strict engineering standards of service, but no standards pertaining to the content and quality of service.

The Act itself establishes that the Commission's powers are *not* limited to the engineering and technical aspects of regulation of radio communication. Yet we are asked to regard the Commission as a kind of traffic officer, policing the wave lengths to prevent stations from interfering with each other. But the Act does not restrict the Commission merely to supervision of the traffic. It puts upon the Commission the burden of determining the composition of that traffic. The facilities of radio are not large enough to accommodate all who wish to use them. Methods must be devised *for choosing from among the many who apply* (*National Broadcasting Company* v. *United States*).[10]

The Court thinks, in other words, that if it has to make a choice, it may as well make an intelligent one. And no intelligent choice would be possible if, in the selection of prospective trustees of a mass communication service, their intellectual and moral qualifications were barred from the consideration of the selecting agency. It is just because the Commission may not directly control the veracity of the individual statements before they are broadcasted from a

---

[10] All emphasis in quotations appearing in this Memorandum has been added by the author, unless otherwise indicated.

station (this would be censorship) that "caution must be exercised to grant station licenses only to those persons whose statements are trustworthy" (*In re Western Gateway Corp.*[11]).

The Commission has often asserted its power to go beyond the merely technical and financial qualifications. Its report, *Public Service Responsibility of Broadcast Licenses* (March 7, 1946), contains a complete collection of legislative, administrative, and judicial authority on this point and it would serve no useful purpose to set them forth again. From the Commission's first Annual Report (1928, p. 161) to the express statements of congressional leaders who, in introducing the 1934 Communications Act, called upon the Commission "to take the steps it ought to take to see to it that a larger use is made of radio facilities for education and religious purposes" (78 Cong. Rec. 8843); from the discussions of the Commission and federal courts calling for examination of the "nature and character of the program service rendered" and asserting the "duty" of the Commission "to take notice of the [applicant's] conduct" (*Trinity Methodist Church* v. *F.C.C.*[12]), to such rhetorical questions asked by the Supreme Court as "how could the Commission choose between two applicants" equally qualified from the financial and technical viewpoint "if the criterion of public interest were limited to such matters"—the authorities represent one unbroken line tending to make sure that the Federal Communications Commission is put in the position of being able to select licensees from whom service in the public interest can be expected.

It is noteworthy that the radio industry itself has not doubted the power of the Commission to take into account program service. In testifying before the House Committee on Interstate Commerce, the National Association of Broadcasters stated:

It is the manifest duty of the licensing authority, in passing upon applications for licenses or the renewal thereof, to determine whether or not the applicant is rendering or can render an adequate public service. Such *service necessarily includes* broadcasting of a considerable proportion of *programs devoted to* educational, religion, labor, agricultural and

[11] 9 F.C.C. 92.
[12] 62 F. 2d 850.

similar activities concerned with *human betterment* (Hearings on H.R. 8301, 73rd Cong., p. 117).

The *Daily News* itself has not doubted the relevance of its broadcasting policies and has made ample representation as to the type of programs it intends to broadcast and as to the general civic policy it intends to follow. It was not until the credibility of the *Daily News* allegations, representations, and promises was challenged by our petition to intervene that the *Daily News* has advanced the claim of inadmissibility of the policy and character questions it had itself put in issue.

Original Grants and Prior Conduct

We have thus seen not only that the constitutional objection raised by the *Daily News* cannot be directed against the mere fact of denial of a license to broadcast, but also that it cannot be directed against the examination of the content of the prospective service by the applicants.

It is equally obvious, however, that the *Daily News* cannot object to an inquiry into past conduct in order to test the qualifications of the applicants and the degree of reliance that can be placed on their promises. If a judgment about the future performance is to be made, past conduct must be considered. There can be, of course, no evidence of future conduct except that based on inferences drawn from the past. The exclusion of past conduct from the Commission's consideration would necessarily reduce the whole proceeding to a perfunctory finding that the applicant does now make certain allegations and promises, all investigation of the performance of past promises being strictly irrelevant!

This conclusion being obviously absurd, we must now examine the possibility that the original broad constitutional objection of the *Daily News* can be construed as contending only the inadmissibility of evidence of past conduct in fields other than broadcasting.

This contention is, however, untenable mainly because it would of necessity limit the Commission's power of informed and intelligent selection to the renewal application, excluding it from the all-important field of original grants. The theory would violate the Act itself, which does not distinguish between grant and renewal and certainly does not limit the requirement of "public interest, convenience and necessity" to renewals. Counsel for the *Daily News* has put it very well when he said: "The Act says that the same principles shall apply on renewal as apply on original grants." He will not disagree with us when we say, conversely, that the same principles shall apply on original grants as apply on renewals: the applicant's past conduct must be taken into account in order to determine his willingness and ability to serve the public interest.

The broadcasting industry has also expressly asserted that no distinction can be made between renewals and original grants. In the already quoted passage of its statement to the House Committee on Interstate Commerce, the National Association of Broadcasters said:

It is the manifest duty of the licensing authority, *in passing upon applications for licenses or renewal thereof*, to determine whether or not the applicant *is rendering or can render* adequate public service. Such service necessarily includes broadcasting . . . devoted to . . . human betterment (Hearings on H.R. 8301, 73rd Cong., p. 117).

If the capacity of a new applicant who has no broadcasting record to render public service by adequately informing the public and promoting cultural and moral human betterment is to be tested, how can it be done except by examining his conduct in fields other than broadcasting?

The Renewal Inertia

It will certainly not do to give every new applicant a chance to operate the station and then judge him by his performance. First of all, the problem of who should get that "chance," the *Daily News* or another applicant, would still have to be solved. Second, it would be wasteful and dangerous to make first grants indiscriminately and then try to remedy the situation by refusals to renew. Finally, the lack of discrimination in original grants would in itself lower the general level of performance, and the natural desire not to upset existing patterns too radically by frequent refusals to renew and not to destroy important financial investment would tend to perpetuate lower standards. The inevitable tendency in a renewal proceeding is to ascertain whether or not the license holder has abused its grant, not whether or not he is the best possible licensee available. The radio industry has done its level best to further that tendency. In the words of the American Civil Liberties Union, "the opposition of the industry is evidently based not so much on fear of censorship, as its spokesmen allege, as on the idea that radio licenses once granted become a vested private interest over which licensees alone should have control, except in cases of flagrant mis-use of their privileges" (Radio Programs in the Public Interest, American Civil Liberties Union, July, 1946). While obviously this approach must be opposed, it would be unrealistic not to count on the existence of a natural renewal inertia, and neglect the strongest and most direct means to assure service in the public interest, i.e., the selection of *original grantees* whose capacity for public service is beyond reasonable doubt.

Special Privilege for the Fourth Estate?

Having shown that it is impossible and legally unsound to limit examination of the applicants' qualifications to their past use of radio licenses, we are now faced with the *minimum residual meaning* of the *Daily News*'s sweeping challenge, i.e., with the contention that the examination of the editorial policies or patterns of news selections of *newspaper applicants* for radio stations is a violation of their constitutional immunity from censorship.

If this contention were accepted by the Commission it would create the paradoxical situation that newspapers alone, among all applicants, would be exempted from the obligation to show that they are intellectually and morally qualified to become the holders of an important public trust. We are not here concerned with the desirability of concentrating in the same hands several major media of communication. It may or may not be desirable that a newspaper should own and control AM, FM, and television and fac-simile channels. *But it is certainly inconceivable that the position of power* which newspapers hold in the field of public information and formation of public taste and opinion *should be used as an argument for their exemption* from an inquiry to which all other applicants would be subjected. After all, the First Amendment applies not only to newspapers. All citizens—and aliens as well, for that matter—enjoy the right of voicing their opinions and exchanging news and ideas. No one can be deprived of that freedom except in the case of a "clear and present danger of substantive evil." But everyone's use of that freedom can be examined when a selection must be made and a public trust confided to those who have given evidence of higher standards of accuracy, veracity, and objectivity. Newspapers have applied for and obtained a growing number of available radio channels. The whole system of inquiry into the intellectual and moral qualifications of original grantees would break down if so important a segment of licensees as the newspapers were granted an exemption. Newspapers—and the rest of us as well—may have a constitutional right to be prejudiced, biased, unfair, inaccurate, and, within limits, even mendacious. But none of us—not even newspapers—have a constitutional right to obtain a public trust despite such prejudice, bias, unfairness, inaccuracy, and mendacity. As Justice Holmes has put it once—and in a much more questionable case—"he has a constitutional right to talk politics, but he has no constitutional right to be a policeman" (*McAuliffe* v. *Mayor of New Bedford* [13]).

A man may have a constitutional right to try to misinform, mislead, and miseducate the public as long as he operates in a competitive field open to anyone who wishes to pursue a different policy. But he has no constitutional right to be preferred in his demand for a monopolistic or oligopolistic public franchise in a field of a restricted communications media.

"Our Policy Will Carry Over"

Quite aside from the general principle of relevancy of newspaper policies, the *Daily News* has made the examination of its policies inevitable in the present proceeding. By the manner in which it has tried to support its application, it has, here again, put its newspaper activities and performances in issue and cannot now escape

---

[13] 155 Mass. 216 (1892).

their examination. This is not, as counsel for the *Daily News* thought, a "technical question of cross-examination." It goes to the very heart of the *Daily News* direct case which is based on its newspaper performances and which must fail if evidence of these performances is withdrawn or if they are shown to fall below certain minimum standards. Section 8 of *Daily News* Exhibit 2 opens with the following solemn statement: "We consider the right to operate a broadcast station as a responsibility as well as an opportunity. Our policy on the News has been that we are a medium for public welfare and community interest, as well as a dispenser of news. THIS POLICY WILL CARRY OVER TO THE RADIO STATION."

The *Daily News* sought to persuade the Commission that *its service as a newspaper* justified the granting of an FM license. Since the *Daily News* relies upon such service as justification for the granting of the permit and since it promises that *"This policy will carry over to the radio station,"* it is eminently appropriate to examine its record to determine whether it has the qualifications justifying the granting of a construction permit. The Presiding Officer, in overruling the *Daily News*'s constitutional objection, thus summarized the situation:

I can only say, gentlemen, that the applicant, News Syndicate Co., Inc., has presented a case, a substantial portion of which does deal with the circulation of the Daily News throughout the country, the Daily News in public service, and it has introduced evidence of its participation in the many worth-while and worthy causes. A good portion of the direct case constituted a presentation of material designed to show why the News Syndicate Co., Inc., would be qualified to run a radio station. It seems to me that it is perfectly appropriate to examine into what the applicant, who is a newspaper, does with his newspaper.

On cross-examination the *Daily News* executives made it clear that they would be responsible for carrying out the policies of the television and FM stations if those licenses were granted.

In answer to a specific question, F. M. Flynn, the general manager of the *Daily News*, stated that the *News* *"undoubtedly* would set the broad policies" of the FM station and has also, in substance, agreed that it expects to achieve there *"the same standards* of truthfulness and accuracy and freedom from bias" achieved in the *Daily News*'s newspaper activity.

The examination of Carl Warren, the *Daily News* "broadcast editor" responsible for the WNEW copy, has thrown further light on the chain of continuity that links the *Daily News* to the WNEW newscasts and would link the latter to the FM station. In response to a question from the Presiding Officer, Mr. Warren testified that a news story originating in the Washington office of the *Daily News* is put on a "leased wire" in Washington and that it comes "right to [our] broadcast room in the Daily News building"; that "it arrives over a teletypewriter machine . . . and is available to the broadcast desk as well as to the telegraph desk and other desks which handle it." It is thus clear that the WNEW newcasts are fed from the general newspaper sources of the *Daily News*. In its turn, the staff of the WNEW newscast is destined to service the *Daily News*'s FM station. "The same men who now service WNEW would service the newscast portion of the FM station, if the Daily News ever gets one." Mr. Warren who now "assumes responsibility for the copy on the WNEW newscasts" expects "to achieve *the same* high standards of accuracy and freedom from bias in the operation of the newscasts on the FM."

The record is replete with similar statements showing the close connection, asserted by the *Daily News* itself, between its past and present newspaper patterns, performances, standards, and policies and the future policies of the prospective FM station. It would serve no useful purpose to quote them all; they are but illustrations of the basic confession made by the *News* itself: "This policy will carry over to the radio station." Can it be seriously maintained that, before letting that policy "carry over," the Commission is entitled to find out *what* that policy is and to decide whether it is consistent with certain minimum standards of service in the public interest?

Drawing the Line: An Unreal Issue

What are then, finally, these minimum standards of public service to which the applicant for a franchise must be expected to adhere? We are fully aware that it is on this issue that the line must be drawn between an odious political or partisan censorship leading to the domination of the air by an oligarchic government-sponsored group, on the one hand, and an honest and impartial effort to assure genuine freedom of the air *despite* the technologically inevitable oligopolistic structure of the broadcasting industry, on the other.

The difficulty of drawing the line pursues every student of law from his first classes in Torts, where he tries to master the law of negligence, through the quicksands of equity to the problems of due process. At times the difficulties in drawing the line and the fear of arbitrariness by administrators, jurors, or judges are such that society is tempted to do nothing rather than do something imperfectly or crudely; to choose the legal certainty of inaction rather than risk an intervention based on discretion. Judges and administrators feel this escapist temptation frequently, but yield to it only rarely—and even more rarely with good results. In no case, at any rate, could the results of an "escape into the certainties of inaction" be more disastrous than in the field of minimum fair broadcasting standards. The inevitable result would be that a broadcasting of business, by business, and for business would take over a task entrusted by Congress to a responsible public agency.

Moreover, the hue and cry of people who do not know where to draw the line often refers to wholly imaginary difficulties which arise only in a few borderline cases, while the bulk can be adjudged without difficulty. It is clear, for instance, that the Commission would violate the First Amendment if it made the grant of a license dependent on whether or not a newspaper has supported a Republican or Democratic candidate or been for or against the New Deal. But is it not equally clear that the First Amendment is not violated if the grant of a public trust is made dependent on whether or not a newspaper is trustworthy, truthful, devoted to public welfare, and free from racial or religious bias? The fact that difficult borderline cases may arise here, as elsewhere, in the future is certainly no reason to deny a clear answer in the clear "polar" case.

[156]

Ex ore tuo te judico

That this is a "polar" case is made fully apparent by the fact that the Commission could accept without hesitation the minimum fair standards and policies of decent broadcasting set forth by the *Daily News* itself. We certainly would be ready to stipulate that its past performances be judged exclusively on the basis of the criteria of its own making.

Whatever the difficulties of hypothetical cases, the *Daily News* can have no avowable reason to oppose an investigation based on criteria, the promised adherence to which has been set forth by the *Daily News* itself as the compelling reason in support of an application for a radio station. *Ex ore tuo te judico*, we say to the *Daily News:* we judge you by your own words.

The *Daily News* used effective language in its application when it said that "the important position of a radio station in the life of the community with *its power to entertain, instruct and inform,* necessitates a policy of operation that is progressive, instructive, entertaining, *without bias* and always in good taste." It has also listed the following pertinent "Basic Program Policies":

(1) The name and word of God must be used with reverence.
(2) Treat all races, colors and creeds fairly, without prejudice or ridicule.
(3) Bar all profanity and salacious material from all productions.
(4) Avoid detail of murder or suicide.
(5) Avoid all forms of misrepresentation and false and misleading statements.

We accept these standards and submit that our evidence will show that in its past newspaper performances the *Daily News* has failed to live up to them, and that it, as a newspaper, has (a) indulged in inaccurate, malicious, and biased misrepresentations of the role of ethnic minorities in American life, and (b) has printed about them more unfavorable and less favorable news than the other New York City morning newspapers. We believe that these facts, if proved, would show a clear violation of the second and fifth principles stated by the *Daily News*, being respectively fair treatment of all races,

[157]

colors, and creeds and avoidance of false or misleading statements. Therefore, and since the *Daily News* has promised, or rather threatened, that its policy "will carry over to the radio station," the grant of a franchise would not be, on the strength of the *News's* own standards, in the "public interest, convenience and necessity," and should therefore be denied.

Past Performances and Present Beliefs

We must, finally, call the attention of the Commission to the fact that our evidence deals not only with *past* performances of the *Daily News*, against which the objection of inadmissibility has been raised, but tends also to point out some of the *present* beliefs and conceptions of the *Daily News* executives with respect to what constitute proper standards of radio performance. These beliefs and conceptions, admitted and confessed by the *Daily News* representatives themselves, are concededly admissible and relevant evidence. To the extent to which they contradict the initial assurances and representations of the *Daily News* they are in themselves sufficient to show the lack of necessary qualifications and, because of their gross departure from the generally accepted standards of fairness, must inevitably lead to the denial of the *Daily News* application.

Compulsory Racial Segregation and the Constitution

[Regulations of the public school authorities of Orange County, California, required the segregation of children of Mexican and Latin descent. Parents challenged the constitutionality of the regulation. The Federal District Court declared the segregation unconstitutional. The case was appealed to the Circuit Court of Appeals sitting in San Francisco. This court invalidated the regulations but not on broad constitutional grounds. It held that the segregation had not been authorized by state legislation (*Westminster School District* v. *Mendez*, 161 F. 2d 774). The American Jewish Congress filed a brief *amicus curiae*, prepared by Pekelis, in which the Circuit Court of Appeals was asked to review the "separate but equal facilities" doctrine and to declare it unconstitutional. Since this doctrine had received constitutional status in some previous Supreme Court opinions and decisions, the Pekelis brief was a bit on the daring side. The brief deserves to become famous.—Ed.]

GONZALO MENDEZ, the appellees, as citizens of the United States and on behalf of their minor children and some 5,000 persons similarly affected, all of Mexican or Latin descent, filed a class suit pursuant to Rule 23 of Federal Rules of Civil Procedure in the District Court of the United States for the Southern District of California against the appellants, the Westminster Garden Grove and El Modeno School Districts and the Santa Ana Schools, all of Orange County, California, and the respective trustees and superintendents of these Districts. The appellees' petition, based upon the Fourteenth Amendment to the Constitution of the

United States and Subdivision Fourteen, Section 24 of the Judicial Code (Title 28, Section 41, subdivision 14, U.S.C.A.), alleged (1) that the appellants had adopted and enforced certain regulations which prohibited children of Mexican or Latin descent or extraction from attending certain schools in the respective districts, (2) segregated and required them to attend schools reserved exclusively for children or persons of Mexican and Latin descent, and (3) that such regulations and usages resulted in a denial of the equal protection of the laws in violation of the Fourteenth Amendment. The petition demanded that the regulations and usages be declared unconstitutional and that the appellants be enjoined from further application thereof.

Upon trial of the issues before the United States District Court, Judge Paul J. McCormick rendered judgment against the appellants on the ground that the "pattern of public education promulgated in the Constitution of California and effectuated by provisions of the Education Code of the State, prohibits segregation of the pupils of Mexican ancestry in the elementary schools." The Court also held that the segregation practices of the appellants' school districts show "a clear purpose to arbitrarily discriminate against the pupils of Mexican ancestry and to deny them the equal protection of the laws," and were therefore a violation of the Fourteenth Amendment to the Constitution of the United States.

The present brief is being filed after the presentation of the briefs of the appellants, of the appellees, and of the National Association for the Advancement of Colored People as friend of the Court. To avoid duplication, we shall confine ourselves to the discussion of the additional points listed below.

We should like, however, to emphasize that we fully agree with the main point made and documented by the National Association for Advancement of Colored People to the effect that, as long as racial segregation prevails, no equality of even physical facilities is in fact possible: If the facilities were really duplicated, financial ruin of the local bodies or the states would ensue. If financial disaster is to be avoided, the facilities granted to minorities are bound to be physically inferior.

[160]

For the purposes of this brief, however, we shall proceed on the assumption that the physical facilities furnished to the appellees are identical with those furnished to the English-speaking group.

Whenever a group, considered as "inferior" by the prevailing standards of a community, is segregated by official action from the socially dominant group, the very fact of official segregation, whether or not "equal" physical facilities are being furnished to both groups, is a humiliating and discriminatory denial of equality to the group considered "inferior" and a violation of the Constitution of the United States and of treaties duly entered into under its authority.

1. It is not disputed that the furnishing by an official body of inferior physical facilities to any given ethnic group would represent an unlawful and discriminatory denial of equality to such group (*Plessy v. Ferguson* [1]).

2. Mere identity of physical facilities, however, does not necessarily amount to equality either in the economic, political, or legal sense. (The law would not recognize, for example, that an estate has been divided *equally* between two children each receiving one of the two identical houses comprising the estate, if one of the houses were located in a busy banking district and the other fifty miles from the nearest railroad station. Nor would a probate court accept the division as *equal* even if the two identical houses were located on the same street, opposite each other, but if, for some known or unknown, valid or invalid, reason, one side of that street were fashionable and sought after, the other neglected and rejected.) Equality is indeed determined, in fact and in law, not by the physical identity of things assigned in ownership use or enjoyment, but by identity or substantial similarity of their *values*.

In their turn, values do not depend solely or even primarily on the physical properties of things or facilities to be valued but also on the "social location" of these things or facilities, on their social significance and psychological context, or, in short, on the community judgment attached to them.

---

[1] 163 U.S. 537 (1896).

The recognition of these legal principles of evaluation is not confined to the field of property. Law is no more blind to realities when political or civil rights are involved than when it deals with real estate or chattel. American law demands, in the enjoyment by persons of government-furnished facilities, an equality not less real and substantial than the one it exacts for the protection of heirs, partners, or stockholders. In calling for "equal protection," or for "equal facilities," or for the "outlawing of discrimination," the Constitution and the laws of the United States call for genuine equality of protection and not for a merely formal or physical identity of treatment.

3. It is a well-known fact that the value and desirability of many objects, facilities, traits, or characteristics may depend not so much upon their intrinsic qualities or defects, advantages or shortcomings, as upon their association with or use by persons enjoying a certain reputation. The value of a mediocre type of fabric may be enhanced by an *arbiter elegantiarum* wearing it; the desirability of a beautiful resort may be lessened by its being visited by people deemed of "low" social standing. If a group considered "inferior" by the prevailing community sentiment adopts any given color of garment, accent of speech, or place of amusement, that color, accent, or place will automatically be shunned by the majority and become less desirable or valuable.

These are, however, phenomena of social stratification productive of *social* inequality against which the law offers no direct remedy.

4. The same depreciation may take place, however, not because of spontaneous adoption of certain places, styles, or objects by a group deemed "inferior" but because of their imposition by the community, organized or otherwise.

If the Nazis, while proclaiming the essential inferiority of the "Jewish race," compelled Jews to wear clothes of one given color while reserving another to the master race, it could not be said that Jews had received equal clothing facilities even if the physical qualities of the clothing were identical to those given to the members of the Aryan race. Nor would the discriminatory and humiliating character of the measure depend on whether the colors were brown for the Jews and black for the others, or vice versa. It is the exclusive allocation of a given color, of *any* color, to a race declared "inferior" that makes the color less desirable. The inferiority thus transmitted from the wearer to the garment destroys the genuine "equality" of the furnished facilities.

Similarly, it could hardly be disputed that an act of a legislature or of a school board expressly declaring that a given group is "inferior" and therefore to be confined to separate parks, schools, or halls is discriminatory and therefore unconstitutional.

This result would be reached not because such act expresses an opinion of inferiority or superiority (the mere expression of an opinion may very well not be within the concept of state *action;* see Brandeis, J., in *Standard Computing Scale Co.* v. *Farrel* [2]), but because discriminatory *action* has followed discriminatory *opinion.* The official assignment to a group of separate parks, schools, or halls based on an officially stated conviction of the group's inferiority would be an assignment of facilities *inferior* per se, regardless of their physical identity with the facilities assigned to the "better" group.

The situation as here described could not be characterized as merely *social* inequality. We may assume that social inequality has antedated the enactment of the assumed statute or regulation. But a legislative or administrative declaration of that pre-existing social inferiority and the ensuing action of assignment of facilities, inferior because segregated, amounts to the creation of a *legally sanctioned* political inequality.

5. This result does not vary when, in the now described chain of (1) pre-existing social inequality; (2) legislative declaration thereof, and (3) assignment of separate, and hence inferior, facilities, the intermediate link, i.e., the overt finding of inferiority, is omitted. Official action will not be allowed to accomplish by indirection what it may not achieve openly (*Yick Wo* v. *Hopkins* [3]).

---

[2] 249 U.S. 571 (1919).
[3] 118 U.S. 356 (1886).

The failure of a statute or regulation expressly to declare a legal inferiority does not protect it from the scrutiny of the courts. When the reasonableness of a legislative classification is in question the courts will look behind the apparent classification to determine the real intent of the law and whether or not, in fact, an illegal classification has been made. Thus, in *Yick Wo* v. *Hopkins* the Court declared:

Though the law be fair on its face and impartial in appearance, yet, if it is applied and administered by public authority with an evil eye and unequal hand, so as practically to make unjust and illegal discriminations between persons in similar circumstances, material to their rights, the denial of equal justice is still within the prohibition of the Constitution.

Any classification adopted by a governmental body as the basis of official action must be viewed not in the abstract but realistically in the social setting in which it operates. The judge

must open his eyes to all those conditions and circumstances . . . in the light of which reasonableness is to be measured. . . . In ascertaining whether challenged action is reasonable, the traditional common-law technique does not rule out but requires some inquiry into the social and economic data to which it is to be applied. Whether action is reasonable or not must always depend upon the particular facts and circumstances in which it is taken.[4]

Furthermore, the Supreme Court has declared that while generally it will not inquire into the motives which led to the enactment of state regulation, yet "where the facts as to the situation and the conditions are such as to oppress or discriminate against a class or an individual the courts may consider and give weight to such purpose in considering the validity of the ordinance" (*Dobbins* v. *Los Angeles*[5]).

It should be pointed out here that in those states which have enacted Civil Rights statutes entitling all citizens and residents to full and equal public accommodations, the separation of persons in a public place is generally deemed to be a discrimination. It has been

---

[4] Harlan F. Stone in 50 *Harv. Law Rev.*, 4, 24 (1936).
[5] 195 U.S. 223 (1904).

held in such states that separation founded on race or color alone can be justified only on the ground that the Negro is inferior to the white and that such separation would do violence to equality before the law. In these cases segregation is synonymous with discrimination.

Segregation of school facilities according to national ancestry has no independent rational justification and no other relation to the purpose of the law than that to be found in a community feeling of the respective superiority and inferiority of the two ethnic groups. Official adoption of social classifications based on such feelings of necessity implies the adoption of the meaning inherent in, and inseparable from, the classifications themselves, that of the respective inferiority and superiority of the groups. It may be doubted whether or not law should take affirmative steps to eliminate social inequality. But it seems certain that law may not adopt, sanction, and enforce it. Whenever law adopts a social classification based on a notion of inferiority it transforms the pre-existing *social* inequality into *legal* inequality. What ensues is official discrimination, a denial of equality before the law, whether or not the statement of inferiority is made openly by the government or inheres in the classification upon which official action is based.

6. Once a social classification based on group inferiority is "adopted" by the law, the ensuing legal inferiority will in its turn intensify and deepen the social inequality from which it stems. Law is, indeed, at the same time the consequence and the cause of social phenomena. In no other field is this truth more apparent than in that of ethnic relations. The undeniable effect of classification by race, color, or ethnic origin has been to enforce an inferior economic and social status upon the nonwhite minority. The actual operation of segregation statutes illustrates this oppressive function of the law. It is well known, for instance, that the doctrine of "separate but equal" facilities has proved to be a mere legal fiction in most cases, that invariably segregation has been accompanied by gross discrimination, and that absolute equality seldom, if ever, exists. The great disparity in the funds expended upon white and colored

schools respectively by those southern states which enforce segregation, the one-sided enforcement of segregation laws, the inferiority of public accommodations reserved for Negroes, the wage differentials and other economic inequalities between the races, the segregated slum areas in which Negroes are forced to live, the neglect of their social needs or complete denial of public services, and the other innumerable burdens and deprivations impressed upon the Negro minority by the oppressive mechanism of segregation all furnish overwhelming testimony that the system of legal separation based upon race was never intended to have and cannot have any result other than one of increasing, through the sanction of the law, that social and economic inferiority in which the law itself originated.

This situation involves at the same time another kind of vicious circularity. The now described effect of segregation laws makes their spontaneous repeal or amendment a practical impossibility. When a more or less inarticulate social feeling of racial superiority is clothed with the dignity of an official law, that feeling acquires a concreteness and assertiveness which it did not possess before. The stricter the law or discriminatory segregation, the stronger and the more articulate the feeling of social distance. And the stronger that feeling, the stricter the law and the more difficult its amendment or repeal. In such a setting the very roots of democratic processes are threatened and no reliance can be placed on their correcting effect. It is this type of situation which Chief Justice Stone had in mind when, in sustaining the constitutionality of an economic measure, he warned that the decision did not foreclose the question whether

legislation which restricts those political processes which can ordinarily be expected to bring about repeal of undesirable legislation, is to be subjected to more exacting judicial scrutiny under the general prohibitions of the Fourteenth Amendment than are most other types of legislation

and whether

similar considerations enter into review of statutes directed at particular religious, . . . or national . . . or racial minorities, . . . whether prejudice against discrete and insular minorities may be a special condition, which lends seriously to curtail the operation of those political processes ordinarily to be relied on to protect minorities and which may call for a correspondingly more searching judicial inquiry (*United States* v. *Carolene Products*[6]).

The importance of Stone's theory of political restraints has been stressed in Dowling, "The Methods of Mr. Justice Stone in Constitutional Cases."[7]

The true function of law, in a constitutional form of government, is to guide society toward higher forms of coexistence rather than to follow the less worthy attitudes of a community. The people of the United States have established a constitution in order to ensure that all government officials will find in the permanent dictates of decency a defense against the transient whims or prejudices of a local or national majority. When, on the contrary, governmental officials follow the lowest level of community thinking, they betray their function of political leadership. Where prejudice is legalized, where bigotry is given official sanction, where prestige of law is lent to bias, there ignorance, narrow-mindness, and hatred assert themselves openly, and operate *as of right*. An official action, born in and based on a discriminatory classification, breeds in turn more inequality and more prejudice. The vicious circle can be broken only if the courts exercise the power which the Constitution has vested in them for the protection of the basic values of our society.

7. Every one of the preceding remarks acquires particular significance and singular strength when applied to segregation of facilities available for the education of children. Indeed:

a. The value and the desirability of an educational institution are particularly dependent on intangible elements. The physical characteristics of the benches and desks of a school shrink into utter insignificance when compared with the social and psychological environment which the school offers to its children.

b. Children are more impressionable and are more impressed than adults by the implied environmental judgments of superiority and inferiority. Those deemed superior are often, in manifesting

---

[6] 304 U.S. 144 (1938).
[7] 41 *Col. L. Rev.* 1160 (1941).

their innocent pride, more cruel than normal adults usually are. On the other side, children who feel that they are treated as inferior are more bitterly humiliated by the social stigma that strikes them than adults can be.

c. The children's acceptance of the reasonableness of official action is often less critical than that of adults. On the other hand, once their respect for community judgments is shaken, their denial of community values is equally sweeping.

d. The official imposition of a segregation pattern based on notions of inferiority and superiority produces its deepest and most lasting social and psychological evil results when applied to children.

Authorities agree that feelings of racial superiority or inferiority are not innate in any child but are instilled in him by adults or by his observation of institutions about him. Since segregation reinforces group isolation and social distance it helps to create conditions in which unhealthy racial attitudes may flourish. By giving official sanction to group separation based upon the assumption of inferiority, we help to perpetuate racial prejudice and contribute to the degradation and humiliation of the minority child. The crippling psychological effects of such segregation are in essence a denial of equality of treatment. In this sense segregation is burdensome and oppressive and comes within the constitutional prohibition.

In this connection great weight should be given to the finding of the court below in the instant case:

The evidence clearly shows that Spanish-speaking children are retarded in their learning English by lack of exposure to its use because of segregation, and that commingling of the entire student body instills and develops a common cultural attitude among the school children which is imperative for the perpetuation of American institutions and ideals. It is also established by the record that the methods of segregation prevalent in the defendant schools foster antagonisms in the children and suggest inferiority among them where none exists.

8. The record of the instant case clearly shows that the segregation of children of Mexican or Latin descent in the Westminster School District of Orange County was based on the prejudiced feel-

ing that these children were inferior to those of the Anglo-Saxon group. The clear significance of the assignment of separate facilities to them was therefore, in the social context in which official actions must be judged, a discriminatory and humiliating assignment of facilities which were "equal," if at all, only in their physical aspects.

Superintendent Kent asserted that the Mexican children are "dirty"; have lice, impetigo, generally dirty hands, face, neck, ears; and are inferior to the white races in the matter of personal hygiene (R. Tr., pp. 116, 121). He admitted that "on account of cleanliness" the children of Mexican descent have been segregated (R. Tr., p. 88).

9. It is a matter of common knowledge, of which many courts have already taken judicial notice, that measures of segregation against Negroes, Mexicans, Chinese, and other minority groups or colored races are due to and predicated solely upon the social notions of national, racial, or religious inferiority and superiority.

Mr. Gunnar Myrdal, social scientist, in his exhaustive two-volume study of Negro-white relationships in the United States, *An American Dilemma*, has described these mores:

In the magical sphere of the white man's mind, the Negro is inferior, totally independent of rational proofs or disproofs. And he is inferior in a deep and mystical sense. *The "reality" of his inferiority is the white man's own indubitable sensing of it, and that feeling applies to every single Negro.* . . . The Negro is believed to be stupid, immoral, diseased, lazy, incompetent, and *dangerous*—dangerous to the white man's virtue and social order.[8]

Segregation of this type may be described as a form of partial ostracism, and its motivation has become the protection of a dominant culture from the threat of an "inferior" culture. Through a variety of complex patterns and social controls it reinforces and guarantees the inferior status of the minority group isolated, and in turn the inferior status becomes a justification for a belief in the inherent inferiority of this group and the wisdom of enforcing segregation.

So completely is the inferior position of the Negro minority

---

[8] P. 100.

guaranteed by legal segregation that numerous southern state courts have held that the word "Negro" or "colored person" when applied to a white person gives rise to a cause of action for defamation, a doctrine which has also been upheld by a federal court.[9]

10. Discriminatory denial of equal governmental facilities is concededly a violation of the equal protection clause of the Fourteenth Amendment to the United States Constitution. The assignment of segregated facilities to a group because of its alleged or real social inferiority is similarly a denial of equal facilities and of the equal protection of the laws.

The leading case in the field, *Plessy* v. *Ferguson*,[10] decided in 1896, exactly a half century ago, accepts in substance the constitutional theory that segregation based on notions of inferiority is invalid. The court declared that "every exercise of the police power must be reasonable and extend only to such laws as are enacted in good faith for the promotion of the public good *and not for the annoyance or oppression of a particular class*" [11] and that, for instance, laws

requiring colored people to walk upon one side of the street, and white people upon the other, or requiring white men's houses to be painted white, and colored men's black, or their vehicles or business signs to be of different colors, upon the theory that one side of the street is as good as the other, or that a house or vehicle of one color is as good as one of another color, would be clearly unconstitutional.

The court found, however, that the law requiring segregation on railroads was constitutional because it proceeded on the factual and sociological assumption that such segregation did *"not necessarily imply the inferiority of either race to the other."* [12]

The court's basic finding reads as follows:

We consider the underlying fallacy of the plaintiff's argument to consist in the *assumption that the enforced separation of the two races stamps the colored race with a badge of inferiority.* If this be so, it is not by reason

---

[9] See Stultz v. Cousins, 242 F. 794 (C.C.A. 6th, 1917).
[10] Cited in note 1, *supra*.
[11] P. 550; italics supplied.
[12] P. 544; italics supplied.

of anything found in the act, but *solely because the colored race chooses to put that construction upon it*. The argument necessarily assumes that if, as has been more than once the case, and is not unlikely to be so again, the colored race should become the dominant power in the state legislature, and should enact a law in precisely similar terms, it would thereby relegate the white race to an inferior position. We imagine that the white race, at least, would not acquiesce in this assumption.[13]

In short, the factual basis of *Plessy* v. *Ferguson* is: The "colored race chooses to put" the construction of inferiority upon the segregation statute. In that construction—the assumption that segregation is predicated on inferiority—"the white race . . . would not acquiesce." Will any court today, in the light of the sociological and psychological findings made in the last fifty years, prove so lacking in candor and so blind to realities as to subscribe to the fiction of benevolent segregation on which *Plessy* v. *Ferguson* relies? That is the issue. Not the legal doctrine of *Plessy* v. *Ferguson* is in question but the factual fallacy on which it rests. Once ascertained that the only real meaning of the distinction between Negroes and whites, Mexicans and Anglo-Saxons, is that of inferiority of one group to another—the legal consequences are not in question. The very doctrine of *Plessy* v. *Ferguson* calls for the outlawing of humiliating and discriminatory laws.

11. In addition to the foregoing considerations, the abolition of discrimination on account of race, creed, or color has now been made a part of national policy by the ratification of international treaties to which the United States of America is a party. This national policy must override any contrary state law and custom in accordance with Article VI, Clause 2, of the Constitution, which provides that "All Treaties made, or which shall be made, under the Authority of the United States, shall be the supreme Law of the Land; and the Judges in every State shall be bound thereby, any thing in the Constitution or Laws of any State to the contrary notwithstanding."

The Charter of the United Nations has been duly signed by the

---

[13] P. 551; italics supplied.

President and ratified by the Senate of the United States. Under the provisions of this charter the United States solemnly undertook together with the other signatories to promote freedom for all without distinction as to race, language, or religion. Thus, Article 55c of the Charter provides:' "The United Nations shall promote . . . uniform respect for, and observance of, human rights and fundamental freedoms for all without distinction as to race, sex, language, and religion." And in conjunction therewith, Article 56 states: "All members pledge themselves to take joint and separate action in cooperation with the Organization for the achievement of the purposes set forth in Article 55."

Furthermore, the United States Government, as a participant of the Inter-American Conference on Problems of War and Peace and in connection with the signing of the Act of Chapultepec in Mexico City on March 6, 1945, joined with other nations in a resolution to recommend that their governments "make every effort to prevent in their respective countries *all acts which may provoke discrimination* among individuals because of race or religion" (italics added), outlawing not only discrimination but also its *potential* causes. The formulation is certainly broad enough to cover *segregation*.

These declarations upon their execution bind the states as well as the federal government. Treaty provisions prevail over state enactments when the latter are inconsistent therewith. "That the treaty power of the United States extends to *all proper subjects of negotiation* between our government and the governments of other nations is clear" (Field, J., in *Geofroy* v. *Riggs* [14]). The courts are bound to take judicial notice of treaty declarations and to enforce the rights of persons growing out of them.

Persuasive precedent is provided by the decision *Re Drummond Wren*,[15] decided by the Supreme Court of Ontario. In that case a restrictive covenant in a deed declaring that the lands involved were not to be sold "to Jews or persons of objectionable nationality" was held invalid as contrary to public policy. In determining the national policy which should govern the case, Judge Mackay relied

---

[14] 133 U.S. 258 (1890).
[15] O.R. 778 (1945).

heavily upon Sections 55c and 56 of the United Nations Charter, of which Canada was a signatory, as well as upon other international compacts and provincial statutes.

12. The theory advocated here does not mean that the federal government can, through the use of its treaty power, invade every field of state activity. We do not say that "the United States has exactly the same range of power in making treaties that it would have if the States did not exist" (Corwin, "The Treaty Making Power" [16]). On the contrary, we believe that in order to fall within the supremacy clause provision a treaty should deal with "objects which in the intercourse of nations had usually been regarded as the proper subjects of negotiation and treaty," [17] with "proper subjects of [international] negotiation," [18] with "subjects which properly pertain to our foreign relations." [19]

While the international treaty-making power of the United States of America has not changed since 1791, the content and nature of international relations have undergone considerable change. It would be, to put it mildly, unfortunate if the United States of America were unable to play a full role in the international relations of the modern world.

The advancement of an interest acknowledged to be of international concern may be regarded by the United States as well as by other States as necessitating restrictions upon the conduct of individuals who inhabit their respective territories in relation to activities which would appear normally to lack international significance and to possess a merely domestic aspect. Thus, matters of occupation, condition of labor, the production and manufacture, and even the transportation of particular articles may suddenly attain an international aspect and to become appropriate objectives of a treaty of the United States. *The constitutionality of the result is not affected by the circumstance that the federal agency is enabled through treaty making to accomplish what congress may remain impotent to achieve* (Hyde, *International Law* [20]).

---

[16] 199 *No. Amer. R.* (1914) 898.
[17] Holden v. Joy, 17 Wall. 211 (1872).
[18] Geofroy v. Riggs, cited note 14, *supra*.
[19] Santovincenzo v. Egan, 284 U.S. 30 (1931).
[20] Vol. II, sec. 500; italics supplied.

The problem in this case is thus whether or not the guarantee of human rights without discrimination is within the United States of America treaty power, whether or not the pertinent provisions of the United Nations Charter are constitutional and thus part of the "supreme law of the land."

The answer can hardly be doubted. The treaty involved is not one concluded casually between two nations. The United Nations representing the civilized international community were unanimous in believing that human rights are a matter of international concern, that individual freedom and international peace are inseparable, that a world in which racial hatred, contempt, discrimination, segregation, or other forms of interracial and intergroup humiliation continue to exist within the various nations is a world in which there can be no lasting peace among nations. In other words, what the United Nations did was not unlike the adoption of an international Fourteenth Amendment. Just as the people of the United States after the Civil War reached the conviction that the preservation of certain basic individual rights within the states was a matter of federal concern and a condition of the national peace, the United Nations after the Second World War reached the conclusion that the preservation of these rights is a condition of the international peace as well. We are sure that no American court will hold this finding unreasonable.

To achieve the dual ideal—of individual equality within, and of peace among the nations—much concerted effort on all levels of domestic and international life will be needed. Modest as the problem of the relations among the Latin and Anglo-Saxon children of Orange County, California, may appear to a superficial observer, in reality that problem is in its nature not dissimilar from those confronting the world at large. The solution of these apparently "small" or "local" problems can have an important cumulative effect. History has assigned a great role and a great responsibility to the United States. Her courts cannot and will not refuse to play their part. Faithful to the traditions of judicial statesmanship they will accept their share of American responsibility.

The Dormant Power
of American Cities

[In this paper Pekelis argues that American cities have the power to act to prevent unfair employment practices which discriminate against persons on account of race, color, creed, or national origin. This paper was written before FEPC acts were adopted by eight states; but even if this development had been foreseen by the author, his argument regarding the powers of cities in this area of civil rights would still have been cogent and relevant. Chicago, Minneapolis, Milwaukee, Philadelphia, and other cities have moved into this area of action by appointing fair employment commissions. More cities are likely to do the same. The basis of this movement is to be seen prefigured in the following paper.—Ed.]

THE LAWMAKING POWER in the United States is not confined to Congress and the state legislatures. To outlaw the practices of discrimination in the fields of housing, education, and employment, the dormant power of the American cities could and should be awakened. To take FEPC as an instance, the default of federal and state legislatures could be to a large extent remedied if a network of municipal ordinances spread over the country and covered the areas that are the key centers of industrial production and ethnic tension.

The preliminary question which arises concerns the existence of a municipal power to outlaw religious and racial discrimination in the fields of housing, education, and employment. To this question there can be no single answer. The situation varies from field to field, from state to state, and from city to city, depending on constitutions,

[175]

statutes, and charters. Still, despite technical diversities, the problem has a common background well worth exploring.

To begin with, many cities in the United States made attempts in the past at regulating ethnic relations. Their underlying philosophy was that racial conflicts could be avoided by segregation ordinances, which forbade residence—or employment—of Negroes outside a fixed zone. State courts of last resort have held such ordinances to be within the scope of the municipal power "to prevent conflict and ill feeling between the white and colored races." True, the federal courts have declared them unconstitutional as a violation of the equal protection clause of the United States Constitution. *But this declaration involved no question of city power.* The housing segregation rules would have been equally invalid if they had been embodied in a state statute.

This constitutional objection could not be invoked against an ordinance which, instead of imposing, would forbid racial discrimination. And as to the problem of municipal power itself, the courts which held that a city has the power to attempt prevention of conflicts through segregation could hardly deny its power to try, for the same end, a scheme of co-operation. In an old story, the high-pressure public relations man answers the church trustees' request for advice with the stunning suggestion: "Why not try religion?" The cities, confronted with racial tensions, may well ask themselves: "Why not try justice?"

The segregation ordinance precedents, relevant as they may be, are of course not conclusive. The problem has wider implications. The examination of the legal background shows that practically every law describing city powers contains some oracular key words, pain and delight of augurs and lawyers. Whether city powers are defined by constitutional, home rule provisions (the first one was adopted in 1875 in Missouri) or are contained in statutes, reference is always made to the city's "police power"; or to the power to provide for the "safety," "prosperity," "peace," "good government," or "welfare" of its inhabitants; or to the power to regulate matters of "local" or "internal" concern; or to take care of "the property, affairs or governments of cities"; or finally to "all powers of local self-government . . . as are not in conflict with the general laws." It is true that some enactments contain a detailed list of powers in addition, and that a rigid and continuous judicial interpretation could have frozen the meaning even of the vaguest clauses and set rigid limits to municipal power. But judicial interpretations of city powers have, by and large, varied from decade to decade and from subject to subject, even with respect to the same city. Our courts, faithful to that delphic tradition which is, after all, the ultimate source of their own power, have done their best not to kill the golden-egg goose and have kept the law in a state of flux.

Thus our problem becomes, once more, one of philosophy rather than of exegesis. The quoted "definitions" provide no answers; they pose questions. They are frameworks open to the contributions of opinion and pressure. The "police power" of an international organization, a national government, a state, a city, or a board of education depends on the notion of what the role of each of these bodies is or ought to be. A "matter of local or internal concern" or the power of "local self-government" is as much a matter of political conception as a matter of "national concern" or the power to regulate "interstate" commerce. The 1930's saw a vigorous American inquiry into the potential scope of the federal power. The result was that many problems until then deemed of state concern only were found, in fact, to be of special concern to an entity larger than a state and therefore, in law, within the power of the federal government—its police, commerce, taxing, bankruptcy, spending, or currency power. Thus a great many problems received a satisfactory solution on the federal level.

New, or old and still unsolved, problems press our generation, but the federal legislature seems unwilling to solve them. Could it not be that some of them could find a solution on an *infra*—rather than *supra*—state level? We could still witness the discovery that problems hitherto deemed of state concern only are, *in fact*, of special and peculiar concern to entities smaller than a state and therefore, *in law*, within the variously described police, welfare, good government, safety powers or local government powers of the cities. The extension of the federal power has proved possible without the need

[177]

of constitutional amendments. A larger use and a more liberal interpretation of city powers could similarly be achieved through a reinterpretation—by city councils and courts—of the existing law.
After all, that law has been written in broad and flexible terms just
because the draftsmen wanted it to be an instrument of welfare,
adaptable to changing conditions, not a political strait jacket for
generations to come.

This expansion will require, however, a technique similar to the
one used in the pioneer federal statutes. Lawmaking power does
not grow on trees. The very modalities of its exercise may determine
whether it exists. The Wagner Act, for instance, begins with an
introductory section that reads like a study of industrial relations
and the incidence of labor disputes on interstate commerce. A city
which ventures into a new field must start with a careful investigation of that field and predicate its measure on careful findings of
facts that make the evil to be fought a matter of specific municipal,
rather than state, concern. *Contemporary racial conflicts are a peculiarly urban phenomenon.*

In the field of ethnic relations such findings require no difficult
investigation. The basic truth is hardly controvertible: contemporary racial conflicts are an urban peculiarity. To begin with statistics,
and to speak of Negroes only, the proportion of Negroes to the total
population of New York City was in 1940 more than twice what it
had been in 1920. A substantially similar change has taken place
during the same period in Chicago, Detroit, and Philadelphia. No
comparable increase in the Negro population of the surrounding
rural areas has occurred. It is, therefore, not surprising that it is
Detroit and Philadelphia, New York and Chicago, not the upstate
or downstate rural counties, that face the ugly danger of race riots.

Even these figures, impressive as they are, do not tell the whole
story. Racial conflicts are in themselves—in their modern form—an
aspect of urbanization, and so is the breakdown of time-honored
devices to cope with them. Topographical and social segregation,
distinct vocational stratification, psychological acceptance of a
"born-in" status, separate "but equally dignified" hierarchies, traditional behavior patterns, and self-centered ghetto autonomies are

[178]

all swept away by the rapidity of social change, the vocational mobility, and the migratory instability of cities. Racial tension, as we know it today, is as urban in nature, and its control is as much within a reasonably modern interpretation of city police, welfare, and safety powers, as street traffic congestion. What is needed to assert that power successfully is a series of carefully drawn ordinances, with specific findings of local evils and legal remedies justified by those findings. Legal ingenuity will also be taxed in the setting up of municipal enforcement machinery consistent with local law and tradition.

Two more points need to be made. A realistic view of the proper city power must take into account the well-known and conveniently forgotten fact that, whatever their numerical strength, our larger cities are dominated, in state legislatures, by the rural counties. This result is achieved through "rotten boroughs," a heavy disproportion between the number of county inhabitants and that of county representatives, or arbitrary limitations written into state constitutions; the constitution of New York is notable in this respect. The result is that New York City, in which 55.3 per cent of the state's total population lives, is entitled to elect only 42 per cent of the Senate and 44 per cent of the Assembly. Inequities in representation are even more acute in other states, as a recent "rotten boroughs" suit brought in Illinois has emphasized.

The need for strengthening the political power of the "infrastate" units has, however, much broader implications. The existence of a federal structure in the United States is justly regarded as a condition of freedom, and hardly anybody would welcome the rise of a centralized leviathan American regime. But is the often advocated renascence of state power the best and most sufficient answer?

It has been remarked by Jerome Frank and P. J. McEvoy that the degree of newspaper information a citizen gets about the happenings in the state capitols is negligible as compared to that available about federal and municipal affairs. I have recently discovered that no verbatim transcript of proceedings in the New York State Legislature is available in New York City to laymen or lawyers. Do our states come anywhere near the optimum size of political units in a federalistic, pluralistic society? Or are they in one sense too small and in another sense too large to assure the best functioning of political processes?

Democracy on the European Continent has never known genuine local home rule, and this was probably its main single and fatal weakness. In his *Democracy in America,* De Tocqueville saw the basis of American democracy in the vitality of smaller political units of city and county governments. I am convinced that this vitality must be deepened if the main condition of freedom, the liveliness of the individual's participation in public affairs, is to be secured.

It is fashionable nowadays to speak of "our atomic age" and to advocate a world government. But unless loyalty to smaller political units—and the primary ones must be much smaller than a nation or a state—is assured, no universal government is possible. There can be no world peace without peace inside our cities. There can be no world government without a home rule for villages.

To work for a better world on a village level is rarely a glamorous enterprise. Man's impatience is with miles; but—as Emerson has it —it is for the best that each mile be made of one thousand seven hundred and sixty yards.

Human Rights:
Bill or Agency?

[This paper was prepared before the adoption of the Universal Declaration of Human Rights by the United Nations General Assembly on December 10, 1948, but the point of view it expresses is still relevant and significant, for the problem of the enforcement of human rights is still unsolved.—Ed.]

THE PROTECTION of human rights is a task that bulks large among those confronting the San Francisco Conference. The Dumbarton Oaks Proposals confine it, in Chapter IX, to the secondary functions of an advisory Economic and Social Council. Those who still hold "that to secure these rights governments are instituted among men" would like to see it included in Chapter III among the essential aims of the international organization. So would those who know that individual freedom and international peace are indivisible. But the question is not what the United Nations Charter will say about human rights, and even less in which chapter it will say it. The critical question is whether anything at all can be done about it.

General agreement on the essentials of human rights seems to exist among the United Nations. Whether or not all of them are equally sincere about it is doubtful. Hardly any of them would refuse to join in a general statement of respect for fundamental freedoms, but it would be very difficult to formulate detailed provisions dealing with human rights which would prove acceptable to everybody at this time.

It is also the consensus that the international community has some interest in the preservation of certain minimum standards of individual freedom. But attempts at an outright international enforcement of these standards would be blocked by reluctance to recognize a superior international power in a sphere long a jealously guarded domain of internal jurisdiction.

If this appraisal is correct, the way, if any, of assuring some concrete protection of human rights at this time must be found in a scheme that would make use of the general, although vague, agreement on the existence of some basic human rights and their international significance, but at the same time avoid the difficulty of a detailed definition of such rights and thus sidetrack the opposition to superior international enforcement which deems it a challenge to national sovereignty.

This dilemma can be solved through (1) the avoidance of every attempt at the formulation of a detailed Bill of Rights at this time, and (2) the immediate creation of an international agency that will operate within the framework of the national sovereignties. Such an agency should, in the first instance, use whatever machinery, legal or otherwise, is provided for by the several nations in order to further and protect the basic human rights already recognized by their internal laws.

The creation of the agency should not be contingent upon the promulgation of a detailed Bill of Rights. The San Francisco Conference obviously would be unable to formulate it. Every attempt to force such an action would result in a reference to a special committee with the consequent postponement of all action in the field of human rights. On the other hand, the fundamental rules of an international Bill of Rights are already on the lawbooks of the various countries. Thus, for instance, Rumania has never repealed the constitutional provisions guaranteeing the enjoyment "without discrimination as regards racial origin, language or religion" of "liberty of conscience, freedom of instruction, freedom of the press, freedom of assembly and freedom of association." The Spanish constitution still assures that "any individual has the right freely to express his ideas and opinions, availing himself of any method of dissemination without being subject to prior censorship"; and Argentina goes beyond the classical freedoms in adding the freedom "to teach and to study" and in proclaiming as a matter of constitutional law that "the national jails shall be healthful and clean, intended for the safekeeping and not for the punishment of the offenders detained therein."

It is, of course, true that most of these solemn proclamations have been honored more in the breach than in the observance. But the mere adoption of an international Bill of Rights would not change the situation. The main effort must be made in the direction of international *enforcement* rather than promulgation of additional *substantive rules.*

The first function of the agency should be the study of the conditions prevailing in the various countries in respect to the protection of human rights. Such studies, based on reports of the governments concerned and field observations made by representatives of the agency, should be made available to the general public.

In the second place, the agency should have the right to appear before legislatures, administrative agencies, and national courts as *amicus curiae* whenever it feels that the cases or problems before these bodies are of concern to the international community at large.

Third, the agency should be granted the right of independent petition. Most people in areas of impairment of civil liberties do not know how to ask for their rights. To ensure the effective protection of the inarticulate, the agency should have the right of initiative, independent of the complaint of interested private parties. And to remedy possible inhibitions of local attorneys in critical areas, the various member nations should, on reciprocal terms, grant to the members of the bar of a sister nation the right to represent the agency before their courts.

Finally, the agency should attempt the application of the technique of "yardstick regulation" in the field of civil liberties. The agency should organize an Office of Peace Information and, complying with local regulations, should approach the peoples of the various countries through the channels of the press, radio, and film. The publication of a newspaper or the furnishing of news facilities would give the agency more firsthand data on the actual scope of freedom in a country than volumes of investigation. And the presence of a free news periodical could do more to free the spirit of a country than scores of injunctions.

In none of these activities will the agency act as a superior international power, but appear before the various branches of a national government as a witness, a petitioner, or a corporation. It will operate from within the framework of an unimpaired national sovereignty. The only privileges and immunities the agency should claim are those customarily granted by all sovereigns to the agents of their sister nations.

These privileges should include the recognition of the agency's juristic personality; the diplomatic immunity of its agents; their right to free travel; and the extraterritoriality of premises. The extension of such privileges to international bodies has already a number of precedents. For example, the constitution of the Food and Agriculture Organization provides for the grant "of all the immunities and facilities which each member nation accords to diplomatic missions, including inviolability of premises, immunity from suit and exemption from taxation." The signatories of this constitution thought that further extension of privileges to international organizations was not unlikely, and introduced, as an alternative means of determining the privilege of employees of the Food Organization, the reference to the "immunities and facilities which may thereafter be accorded to equivalent members of the staffs of other public international organizations."

The human-rights agency should be an independent functional agency. Modern experience has shown the great advantages of independent regulatory agencies on the domestic plane. Chapter IX of the Dumbarton Oaks Proposals provides—in Section A (2) and in Section D (1), respectively—for the two distinct types of international bodies, the specialized agencies independent in nature and the commissions of experts, being part of the Economic and Social Council. Whether or not an expert study and research group on human rights is created, it is important that the main task of protection of individual freedom be entrusted to a functional, active, independent agency detached from power politics and having a much greater capacity for flexible local action than the Council or its committees are likely to possess.

The human-rights agency should not only decentralize its activities as much as possible, but also attempt close co-operation with responsible unofficial national organizations. A number of associations intent upon promoting civil-liberties standards could co-operate with local branches of the agency and act, in some countries, as the first stage in sifting the multitude of complaints.

The Dumbarton Oaks Proposals provide that all specialized agencies shall be brought into relationship with the general international organization. The human-rights agency would thus be called upon to make reports and recommendations to the Assembly, its Councils, and Commissions. It should also be empowered, when necessary, to bring suit for declaratory or remedial judgment in the Permanent Court of International Justice.

It is, of course, far from certain that all the governments concerned will be ready to accept even this minimum program for international action. In fact, it is possible that some of them will refuse to consent to the creation of an international agency at this time, while claiming their readiness to enter into thorough—and lengthy—negotiations aimed at the formulation of a code of substantive international law. But it seems likely that no nation prepared for bona fide recognition of the international interest in human rights will reject a program which calls for no more than an agency operating primarily, if not exclusively, on the basis of that nation's own laws and before that nation's own tribunals.

Neither should it be assumed that, once created, the agency will achieve the millennium. It must be recalled, however, that the usual pattern of a dictator's career shows, at the beginning, a decided reluctance to break international ties or to defy public opinion abroad. Even after the fury of a war, civil or otherwise, has swept a country, some humanitarian devices have been known to afford a minimum of protection.

The present proposal, far from being new, is nothing else than an application of basic lessons of the history of freedom to the field of international law. These lessons point to the overwhelming importance of procedural institutions over substantive rights. The humanization of English law has not been the work of a council charged with the formulation of the code of equity; it has been the result of a procedural device, the creation of a Court of Chancery. The recent growth of administrative agencies is but a manifestation of the same institutional trend. The United States Federal Trade Commission Act, for instance, does not contain any more precise mandate than the outlawing of "unfair" methods of competition, but this has not prevented the Commission from evolving a consistent and important body of trade regulations. It would be easy to multiply instances of statutes successfully entrusting important and delicate functions to administrative agencies with the help solely of criteria such as "fair, equitable and feasible," or consistent with "public convenience and necessity." And it should not be forgotten that in the United States the least specific of constitutional provisions, the "due-process" clause, proved to be a great safeguard of individual liberties.

The time seems ripe for a reception of similar, common-law techniques in international law and politics. The recent recourse to the creation of specialized agencies is an instance of this new spirit. The Dumbarton Oaks Proposals are another. The Proposals do not attempt to formulate a body of international public law prior to the creation of the security organization. The same approach must be followed for the protection of human rights.

Progressive public opinion must demand the immediate creation of an international functional agency entrusted with a case-by-case evolution of an international law rooted in the principles already embodied in the various national legal orders. The Scylla of perfectionism that would delay the creation of an agency till a Bill of Rights is accepted and its supremacy recognized by all nations, and the Charybdis of defeatism that would be satisfied with the mere insertion of a formula bare of institutional backing, must be avoided. The United Nations must not let the creative moments of international co-operation go by without building a functional agency whose very existence will be a recognition of the basic liberties of man.

Group Sanctions
against Racism

A SYNDICATED COLUMN by John O'Donnell of the New York *Daily News* charged on October 2, 1945, that

behind the successful drive to disgrace and remove General George S. Patton from his army command in occupied Germany is the secret and astoundingly effective might of this republic's foreign-born political leaders—such as Justice of the Supreme Court Felix Frankfurter, of Vienna; White House administrative assistant Dave (Devious Dave) Niles, alias Neyhus; and the Latvian ex-rabbinical student now known as Sidney Hillman. . . . These boys and their pals decided to go out and get General Patton's hide and rank

because—the columnist "revealed"—the soldier who got slapped by Patton in an army hospital was of Jewish descent. "Then Patton proved himself a great leader and hero in France. But his foes here in Washington never forgot the Sicilian episode."

The story was made out of whole cloth; the soldier slapped by Patton was not a Jew, and no Jewish "political leader" had anything to do with Patton's transfer.[1] But the canard received wide publicity. The New York *Daily News* alone has a daily circulation of more than two million copies. The Jews were shocked, then worried. The Jewish press charged that the Jewish organizations, instead of assuming a militant leadership, confined themselves to a letter to the editor.

Can't the Jewish organizations do better than that? It is easy to

---

[1] O'Donnell made a complete retraction in his column of October 19, 1945.

[187]

say "militant leadership," "war against neo-fascism," etc., but when war is declared, what form shall warfare take?

Among the weapons available in a society built upon the profit motive, there is that of economic action: refusal to patronize, picketing, boycott. Could not a defamed minority refuse to buy or advertise in a publication guilty of attacks which follow the classical pattern of *Mein Kampf?* Could not Jewish organizations ask all decent Americans to support them in their action? Or should they bring a suit for libel and try to get satisfaction through the courts?

The answer is—according to what may be described as legal statics —that they cannot safely do any of these things. Legal dynamics, new trends, or straws in the wind may point in the other direction. But the orthodox "law on the books" seems to be weighted against them. To begin with, in the eyes of the law the Jews do not exist as a group. They may be murdered as a group, but they may not complain about it *as a group*. They can be defamed as a sinister gathering of the Elders of Zion, or of ritual murderers, but there is no effective remedy against their defamation as a group. The harm done to each of them may be far greater than what he could suffer from personal defamation. But neither as a group nor as individuals are Jews entitled to ask that their defamer prove his assertions or be branded a libeler.

This is no accident. It is in keeping with the basic character of modern law which—after having been permeated by Renaissance individualism—has become a law of relations among individuals and has lost its feeling for collective rights or group responsibilities.

This attitude, which is based on the recognition of the value of human personality, has made for much progress in human relations. But in its blindness to group relations it fails to conform with reality. The course of our individual lives often depends more on the fate of the group to which we belong—family, union, class, or race—than on our own individual merits. Even if the trials of war criminals did not abandon the theory of individual guilt, expiation by the Germans—i.e., loss of political or economic independence—had, by its nature, to be collective. When responsibilities are clearly collective, such as in the case of a lynching, attempts to allocate individual guilt lead inevitably to a breakdown of justice.

Of course an individual may stop reading, or advertising in, the *News*. But if a group decided not to patronize that paper and tried to induce others to do likewise, the ghosts of criminal conspiracy, combinations in restraint, or secondary boycott would be raised against them. This is what paralyzes collective action and reduces a number of organizations to the device—welcome to some and odious to others—of writing letters to the editor or to the "sitting down at lunch with the Colonel" technique.

To lay those ghosts vision and courage are needed. At the cost of life and limb, American labor has laid the ghosts of conspiracy and boycott, and invigorating currents have penetrated the American political atmosphere. Those who are responsible for the honor and livelihood of the threatened minorities must persuade the popular, political, and legal opinion of the country that *people singled out for attack as a group have the right to defend themselves as a group.*

This principle has led, in industrial relations, to collective bargaining and has provided a defense against conspiracy charges. The same principle can lead to equally important results in the field of ethnic relations. For instance, the enforcement of antidiscrimination laws should not be left to individual initiative only, but minority organizations should be given the power, analogous to that enjoyed by the unions under the NLRA, to file charges of unfair practices.

Our present problem, however, does not require legislative intervention. Collective bargaining was granted to labor by statute. But its second basic right—to picket and boycott—was won by effecting a change of judicial attitude. This change has removed labor picketing from the inferno of criminal conspiracy, or the purgatory of disorderly conduct, to the constitutionally protected sphere of freedom of speech, and has put labor's right to picket and boycott beyond the reach of unreasonably restrictive municipal ordinances, state statutes, or congressional enactments.

This change in judicial attitude was not the result of the dis-

[189]

covery of a new legal argument. As in all basic constitutional issues, the operative forces were ethical or political rather than strictly legal. It was the recognition of the moral and political importance of the economic issues that labor was presenting to the country. To say that the pickets or boycotters "just spoke" was not enough to afford them constitutional protection. Freedom of speech does not mean freedom to say whatever one pleases. A number of torts, misdemeanors, felonies, and even capital offenses can be committed through speech alone.

Suppliers of a commodity, for instance, could not picket a customer's store or otherwise discourage the public from patronizing him because he refused to pay the suppliers a "fair price." But suppliers of labor have the right to picket the store of an employer who refuses to pay "fair wages." In 1943, Texas declared that solicitation of union membership, like the solicitation of insurance, would be subject to prior licensing by the state. Some members of the Supreme Court argued that unions were business organizations and that the state could subject them to restraints similar to those usually imposed upon economic activities. But a majority held that the statute was unconstitutional. The reason for this decision lies in the recognition of the general value of the ideals for which labor fights, of the general public interest in the problems that it raises, in the need for the citizenship to be informed about the controversy and the opposing arguments. The political and the social value of the aim pursued make the use of the boycott weapon legal.

Do racial and religious tensions have a public importance similar to that recognized in industrial tensions? Does the public need to be enlightened about the various aspects of racial or religious unfairness, such as incitement to hatred or exclusion from employment and educational opportunities? Is not a fair settlement of ethnic relations as important for the general welfare of the country as the fair settlement of industrial relations? If so, then the right to appeal to public solidarity must be upheld even if the appeal results in an individual refusal to patronize or in a mass baycott. *Thornhill* v. *Alabama* was concerned with labor picketing only. But the language of the Court's opinion asserted "the liberty to *discuss* publicly and truthfully *all matters of public concern* without previous restraint or fear of subsequent punishment." [2]

However, the recognition of the right of minorities to confront the American people with the problem of racial justice cannot come from a royal grant or a gracious judicial decree. Assertion must precede recognition. Like every other boundary, the line between lawful and unlawful acts is shaped by the forces active on both sides of the line. The boundary between incitement to boycott and the advocacy of social sanctions against violators of decency is variously drawn by society and its judges in various circumstances. And the result depends, to an overwhelming extent, on the way in which the action is conceived and felt by the actors themselves.

In theory, if a man has a right, he possesses it whether or not he is aware of it. In political reality, however, awareness and assertion of rights can become the condition of their existence. Secrecy and deviousness are incompatible with assertion. An act which is a manifestation of inalienable freedom if performed in a manner consistent with the dignity of a free man may become unlawful if performed surreptitiously. Concealed inducements to advertisers or subscribers to cancel their contracts is secondary boycott. An open appeal to the conscience of advertisers, subscribers, and the public at large is exercise of freedom of speech. And this is as it should be. A public appeal states the issue, recites the accusation, affords an opportunity to refute factual falsehoods and logical fallacies, or opposes an appeal to reason against an appeal to emotion. It transforms a base conspiracy condemned by the law into a trial by public opinion protected by the charter of freedom.

The answer to hatred and oppression is not mere debate, or legislation alone, or half-hearted pressure. Once again, the history of labor affords a lesson: debate *plus* pressure, legislation *plus* picketing, individual protection *plus* group action offer the only chance of success. Nor is the ideal value of the struggle impaired by the injec-

---

[2] 310 U.S. 88 (1940); italics supplied.

tion of an economic motif. On the contrary, a community has the moral duty to see to it that, like any other crime, racial aggression does not pay.

Not that the task is easy. Racial exploitation, discrimination, and defamation have long been good business and their economic bastion is beyond the reach of minority snipers. Only public support can help them. But the recognition of their right to appeal for such support cannot come without an uphill fight. Assertion, we said, must precede recognition. But recognition does not always follow assertion, and almost never does so *at once.* If the minorities want to conquer the right to collective action they must be ready for financial and physical sacrifices—and for setbacks and defeats. No change can be accomplished with a previous license, and no revolution, however peaceful, with a declaratory judgment obtained in advance.

On the other hand, short-range defeats are often long-range victories. The defeat of a righteous cause in a court often becomes an impelling argument for legislative or social change and results in a political victory. Nor can it be expected that the courts will decide this issue without the usual "distinctions." The advocacy of a boycott of an employer guilty of racial or religious discrimination may fall not only within the definition of a labor dispute for the purposes of the Norris–La Guardia Anti-Injunction Act, but also within the scope of freedom of speech. On the other hand, it is conceivable that picketing and boycott may be outlawed as an answer to defamation. It could be that the only constitutional restraint on the defamers' constitutional freedom to advocate religious hatred—and the *News* in an editorial has claimed that right for O'Donnell—is not the freedom of the defamed to advocate a boycott of the defamers, but an action for libel. This, however, should focus attention on the failure of our law to provide the victims of group defamation with an adequate defense against libel and lead to a judicial or legislative reversal of the prevailing policy against group libel actions.

All this is within the realm of political and judicial probabilities. However, one thing is certain: the chances of success cannot really be determined in advance of action. To win or to lose may be a question of luck. But the game must be played according to rules. And the rules of the game now call for neither apologetic propaganda nor economic guerrilla warfare, which the loosely knit American minorities could not afford anyway. The rules of the game and decent respect for American opinion call today for an open declaration of economic war against racial aggression and for a full statement of reasons to be submitted, in each individual case, to public opinion.

American minorities have no other force, no other weapon, and no other hope than America herself. To pit the economic power of the minorities against a powerful newspaper would be no more hopeful than to assume that a Fifth Avenue beauty parlor would go bankrupt if the members of the hairdressers' union stopped patronizing it. The essence of boycott is an appeal to the solidarity of all decent citizens. The American minorities have the right to launch such an appeal. The Jews—and the Negroes—have a right to picket [3] the *News* and the newsstands and call for their boycott by all truth-loving men and women. The Negroes—and the Jews—have the right to picket the DAR's Constitution Hall and to ask all lovers of art and beauty not to cross their line. They have the right to picket and call for the boycott of those New York department stores which, in the teeth of the Ives-Quinn law, are today as lily-white as ever.

This kind of struggle is not without risks. But it is well to remember that those who voyage and take no risks are destined to perish.

---

[3] Cf. Terminiello v. Chicago, 69 S. Ct. 894 (1949).—Ed.

The Supreme Court Today

THE FEDERAL JUDICIARY, led by its Supreme Court, may very well prove to be, in the coming decade, the most liberal of the three branches of the national government. Is this why those who have long been yearning for a swift and unrestrained return to "constitutional normalcy" have recently shown a propensity to attack the Court, its authority, and the fitness of its personnel? Is this why the other side, caught in an ideological lag so frequent in the history of liberalism, is still "fighting the last war," as the French General Staff used to do, the war against judicial supremacy and government by judges? And should we discern an ominous significance in the simultaneous appearance of a learned plea [1] for total abandonment of judicial review of constitutional questions, predicated upon the authority of Thomas Jefferson, who, in a certain period of his life, wrote that "the legislature alone is the exclusive expounder of the sense of the Constitution in every part of it whatever," while the judiciary is "an irresponsible body working like gravity by night and by day . . . advancing its noiseless step like a thief"? Be this as it may, and quite regardless of political preferences or motives, conscious or otherwise, which may have inspired the offensive against the Court, most serious students of the Supreme Court's history would agree that a comparison of the present with its past record does not support the denunciation of its recent activity. And there are good reasons to fear that an impairment of the

---

[1] The reference is probably to *Majority Rule and Minority Rights* (1943), by Henry S. Commager.—Ed.

Court's position in the national life would ultimately prove equally disastrous to those who attack it and to those who fail to defend it.

The charges that one finds most clearly formulated in the present offensive against the Court can be summarized as follows:

1. The Justices of the Court are hopelessly split among themselves, and their continuous disagreement on nearly all vital issues destroys the Court's authority and prestige. As Arthur Krock puts it somewhat sarcastically, "in the interests of democracy at war, dissenting brethren should disagree in silence, or at least eschew personalities."

2. The Court systematically disregards its own precedents and by continuously changing its theories creates a confusion among the lower federal and state courts which it is supposed to serve as a guide on all questions involving federal law. Says G. W. Martin in *Harper's*: "What the members of the Supreme Court will do with matters that are laid before them is as predictable, these days, as what a cage of chimps would do with a bunch of bananas. Inasmuch as the principal function of courts is to enunciate principles so that all men may be treated alike, today and tomorrow, and be able to conduct their affairs accordingly, the simian gymnastics of the judges are not so terribly amusing."

3. The Court fails to confine itself to the interpretation of the law as it is. In the words of a New York *Times* editorial, "The majority of the new appointees came to the Court . . . apparently under the theory that their function was not so much to know and apply the law as it stands, or in case of doubt to interpret it objectively, but to apply a new 'social philosophy' in their decisions. The inevitable effect of such an approach could only be to create uncertainty regarding the law and turn the Supreme Court, in effect, into a third legislative house."

One should not be deceived by these seemingly legitimate and innocuous claims for unity, stability, and certainty voiced by the critics. As usual, the quest for unity of approach, certainty of attitudes, for the "law as it is," is a disguise of the underlying design to prevent the development of an institution or of a body of law in a direction deemed undesirable by the critics. Particularly un-

warranted and inconsistent with the American constitutional practice and, for that matter, with the common-law tradition itself is
the suddenly scandalized attitude toward the presence of a number of dissents among the Justices of the Court.

It must be kept in mind that the very existence of separate
opinions is a characteristic common-law feature. A French judge
who would dare to add the single word "dissenting" to his signa-
ture would be deemed guilty of a grave disciplinary infraction and
subject to removal from office. The only country on the European
continent where the individual opinions of the judges composing
a court are known is Switzerland, which is an island of devotion to
the principles of democratic federalism and to the lawmaking function of the judiciary.

The very conception that a court—or a country—to be dignified,
orderly, and authoritative, must speak as a unit assumes that harmony, progress, and order can be achieved only through unity and
uniformity. Related as it is to this conception, the irritation against
the Justices' frequent and vocal disagreements among themselves
is rooted in a conception profoundly alien to the contrapuntal
common-law approach to law, society, and government. The disagreement among justices of the same court—like the coexistence
of two competing systems of courts, of law and of equity, involving two different and, indeed, conflicting legal systems within the
same governmental framework—is equally deplored by a great
many. Quite possibly the dislike of seeing our Justices manifest
their disagreement on vital issues is rooted in the failure to grasp the
deeper and essential philosophy of which the First Amendment is
only one manifestation.

Carefully and often intelligently drawn statistics have shown
that the number of dissenting opinions has greatly increased in
recent years. Figures substantiate this observation, but no statistics
in the world can show how much of the increase in the number of
dissents is due to the greater care now taken by the Justices in
the selection of the cases which they consent to review. The exercise of the appellate jurisdiction of the Court is made overwhelmingly dependent upon a rule of discretion, exercised through the

denial of petitions for certiorari or the dismissal of appeals for want of a substantial federal question. By wisely using this power the Court has almost entirely succeeded in eliminating from its reports those trite and trifling questions as to which a dissent could scarcely arise but which for this very reason were hardly worthy of the Court's attention. The Justices today "take" a case (and four votes out of nine are necessary for the purpose) only when it reveals an issue worth discussing and deciding.[2]

Other critics finally have berated the form that the disagreement among the present Justices has taken, the form of alleged personal attacks and of unseemly clashes decried as inconsistent with judicial temperament and posture. Most editorials agreed that the Justices "hurl thinly veiled insults at one another," and one of the writers even detected an interesting explanation for the Court's "crisis" in the fact that of the nine Justices now on the Court, seven came there with no previous experience as judges, the tenuous exceptions being those of Mr. Justice Rutledge, who spent two years on the Court of Appeals for the District of Columbia, and of Mr. Justice Black, who "had served eighteen months as a police judge."

The headlines faithfully added their blank strokes to the conventional picture of a turbulent court torn by an internal strife and gave us, in New York alone, on one opinion Monday, such images as "Frankfurter Cries Laxity at Justices," "Stone Is Target," or "Barbs Fly in High Court." Too bad that one who hopefully turns, encouraged by headlines and editorials, to the text of the opinions finds them so disappointingly calm and so impersonally technical! The first statement, indeed, which has been used by the reporters as showing the existence of personal clashes was uttered by Mr. Justice Black in the Hope Natural Gas Company case,[3] where he referred to a "wholly gratuitous assertion as to constitutional law in the dissent of Mr. Justice Frankfurter." This statement has been answered in almost identical terms by the latter Justice in the Gerdes case,[4] where he said that the majority resorted "gratui-

---

[2] See address of Chief Justice Vinson before American Bar Assn., September 7, 1949; 70 S. Ct. Rep., Advance Sheets, November 15, 1949.—Ed.

[3] 320 U.S. 591 (1943).

[4] 321 U.S. 178 (1943).

tously" to another doctrine of constitutional law. Whatever the connotation that the word gratuitous may carry in common language, both Justices, in the opinions which contained the term, took pains to explain that they used it in a technical and narrow sense indicating no more than that the announcement of the doctrine in question was a dictum, since it had been asserted in cases which, as Black has put it, did "not afford a proper occasion to discuss the soundness of that doctrine" and "courts do not discuss issues in abstract" or, as Frankfurter said, could "be disposed of on [a] conclusive ground" not involving constitutional issues. To be sure, the two Judges disagreed as to the merits of the two doctrines in question as well and labeled them respectively as "highly controversial" and "wholly novel." But anyone can see Black and Frankfurter, who sit nearby on the bench, exchange frequent remarks in the most friendly mood and their dissents are not even distantly analogous to what has been written and said in the past by Judges whose judicial aptness and greatness are no longer questioned by newspapers or magazines. To give one instance only, one could point to Mr. Justice Holmes's dissent [5] from an opinion written by the proudly devout Christian and Catholic Mr. Justice Butler: "I would suggest that the Quakers have done their share to make the country what it is, that many citizens share the applicant's belief and that I had not supposed hitherto that we regretted our inability to expel them because *they believe more than some of us do* in the teachings of the Sermon on the Mount." How does this dig compare with the most recent dissents? Consider for instance the following: "That is why we should be uncompromising in observing the limits of our authority and should avoid laxity in assuming jurisdiction." This is the statement which came as such a shock to one newspaper, the New York *Daily News*, that it published the Justice's picture and headlined it, "Frankfurter Cries Laxity to Justices."

To the category of ready-made indignation belongs the sudden naïveté of those who, like the New York *Times*, ask: "Are our Constitution and federal laws so ambiguous or lacking in clarity

---

[5] United States v. Schwimmer, 279 U.S. 644 (1929).

that even experts cannot tell what they mean?" This astounded question completely overlooks what by now is common knowledge, namely, that our Constitution has been phrased in such terms as to avoid the political strait-jacketing of future generations; that the often praised wisdom of the founding fathers consisted in not attempting the precise solution of the infinite number of situations and contingencies which might arise in the future; and that one of the reasons why the American Constitution has survived so many other more recent charters is to be found in the very vagueness, generality, or, if you like so to call it, uncertainty of its constitutional mandates. It is obvious that provisions such as the ones prohibiting "cruel and unusual punishment," "excessive fines," or "unreasonable searches and seizures," or those requiring "just compensation," "due process," or "equal protection," leave the real content of the constitutional guarantees thus created wide open to the changing interpretation of what is cruel, unusual, excessive, unreasonable, just, due, or, for that matter, "equal." Congress might have occasionally tried to give a more specific content to its enactments but, at many strategic points, it preferred to avoid the danger of "freezing the law" and deliberately left it in a state of flux by laying down only general principles of policy rather than attempting the formulation of a perfect statute whose minute paragraphs could lead to *automatic* results in all possible cases. So courts and administrative agencies have often been left with no more precise indication than that methods of competition must not be "unfair," that motor carriers must serve "public convenience and necessity," and that the activity regulated must be one "affecting commerce."

Nor should it be assumed that statutes of this kind are a pernicious invention of the brain-trusters. The prevention of "unfair methods of competition" is the only definition of the scope of the activity of the Federal Trade Commission created in 1914, and it is the Sherman Act, passed in 1890, which still retains the prize for grand generality.

The notion that the Court has recently become a "third legislative house" is equally unwarranted. Of course the Court is not, and should not be, a *legislature,* but does that mean that the Court is not, and should not be, a *lawmaking* agency? Do those who criticize the Court today advocate the shutting off of the most characteristic source of the common law, of the law made by judges? Should the only lawmaking activity in the framework of our government be that of the legislature? If this were or ever became true, an equally radical change would be required in our constitutional and legislative techniques. The very type of constitutional and statutory provisions under which we live calls for a statesmanlike judiciary, politically and socially alert, conscious of its being a living branch of a living government and not an automatic device distinguishing right from wrong with the implacability of a machine for the detection of false coins. The history of the decisions of our Supreme Court is a history of political decisions. And many a landmark in the history of the United States is a great judicial decision.

The present Court has lived up to the best American tradition. Its greatness and its conformity to that tradition are particularly apparent in its refusal to assume the cloak of infallibility. Max Lerner noted recently that "it is good to have Justices on the Supreme Court who pretend to no Olympian infallibility and who can stick their necks out of their enfolding robes." It is noteworthy that the present Court has been quite explicit in this attitude. It has repeatedly stated that "Congress and courts both unhappily may falter or be mistaken in the performance of their constitutional duty"; that problems of justice are not "a question of algebra to which there is a demonstrably right or wrong answer"; that one should not advance "illusory pretenses of exactitude"; that "our own experience vividly demonstrates that careful and competent men frequently reach different conclusions despite the fullest and most careful examination of all available data, including the difference of opinion on the part of their associates."

Law is too serious a business to be left to lawyers. While there are legal questions and legal problems, there are no legal answers or legal solutions. The greatness of the Court is manifested in its growing awareness that the issues which confront it, no matter how legal, must of necessity find a composition social, economic, or political in nature. Thus, various Justices of the Court have again and again put the emphasis upon the necessity to work out a "practical, as distinguished from a theoretical, definition," declared "that practical tests should govern," that the "recognition of the relevance of the economic effects has made the mechanical application of legal formulae no longer feasible"; that "social as well as economic return" must be "taken into account" in the process of regulation; that the Court "should, for the guidance of the regulatory and the regulated, reveal something of the philosophy, be it legal or economic or social, which guides [it]." They know that "this does not satisfy those who seek for mathematical or rigid formulae." But they are blunt and outspoken in stating that such formulae "are not provided by the great concepts of the Constitution such as interstate commerce, due process, equal protection"; that the constitutionality, for instance, of the application of the AAA to a given case can be more properly determined by a reference to the "economics of the wheat industry" than by a measurement of the commerce power based on the mechanical application of any legal formula or nomenclature.

Nor can it be assumed that it does not matter too much what is said about the Court, since, anchored in the Constitution, it is, in a sense, above praise and blame. On the contrary, it must be fully recognized that the constitutional position of the Court is extremely tenuous. Indeed, its jurisdiction upon matters representing more than 95 per cent of its average business depends on the strength with which public opinion would believe in the Court and support it if it came into conflict with a hostile Congress. The Constitution, in this respect, is of an unusual explicitness and provides in Article III, Section 2, that the original jurisdiction of the Court is restricted to the exceptional cases affecting ambassadors, other public ministers and consuls, and those in which a state is a party. In all other cases the Supreme Court shall have jurisdiction only *with such exceptions and under such regulations as Congress shall make.* In other words, even without challenging the doctrine of judicial review as laid down in *Marbury* v. *Madison*, Congress could cut off the Supreme Court of the United States from the power to review the decisions of the lower courts and could also create special courts for the administration of special statutes. Such a court, the United States Emergency Court of Appeals, has recently been created by the Emergency Price Administration Act and it has exclusive jurisdiction to review OPA orders. It is true that the decisions of this court are reviewable by the Supreme Court, but this is only so because, as the Supreme Court itself said, the congressional enactment "has saved" to it such authority. The real basis of the constitutional position of the Supreme Court is in the prestige it enjoys and in the readiness of political public opinion and of the people at large to protect it and to prevent any encroachment upon its powers.

As of all things essential, it is true of the Court that it is infinitely powerful and at the same time frightfully defenseless. The Justices composing the Court and all those who discuss it should therefore be always fully aware of their responsibility. Not all Justices have at all times realized the strength and the frailty of the institution they serve. Some of them have been small and even petty men and have indulged in personal animosities. Others, like bad actors, have thought more about themselves and the effect they were making upon the public than about Hecuba, whose death they were supposed to lament. More than once, however, the people's interest in the Court and the people's respect for it have saved it from the blindness and pettiness of some of its detractors, members or outsiders. It is thus true that the Court owes to its people at least as much as the people owes to its Court. The present Bench, as a whole, is animated by a courageous willingness to cut through legalistic niceties to the living concreteness of the issues debated before it. The very difficulty of the enterprise upon which they have embarked and the passion without which the solution of the real problems presently confronting the country could not have been attempted have inevitably led to a considerable disagreement and even to animosity in its expression. But despite unfortunate and dangerous shortcomings, despite some relapses into technical formalism, despite some yielding to the temptation to avoid an issue by denying its own jurisdiction, the present Bench is on the whole a great court, faithful to the genius of American government and to the tradition of free dissent, remarkably free of partisan politics, aware of its governmental function, able and willing to do its share in the trial which a great nation faces.

A Supreme Court Yearbook

THIS is a proposal for the publication of a yearbook devoted to an annual survey of the activity of the Supreme Court of the United States, seen in its legal significance, in its social and political implications, and in its relation to the general trends of public opinion.

One of the main characteristics of this yearbook would consist in its being devoted to the activity of a single legal institution seen as a whole. Noninstitutional, analytical surveys of legal developments have often been attempted and carried out abroad. In Great Britain, for instance, the London School of Economics and Political Science has been publishing an *Annual Survey of English Law* since 1931.[1] These surveys, however, have always centered on the distinction among the various specific fields into which law has been traditionally divided—contracts, torts, crimes, corporations, and so forth—rather than on the distinctive contributions of individual institutions. A systematic or analytical approach to law is, of course, useful and often indispensable. But it is far more important to recall that institutions have a weight of their own and that this is particularly true of the American courts, with their strong and characteristic individual traditions. In a sense, it could be said of American law as a whole that it is "institutional" rather than "systematic" in nature. It is best studied in its living institutions.

The Supreme Court of the United States seems particularly well suited for, and has often been made the object of, institutional

---

[1] This undertaking is being duplicated in the United States by New York University School of Law, known as *Annual Survey of American Law.*—Ed.

studies. The novel significance of the proposed yearbook, however, lies in its periodical nature. The yearbook will not present merely a portrait of the Court, or a history of its past, or a restatement of the settled law. A yearbook is bound to emphasize the process of continuous change operated in and by the Court and to present an account of the law in the making.

It seems indisputable that there is an emphatic need for such a treatment of American law. American law has no more reached the end of its development than has American society itself. The Supreme Court of the United States renders every year a series of decisions which at the same time reflect and cause far-reaching changes in our political ideas, our economic and social structure, and our system of government. Legal studies have a natural and well-justified tendency to emphasize only those elements of the legal system which have already acquired considerable stability. Only too often they furnish to the reader an account limited to legal and social statics. Stability is, of course, the essence of the law, just as the force of inertia is the essence of the materials used by builders. But, if nothing can be built without stability, nothing can be built by stability alone. A widespread understanding of legal dynamics, of the direction, the meaning, and the rhythm of the major institutional changes that are taking place under the impact of judicial decisions, is essential for an enlightened building of a free society. A yearbook, an annual survey, will be prevented, by its very nature, from taking refuge in the pleasant sphere of "well-settled maxims" and neglecting those dynamic elements in the American law which have made for the continuing vitality and usefulness of its basic principles.

The main significance of the proposed yearbook would, therefore, lie in an earnest attempt to put the political, social, and economic significance of major current developments in the law within the easy reach of economists, social scientists, and, indeed, all intelligent laymen interested in the political life of the country. The yearbook ought to be written in nontechnical terms, intelligible to readers without previous law school training. Such translation of the law into English would not only help laymen to understand the law that governs them; it would help the lawyers themselves as well. It would subject technical legal doctrines to the acid test of common sense. It might even compel some lawyers or judges to face the core of their problems stripped of the helpful trappings of a conventional terminology.

Difficult as this task may be, it is not an impossible one. American law, and particularly American constitutional law, has not reached—and never should reach—such a degree of technical refinement as to be impervious to a translation into terms intelligible to the educated citizen. A historical precedent—*si parva licet magnis componere*—suggests that the attempt itself may be rewarding. One of the main single reasons for the successful operation of our Constitution lies—we suggest—in the fact that our most authoritative constitutional treatise, *The Federalist*, was written not as a book of legal science but as a series of propaganda pamphlets destined for the eyes of the intelligent voter, not of the technical lawyer.

To achieve this broader result, however, the yearbook must, in the first place, be a "lawyerlike" document. The so-called political or sociological treatments of legal problems only too often fail on their own ground and fall short of their political and social objectives because they are undertaken with means which, at best, look amateurish to lawyers and judges engaged in the daily administration of the legal rituals that form the lawmaking process of a country.

The yearbook will be of no use to society if lawyers and judges will not use it. And to be useful to them, in turn, it must be a reliable, responsible, technically accurate, fully documented, and thus authoritative statement. It must cover both the exact scope of the changes in the law that have taken place as a result of the Court's decisions and their legal and social background. To be used where law is made, and often made in a hurry—in law offices no less than in courtrooms—the yearbook must be a book of easy consultation. It needs a carefully thought-out pattern calculated to meet modern legal problems and flexible enough to permit continuous adherence to it. (An attempt to evolve such a pattern can be found in the Table of Contents of a Supreme Court survey published in 43 *Columbia Law Review* 837–955.) A consistent pattern will not only highlight the continuity of thought throughout the yearbook's series. It will—and this is essential—enable a lawyer to refer to the same chapter or section in the various volumes and, without waste of effort, to grasp the evolution of the Court's attitude on the specific problem he is facing at the time.

The attempt to reconcile the technically accurate with the politically intelligible should at all times remain the main purpose and distinctive trait of the yearbook. But many other important features could be developed and included within its general framework. Some of them would influence its basic editorial structure; others would have only a secondary function or could be adopted only at a future time. Their rank and priority cannot be determined now. The simple listing of some of them must suffice for present purposes.

The Court does not devote all of its activity to what is known as decision of cases. A considerable part of its time is spent in considering whether or not a given case should be "taken" for review and decision. The number of cases which the Court refuses to review is about four times as large as that of cases actually decided by it.[2] It is obvious, however, that the refusal to review and decide implies a preliminary judgment and is in itself a decision. Comparatively little attention is paid to this aspect of the Court's activity. We know of no attempt at a systematic study of the cases "rejected" by the Supreme Court. Yet, by considering those cases together, it may be possible to detect important attitudes in the Court's thinking. The Court [generally] gives no reasons for its refusal to review, and its refusals are often based on technical grounds. While it is, therefore, dangerous to draw conclusions from a single refusal, a series of refusals in the same field, studied together, may become a legitimate basis for relevant inferences.

It may or may not be true that the Court is interested in public

---

[2] In an address made on September 7, 1949, Chief Justice Vinson stated that during the previous term of the Court only about 15 per cent of the petitions for certiorari were granted.—Ed.

opinion and studies election returns more carefully than it ponders its own precedents. Certain it is that the country is interested in the Court. The newspapers, and especially the small-town dailies, carry a surprisingly large number of comments, often of doubtful accuracy, to be sure, on the Supreme Court's decisions. National magazines have lately been publishing many stories on the Court and the individual Justices. Law and public opinion are not unrelated. But can their relations be ascertained with any degree of accuracy? The yearbook could attempt a weighted content analysis of published comments and thus reveal the degree of the writers' understanding and misunderstanding, approval and disapproval, of the Court's decisions. It could, furthermore, utilize other devices for the measurement of public opinion at large in order to test the reactions of the reading public. Finally, it should endeavor to ascertain the degree, real or assumed, to which public opinion influences, if at all, the major policies of the Court.

Last but not least, the yearbook could exercise a far from negligible influence in international affairs. The world is engaged today in a revision of its political and social institutions. The process of political reconstruction in Europe and Asia is about to enter its decisive phase. Statesmen and lawyers, politicians and draftsmen will think of America, of the American pattern, of the American experience. Our generation may very well witness a new "Reception of the Common Law"—a reception of constitutional principles evolved in common law countries.

It would be unfortunate if that reception were to follow the line of least resistance and limit itself—as some of the new drafts do—to the facile adoption of our constitutional phraseology. It must be remembered that American institutions owe their political success not to a more or less felicitous wording of our main constitutional and legislative provisions, but to the techniques and policies that have inspired their judicial and administrative construction. It is the Supreme Court that has made our Constitution a living instrument of progress and prevented it from becoming a political strait jacket, an impotent document of good will, or an obsolete historical monument.

What civil law mentality and practice need most are not the—alas! so often imperfect—formulas of American law, but an insight into the American way of handling them. American cases rather than American texts of freedom should become the focus of attention of foreign jurists and statesmen.

To achieve this result, a problem of translation must be solved, a problem which is, once again, legal and political rather than merely philological in nature. A *genuinely comparative* case treatment written in English may give real insight to a foreign lawyer even if he should know no more than the rudiments of this language. On the other hand, even the most perfect literal translation of a case in that lawyer's own language could remain a dead letter if it failed to disclose the tacit indigenous assumption on which the decision was based or omitted the reference to comparable although differently classified phenomena of foreign law.

Which Comes First:

Law or State?

[While the following paper is concerned with the relations between law and state in an Israeli commonwealth, its implications are deep, for they raise fundamental questions concerning the basis of law and the basis of political authority. At the end of the article Pekelis raises questions which he intended to answer in a subsequent article, but he died before he was able to prepare the article.—Ed.]

THE ORTHODOX NOTION of the genetic relation between Law and Society, organized in a State, is that the State is the source of Law. Nineteenth century Europe, with its growth of strong centralized national states, quickly mooted Savigny's dilemma— Legislation or legal science?—and asserted the State's monopoly in the making of Law. In the ensuing classical debate on the *Rechtsquellen,* most continental jurists—despite infinite variety in the formulation and application of their ideas—kept faith with the fundamental persuasion that the primary source of Law is the Sovereign State. The primacy of State over Law was believed to be both logical and chronological: unless you had a State you could not conceivably have a Law of any kind.

Philosophical and political realism require the inversion of this proposition. Both logically and chronologically, it is Law that is the source of State and Society. Law is a pattern of human behavior and, philosophically speaking, it is nothing else than the idea that human behavior (both of those who govern or administer and of those who are governed or administered) ought to conform to some pattern, rather than be entirely capricious and unpredictable. Not even the most elementary society, limited to two beings, could come into existence unless the participants had reached a stage of ethical development in which *some* pattern was recognizable in their wills, unless they had achieved the conviction that their actions *ought* to conform to some recognizable order. In the words of the Bible, two cannot even "walk together except they be agreed" (Amos 3:3). Society cannot generate the idea of law in the minds of men for the simple reason that unless the notion of orderly action, of a pattern of will and behavior—that is to say, the "idea of law"—already exists in the minds of men, no Society can subsist among them. Men cannot form a community, no matter how primitive, unless they have something in common in their actions and reactions. And this very requisite of "commonness" presupposes some orderliness. Unless an order, a conformity to at least a rudimentary law can be detected in one man's actions, there is no possibility of its being compared with, adjusted to, or inserted into the pattern of other men's actions in order that a community may be formed among them. Only from Law can Society be born.

Politically, the notion of the State's primacy over Law is equally fallacious. It has been one of the theoretical factors that have hampered the progress of international law. Despite the often expressed contrary conviction, the truth is that International Law need not and cannot wait for the birth of an International State. In fact, such a State can come into being only if and when its potential components bring about a sufficiently high development of the *Law* of Nations and become convinced that their national actions must conform to an international pattern. A greater awareness of this truth could largely contribute to ideological clarity on the issues involved in the growth of international law and free international law scholars from their present poor-relatives complex. Similarly, if the existence of a political commonwealth is, at least to some extent, a *state of mind*, greater self-awareness could do much to speed the growth of the Jewish Commonwealth.

Jewish Law and Jewish State

The Jews should be the last people to believe in the primacy of State over Law, or in the dogma that the State is the *necessary* source of Law. If, to prove the contrary, the historical evidence of the existence of a People deprived of a State but endowed with a Law were needed, many centuries of Jewish history could be offered as an example. Jewish Law—without the paraphernalia of State power —has kept together the Jewish people, preserved its individuality, and made its present attempt at Statehood possible. This source of Jewish personality and of Jewish unity should not be neglected today, lest a powerful source of the estatification process be impaired.

More than any other group of Jews, those of Palestine should be and, in fact, are free from the fallacious belief in the primacy of the State or any other political community over the free agreement of people. Observations which have been made about the fundamental political beliefs and institutions of frontier Americans could equally well be applied to the Jewish frontier. R. B. Marcy's instructions to *The Prairie Traveller* state that "their first business should be to organize themselves into a company and elect a commander"—to convert themselves, as Ralph Barton Perry says, at once from a mere aggregation of chance arrivals into a political and legal entity. Arthur Ruppin makes a similar observation regarding the Palestine frontier when he says that the early settlers were confronted with the alternative of "settlement in groups or no settlement at all." One need not subscribe to Turner's theory as a whole—and even less to the frequent overworking of the "frontier explanation" by some American historians—to recognize that the Jewish frontier has created a number of political attitudes which we have long known prevailed among early American settlers. Who knows, indeed, whether the agreements that led to the foundation of Kvutza Dagania may not one day be hailed as the Mayflower Compact of a New Commonwealth. Palestinian settlers—no less than their American forerunners—have always been ready to resort to free association to meet the needs of the moment.

"The notion that social institutions are prior to individuals, being impersonal organisms or products of immemorial growth, could have no relevance to this practice" is another statement written about the American frontier and applicable to the Jewish pioneers. The Jewish conception of society is that of a man-made society, of a planned society, erected and maintained by men for men, of an *organization* rather than of an *organism*. From the Book of Samuel to Franz Oppenheimer's plan for Merkhavia, the line is unmistakably plain and reveals both the reliance on a conscious, planned human effort and the belief that agreement, social compact, and law antedate society and state. Jewish Palestine would be less than faithful to itself and to Jewish tradition if it did not attempt to bring about an immediate revival and development of a Jewish Law regardless of whether or not an official Jewish State is at once created.

Renaissance of Jewish Law: The Basic End

In the most tragic hours, Jewish leaders, the doctors of the Law, have seen in a Revival of Legal Studies the anchor of the People's survival. Today, too, this Revival must be invoked in order to secure an expansion of the Jewish Commonwealth, its greater internal cohesion, and its genuine independence and to arm it against the day of its inevitable recognition, as well as for the coming centuries of Jewish freedom.

The main lines of this Revival are set by the history and the present situation of the Jewish people in Palestine. The Jewish Law of the future must be deeply rooted in the Jewish Law of the past. Indeed, it must form an indestructible unity, the powerful source of the "transcendental unity" of Jewish past and Jewish future. It must at the same time recognize the ethical bases of the advanced modern political and social conceptions common to the large pioneer element among Palestinian Jewry.

The problem before the Jewish people is indeed a momentous

[213]

one: to reconcile the immutability of the basic truths of Revealed Law with the eternal progression of Life; to bridge the gap, created by centuries of Ghetto existence, between legal abstraction and living law; to re-establish the harmonious consistency of the totality of Jewish Law with a dynamic conception of society and with that Messianic idea of history which is the common foundation of Israel's traditions and of its contemporary aspirations toward a Co-operative Commonwealth.

Jewish tradition is not a recital of the past or a spiritual strait jacket for a chain of generations; it is a means of advancement, a seed of the future, an instrument of freedom.

The Available Means: A Court and a Restatement of Jewish Law

The Jewish Legal Renaissance can be achieved through the simultaneous utilization of two fundamental devices, neither of which presupposes the existence of an officially recognized state and both of which would further the process of Jewish estatification. The first of them is the creation in Palestine of a *Central Arbitration Court of Jewish Law*; the second, *Restatement of Jewish Law*. Before we discuss the implementation of these two devices we must emphasize that they are complementary in nature. The arbitration tribunal will perform its true function and become a genuine Court of Jewish Law only if it strives not simply for an isolated solution of the individual controversy, nor merely toward the adjustment of the rights of individual litigants. It must also attempt always to adjust such controversies on the basis of a maxim capable of becoming a law. A private arbitrator grows in stature and becomes a political figure, a member of the judicial branch of a *de facto* government, only if he is guided by considerations of common welfare rather than of transient expediency; when he asks himself not simply what is the best solution of the individual contest before him, but what is the general *rule* through the application of which that individual contest could best be solved; when he acts on the basis of a rule that he would have adopted if he had been legislating in the subject matter; when he thus contributes the creation of a body of Jewish judge-made law, resulting from the reaction of a thoughtful Jewish judicial mind to the present realities of a living Jewish community.

Such results will never be achieved unless this growing Jewish jurisprudence is enabled to draw its inspiration from the work of a body of students engaged in the attempt of a modern reformulation, a modern restatement of traditional Jewish Law. In turn, these scholars should not be allowed to confine themselves to the ivory tower of a self-contained and self-sufficient law, and to become engrossed in tempting games of abstract logic, in the niceties of construction, the intellectual delight of resolving ambiguities. They must work in the midst of their land and in the midst of their people, in close contact with the Arbitration Court, as its members and counselors and advisers. They must constantly check the traditional rule against the peculiarities of individual cases and the needs of a modern community. They must decide those cases and adjust those needs, on the other hand, with reference to the framework of basic Jewish ethical and legal principles governing the rights of a community and the dignity of an individual.

A Summary of Objections

This scheme, which would promote, through the dual device of Arbitration and Restatement of Law, a Jewish legal renaissance regardless of whether or not an official Jewish State is at once created, may appear open to many objections. They can be grouped in four main categories.

ENFORCEMENT

In the first place, it may be remarked that a Jewish Arbitration Court would have to rely upon the voluntary submission and spontaneous performance of interested parties, for in the absence of an official coercive power it would be unable to secure enforcement of its awards; that a number of arbitration tribunals already exist, but do not flourish, in Palestine; that the more ambitious political and juridical purposes assigned to the Central Arbitration Court are more likely to detract from, than add to, its prestige and popularity among litigants, who generally seek in an arbitration tribunal an equitable, speedy, and businesslike solution of their difficulties and would rightly be afraid of a Court preoccupied with general welfare considerations or inclined to evolve subtle, legal, or, even worse, "talmudical" distinctions. In sum, it may be contended that a Jewish Court could be created in the interest of the community as a whole only if it had the backing of a Jewish State, endowed with the coercive powers that constitute the basis of every governmental organization. This alone could compel the individual parties to a dispute to go through the cumbersome legalistic process of litigation. No legal renaissance can be expected from a Court which would unite the unpopular features of official procedure with the powerlessness of a friendly arbitration.

THE NEED FOR LEGAL CERTAINTY

In the second place, it could be argued that even if a Jewish State were created at once, it would be dangerous or, at least, inappropriate to leave the solution of individual disputes to tribunals and courts not guided by a well-established and, possibly, codified system of rules, statutory in nature; that justice, the prime foundation of every state, would be ill-assured if, instead of offering to the litigants the rock-bottom certainty of a rule of law, the new state, abandoning the *Rechstaat* ideal, invited them to tread on the shifting sands of individual judicial discretion and to appear before magistrates who, instead of being the mere voices of an objective law, would be legislators and judges at the same time, open to group pressures and individual bias.

TALMUD AND KVUTZOT

In the third place, the objection could be voiced that the reconciliation of the past and future in a *modern* restatement of *traditional* Jewish Law is but an empty formula, easy to announce but impossible to give substance to; that it can result only in a hybrid compromise that would be repudiated by both orthodox and progressive groups. The former would indeed have to condemn every deviation, no matter how slight, from the revealed Law or the tradition based on it; and on the other hand, progressive legal and social thinkers could not conceive for a second that the new commonwealth should be entangled in, and handicapped by, the tight net of rigid talmudic prescriptions which generations of enlightenment and political Zionism have escaped.

AND THE ARABS?

Finally, it is possible that doubts may arise as to the wisdom of emphasizing the traditional, religious-Jewish flavor of the laws of a commonwealth that seems destined to include a number of widely different ethnic and religious groups; that the theocratic aspects of a legal system that would claim to be rooted in a religious tradition would foment rather than appease the fanatic rebellion of groups that do not happen to belong to that tradition; and that a net separation of things governmental and secular from things ethnic and religious can better serve the purpose of uniting a country in which many ethnic and religious groups must live and prosper together.

I shall try to deal with these objections in subsequent articles. But I must honestly warn the readers not to expect any logical magic that would do away with the difficulties I have tried to list here. Candor requires me to state that these are valid—although not insuperable—objections. They *can* be overcome—in life, not just on paper. But it is only by being constantly alive to their intrinsic validity that the workers for the Renaissance of Jewish Law and the builders of a Jewish Society will reach that higher level of thought and action on which alone the difficulties outlined can be resolved.

Full Equality

in a Free Society:

A PROGRAM FOR JEWISH ACTION

[Early in 1945 Pekelis was appointed Director of the Commission on Law and Legislation of the American Jewish Congress. In August 1945 the staff of this Commission was merged with another agency of the American Jewish Congress, namely, the Commission on Economic Discrimination. The merger resulted in the formation of the Commission on Law and Social Action (CLSA). The officers of the AJC, with Dr. Stephen S. Wise as President, asked Pekelis to prepare a program of action for CLSA. The result was the paper published below, which Dr. Wise hailed as a "historic document." The paper has served as the "constitution" of CLSA, as a chart of its program and a statement of its philosophy. Directly and indirectly it has influenced the thoughts and actions of many American Jews. The document has its bases in the commitments of Pekelis to cultural pluralism, the religion of the Jewish Prophets, and the political theory of the Declaration of Independence and the Bill of Rights.—Ed.]

I. THE COMMISSION'S AIM

Sec. 1. *Jewish equality and Jewish distinctiveness*

A decent respect for the opinions of Jews and non-Jews alike requires that we should declare at the outset, in some detail and with utmost candor, the ideological fundamentals that underlie this program of ours. These fundamentals embody the paramount aim that will inspire all our activity. Their acceptance or rejection will inevitably lead, we believe, to the acceptance or rejection of the main principles of action formulated in this program.

[218]

To state our basic belief at first negatively, we do not intend to define our task as that of a Jewish "defense agency" or to confine it to the attempt of painless integration of individuals of Jewish faith or descent into the society in which they live. Ours is a much more complex, delicate, and difficult task. It is true that many Jews, and some Jewish organizations as well, would be content if every single Jew—or at least those in the United States—were permitted to enjoy full and genuine political, economic, and social equality. Nor would they regret it if, to achieve this result, the Jews became perfectly assimilated into the rest of the population, at most preserving their right—should some of them so desire—to profess their own religious beliefs and worship according to their rites.

This is not the viewpoint of the American Jewish Congress. In our basic aim—full equality in a free society—the term *freedom* is, if anything, more important than the term *equality*. And no society is free unless it assures its components the freedom of individual and collective self-expression. Jewish equality and Jewish distinctiveness, the integrity of the Jews as a people and their dignity as individuals comprise the twofold but indivisible aim of Congress. We would reject individual equality if its price were renunciation of our collective individuality. We would do so not only because equality conditioned on uniformity is not genuine equality, but also because we believe that, by acting otherwise, we would betray our place in human history and our duty to mankind.

We believe, indeed, that the Jewish people are the bearers of cultural and ideal values the loss of which would make mankind the poorer. We believe that the fate of the oppressed and persecuted, of those who suffer and have no other hope than justice, is preferable to the fate of the oppressors and persecutors and of those who are continuously tempted by might and power to forsake right and justice. And we believe that is why our rites call us thrice daily to exult over our destiny, so unlike that of other peoples, and over our fate, so different from that of kingdoms and empires.

We believe that the endless suffering of our people is not meaningless. We believe that there is a place in history for those whose survival is indissolubly bound to the triumph of their ideals. We believe that we have been chosen as a living test of righteousness, as a test of peoples' ability to forego persecution, not only of Jews but of all those who refuse to conform to a compulsory pattern of uniform folk behavior. And we believe that we would betray our mission if we tried to escape suffering by relinquishing our diversity, if we became ready *propter vitam vivendi perdere causas*, for life's sake, to give up the reasons for living.

We also believe that the inexplicable continued existence of the Jewish people, as a people, is in itself a historical symbol of immeasurable significance, a manifestation of the mysterious superiority of weaponless spirit over the physical forces which apparently dominate the world. And we believe that the disappearance of the Jewish people from the scene of Western civilization—be it through cruelty of persecutors or through our surrender to them—would mark an apocalyptic victory of the forces which, for thousands and thousands of years, have in vain hounded Israel and the ideals for which it stands.

We finally believe that the simple historical facts that have imposed a common group destiny upon us call for an affirmative recognition and active expression of the full extent of our group existence. And we know that every attempt to confine Judaism to a mere religious belief is futile, because our religion is inseparable from our collective existence and our religious precepts from our duty to strive for the survival of Israel.

Sec. 2. *Jewish autonomy and the emancipation*

This survival cannot be taken for granted. The unique and miraculous phenomenon of a people which endured as a people for thousands of years without a land of its own, without a state of its own, has been at all times characterized by certain institutions which have all but disappeared from contemporary Jewish life. These institutions had taken various forms but they were the manifestation of one principle—that of Jewish communal autonomy. It is hard for us to imagine nowadays the degree to which this autonomy was real and effective. Bred as we are in the ultra-individualistic spirit pervading the Renaissance, the Revolution, and the Emancipation, we all profess the official credo of our era according to which society and state are composed of single individuals rather than of groups and individuals. We all somehow share—in most cases uncritically—in the notion that the freedom of a society can be fully achieved by a respect for the basic rights with which individuals, as individuals, have been endowed by their Creator. We forget that groups have a reality of their own, rights of their own, and that the exclusive emphasis on individual rights runs the risk of atomizing society, of creating a centralized organization of isolated and helpless individuals, and of ultimately impairing the delicate network of primary communities—this basic source of individual freedom and individual happiness.

By linking this individualistic movement to the glorious names of the Renaissance and the Revolution we have already recognized its great and beneficial significance in the history of human progress. The oppressive arbitrariness of a community of groups rather than of individuals—and this is what the medieval society was—has not served the ideal of freedom. The guilds were a legitimate object of the hatred of the people rising to power. And the Chapelier Law which forbade "citizens of the same . . . profession . . . when they find themselves together, nominate president, secretary or syndic, keep registers, pass resolutions, make regulations for what they claim to be their common interests . . ." was a legitimate weapon in the struggle against the precapitalistic monopolies of a restrictive economic system. It was inspired, however, by the individualistic laissez-faire belief that unorganized and free activity of single individuals would produce an automatic economic equilibrium. It is well known that that belief has proved to be a half-truth unable to provide a total answer. No economic equilibrium can be achieved without the recognition and regulation of the reality of groups, be they business or labor, farmers or consumers. What must be remembered is that the laissez-faire political counterpart of Jewish history, Emancipation, despite its equally noble in-

[221]

spiration, was also no more than a half-truth and did not provide a total answer. No more than the economic can political equilibrium be achieved without the recognition of group reality.

The demands presented by the agents of the Emperor to the carefully gleaned members of the Sanhedrin called by Napoleon were not due to a feeling of hostility toward the Jews. On the contrary, these demands only mirrored the new policy of the era which has found an even more violent expression in the Loi Chapelier which we have just quoted. But the acceptance of those demands destroyed an age-old Jewish tradition that had represented the main single secular factor of the survival of a landless and stateless people. That tradition, the tradition of communal autonomy, antedated the destruction of the Jewish State. Already, in the Hellenistic period, the Jewish gerusia abroad had powers similar to those of the Greek city councils. Flavius Josephus reports that in the first century B.C. the Jewish ethnarchs of Alexandria ruled their people as the rule "*of a free politeia.*" The Roman proconsuls of Asia Minor were ordered to leave Jewish communal autonomy unimpaired. In Mesopotamia, Persia, and later in the Caliphate of Bagdad, the Jewish communities were ruled by their own *rosh galuth* and *roshejeshiboth*. During the Arab rule in Babylonia and Palestine the *geonim*, and in Arabic Egypt the *magidim*, performed the same functions. Spanish Jewry was organized in a powerful *aljama*, Italian Jews in autonomous *congrege*, Polish and Lithuanian Jews in a complex institutional network rooted in the local *kahal* and developed into *medinoth* and *arotzoth*, crowned by a general Kahalic union. A modern observer is astonished by the amount of legislative, judicial, and administrative power wielded at all times by the Jewish communities and their leaders in matters both secular and spiritual. This astonishment can be but a source of preoccupation. It shows that a very important and age-old factor of Jewish survival itself can no more be taken for granted.

Nor should we forget that the millions whom we still mourn fell victims of an exasperated expression of the same trend which led to the creation of centralized, "groupless," monistic national European states. These states looked with hostility upon every unofficial autonomous group, suspecting it to be a "State within the State."

From their inception, they exacted the relinquishment of Jewish group autonomy as the price of equality. It was written in the Book of Fate that the ultimate extreme and totalitarian expression of that monistic trend should prove incompatible with the physical existence of individual Jews or, for that matter, of members of any nonconformist group.

Sec. 3. *Jewish survival in modern America*

The structure of modern societies makes the resurrection of Jewish autonomy in its traditional, *kahalistic* form as utterly impossible as it is undesirable. No matter how frankly we may recognize certain values inherent in the pluralistic structure of medieval societies, our stake and our share in the great struggles for individual freedom, the Renaissance and the Revolution, guarantee our immunity from the romantic virus of neomedievalism. But, on the other hand, our devotion to the ideals of individual human dignity should not prevent us from realizing the limitations of individualism and emancipation or from recognizing the lasting value of the fundamental pluralistic traits of American society. Only to the extent, indeed, to which the United States is not a monolithic block, or a mere aggregate of individuals and not even a "melting pot," does it offer to the Jewish community, as such, a chance for survival in a modern setting.

The philosophy and practice of cultural pluralism offer the opportunity for a new form of Jewish autonomy. Not as an "official" institution but as a private group, the Jewish community has a legitimate place in an essentially federalistic country, and can perform a wide variety of vital functions which in rigidly regimented societies are reserved either to governmental or at least to officially recognized agencies. To the extent to which the belief is preserved that American unity is achieved through a wide cultural and national diversity; to the extent that the United States guarantees to its minorities their first and basic right, that of fully preserving their minority characteristics; to the extent to which it is thus, in some sense, a multinational state; to the extent to which its centripetal forces do not destroy the autonomy of the social units comprising it —to the extent to which all this is true, America is immune to the totalitarian danger of rigid uniformity and American Jewry has a fighting chance for survival. Nor should we ever forget that if the situation were reversed, and the centrifugal forces were doomed, American Jewry would have to choose, as did so many other groups in the course of centuries, between total spiritual assimilation and the threat of total physical destruction.

The Jewish cause in the United States thus depends on the traditional American aversion to a leveling centralized government and to the compulsory uniformity of all members of a society. It partakes of all the difficulties and complexities inherent in a pluralistic conception of society and—which may be but another way of putting it—a pluralistic conception of human personality. Congress's philosophy of Jewish life rejects the three simple, total solutions of the Jewish problem: total assimilation, total emigration, or total isolation. It also rejects every attempt to pigeonhole a human personality into a single definition, constrain it to a single allegiance, confine it to a single and uniform pattern of conduct. It claims our right to be, at the same time, loyal, devoted, and selfless members of a great variety of overlapping groups—American citizens and citizens of the world; American Jews and members of a world Jewish community; citizens of a state and citizens of a village; members of a political party and members of a religious association. This is a right unthinkable in a simplified, monolithic society, a right dreaded by all kinds of totalitarian tyrants but truly inestimable to free men. It is, strictly speaking, not even a collective or group right; it is the right to a full expression of the manifold potentialities of individual human beings who only as members of a variety of groups are fully and freely individuals.

II. THE COMMISSION'S TASKS

Sec. 4. *Introduction*

We have described, as frankly as we could, the aim that inspires us and our conception of the general social and political setting in which we might operate. What we have said shows that we do not purport to hold the key to a "simple" solution. We know that all truth is complex. And we know that the condition of Jews is more difficult and complex than that of other peoples.

We are aware of the difficulty of achieving our aims of a full equality in a free society. (We know that to achieve it we must claim, at the same time, individual equality and group distinctiveness.) We know that it is not enough to say that a society cannot be free unless the reality and the legitimacy of the groups comprising it are recognized. We know that, at the same time, no society is free unless it denies unlimited freedom to its component groups and subjects them to the restraints of decency and fairness. While we assert the existence of a Jewish community, and claim its right to collective group action, legal, administrative, and social, we do not forget that collective rights are unthinkable without collective duties and responsibilities. While ours is a call for autonomous Jewish action, we do not forget that the peculiarity of Jewish interests lies in their inseparability from the universal cause of general human welfare. We intend to fight the forces of evil—discrimination and exploitation, defamation and violence—and we trust our fighting chances. But rather than rely upon their ultimate disappearance, rather than discount or neglect the existence of danger or the strength of outside pressure, we shall attempt to transform that outside pressure from a factor *against* into a factor *for* our survival.

It is thus with the awareness of the complexity of our various tasks and of their inherent interdependence that we are beginning the description of our specific activities in the five major fields of our endeavor.

These major fields are:

First, struggle for Jewish equality at home, equality in law, and equality in fact;

Second, protection of our civil liberties from the violent and fraudulent manipulations of neofascists and anti-Semites;

Third, active alliance with all progressive and minority groups engaged in the building of a better America;

Fourth, participation in the Congress's attempt to protect the lives and secure the rights of what remains of the Jews all over the world; and

Last, but not least, action within the Jewish community aimed at communal self-knowledge, communal self-control, and communal revival.

A. STRUGGLE FOR JEWISH EQUALITY

General Remarks

Sec. 5. *Anti-Semitism, American variety*

The struggle for Jewish equality—equality in law and equality in fact—is entering its critical stages in the United States. This is due not to the peculiarities of the development of the American Jewish community or to any special endeavor of Jewish organizations. It is due to the historical evolution of American society at large. An analysis of the situation may prove helpful in appraising the task before us.

Anti-Semitism in America differs fundamentally from the classical, European, prewar varieties of anti-Semitism in that it has its sources not in governmental restraints but in certain patterns of social behavior. The forces that limit the Jews in the full enjoyment of equality are not the forces of government but those of industry and trade, of banking and insurance companies, of real estate boards and neighborhood associations, of college faculties and university trustees—in a word, the forces of what could be called the "private governments" of America. In Czarist Russia it was the Ministry of Education and the Ministry of Justice that put a ceiling on the number of Jews to be registered in schools of medicine or engineering, or to be admitted to the bar. In the United States these ceilings are imposed by our "private" medical schools or personnel directors. In America, all Americans are equal—in the eyes of the law. The main threat to Jewish equality, the main danger to the American way of life, with liberty and justice for all, comes not from the police or the bureaucracy, as it used to come in Russia, or Poland, or Germany —it comes from the forces of society itself. Anti-Semitism here is private or communal, not public or governmental in nature.

The causes and dangers of this peculiar situation are well known and are part and parcel of the American tradition. They are found, on the one hand, in the traditional American restraints on governmental power and, on the other, in the already discussed pluralistic structure of our society, that is to say, in the exceptionally extensive role that private groups and social, as distinguished from governmental, institutions play in the life of the country. And if the struggle for Jewish equality enters into its decisive phases, this is due, we repeat, to the fact that the United States has reached a stage of evolution in which group existence and group responsibility, social discrimination, and private injustice have become crucial political and legal and, in some senses, even constitutional problems.

Sec. 6. *Private governments: the dilemma of our generation*

The original and, by and large, still prevailing, American concept of freedom and equality is that of freedom from, and equality before, the government, particularly the national government. The main preoccupation of the framers of our fundamental charter of freedom was the protection of individuals from the encroachment of the federal government. The Bill of Rights begins with the words "Congress shall make no law," and if states-righters of the eighteenth century had had their way, they would have put a period right there. The point may be illustrated by recalling that, strictly speaking, the first freedom guaranteed by the Bill is not the freedom of religion, but a freedom from religion, that is to say, from a federal governmental imposition of religion: "Congress shall make no law respecting an establishment of religion."

The Bill of Rights ran only against the federal government. No federal protection against state or county or city governments was thought necessary by the generation of the Revolutionary War. It took the Civil War to get "due process" and "equal protection" clauses which would limit the unrestricted freedom of these local governments. And it took the convulsions of the period following World War I to have the guarantees of the First Amendment read into the constitutional provisions restraining state power.

How will the Second World War contribute to the evolution of the American political and legal structure? Is the "due process" clause going to expand further? Are constitutional or quasi-constitutional restraints going to limit not only the power of the federal and state governments and their political subdivisions, but also that of our private governments? Or shall we stick to the maxim that "the Constitution runs against governments only" and permit private governments to perform—without constitutional restraints —the functions upon which the freedom and happiness of members of a community depend *in fact?* Are we, perchance, so willing to subject the conduct of our state governments to the exacting test of "equal protection" only because we have left the performance of many essential functions to private groups which are exempt from the requirements of fairness? Are we ready to let freedom ring and equality reign—where they do not matter?

The children of the Jew who escaped from Russia, where the state barred him from state-controlled medical schools, have nothing to fear from the state of New York or that of Massachusetts. If these states operated medical schools, more than one constitution would guarantee nondiscriminatory admission. Unfortunately, most states do not operate medical schools. And against those persons who do operate these schools and determine their admission policies, the Constitution does not run.

This is true unless, of course, we are able and willing to extend the basic philosophy, if not the direct application, of our Constitution and subject to its power not only the political microcosms but the social microcosms as well. Such a course of action is big with hope and danger. How far will we, can we, or should we go in this direction? That is the question. That is the dilemma of our generation.

Sec. 7. *The new trend*

This generation of Americans has grown impatient with a situation in which private governments hollow out the content of freedom and equality, leaving a well-polished shell. They are unwilling to see a press association limit the freedom of the press; a cartel impose what amounts to retrogressive consumption taxes through a well-planned system of basing point plus prices; a political party restrict the electoral franchise; a union and a railroad combine to expel an entire race from the industry—all this under the pretext of being "private" organizations.

It is this impatience that has brought the problem of social and private discrimination, because of race, creed, color, or national origin, to the foreground. The struggle is a major one and the forces of progress have already scored a number of victories. In analyzing recent legislative and judicial developments from this viewpoint, one finds numerous instances of a growing extension of constitutional philosophy to the areas of private power. The Ives-Quinn Act, which makes the right to private employment a civil right, and the Associated Press decision where the Sherman Act was used to curb private encroachments upon the freedoms of the First Amendment; the statement in *Classic* v. *United States* [1] that so long as a primary controls the outcome of an election in fact, it cannot escape constitutional restraints, even if it is denied legal status by the state; the decision that unions are subject to "at least as exacting a duty . . . as the Constitution imposes upon a legislature to give equal protection to the interest of those for whom it legislates"; and even the half-hearted Taft bill (S. 459, 79th Congress) which states that discrimination in private employment is incompatible with the provisions of the Federal Constitution—all these and many more fall into the same pattern and testify to the existence of a major political and legal trend.

It is, of course, not to be expected that the maxim "the Constitution runs against governments only" will be flatly abandoned. A much more subtle process of inclusion and exclusion is both probable and desirable. It is the task of the Commission to explore the avenues along which the expansion of the new trend could progress —from the adoption of a new approach to statutory interpretation to the evolution of constructive conditions in grants, licenses, and franchises; from the application of the doctrine of conspiracy against what is, in substance, the boycott of a race to the assertion of the public function of monopolies; from the enlargement of the notion of the arm of government to the inclusion of governmental omissions into the concept of state action. A trend toward the extension

[1] 313 U.S. 299 (1941).

of the "doctrine of equality" upon which, in the words of the Chief Justice in *Hirabayashi* v. *United States*,[2] "the institutions of a free people are based," to include the powerful network of private institutions is a hopeful and important trend. It is our task to strengthen it, make it articulate and use all the available skills for its technical implementation.

Sec. 8. *Full equality in a free society: possibilities and limitations*

The existence of such a trend is, however, the source not only of much legitimate hope but also of some justified concern. We have already stated our belief that the fabric of freedom must not be too compact in texture and that the pluralistic structure of a society is, by and large, the main single condition of an association of free individuals. America's federalism at any rate goes far beyond the existence of more than two score official jurisdictions and extends into the vast network of fraternities and trade associations, benevolent orders and labor unions, schools and churches. The jealous concern for the rights of the states and the extraordinary strength of private centers of power, mainsprings of American history and many hopes—including that for the survival of the Jewish people of America as a cultural and spiritual unit—are hinged on the preservation of American pluralism. How far should the federal government be allowed to go in defining the right to social and economic equality as a citizen's immunity or in treating private encroachment upon one's life, liberty, or property as an abridgment of a right guaranteed by the Federal Constitution? What would remain of state power if the federal government were allowed to punish murder because it deprives people of life without due process of law? And how far should state governments themselves be allowed to go? Can social pluralism survive if intruding administrative agencies control the policies governing the admission to, and life within, fraternities and factories, summer resorts and schools, clubs and residential sections, churches and theaters, lecture centers and railroads? This is a major social and legal problem comparable to the great economic problem of our time, that of full employment. We

---

[2] 320 U.S. 81 (1943).

can indeed summarize both by asking ourselves what are the possibilities and limitations of full equality and full employment in a free society.

Sec. 9. *The policy of concentration*

The magnitude of the problem is not, however, an indication of its novelty. As a matter of fact, its logical form is familiar to lawyers and is best expressed by the long-framed question: "Where are you going to draw the line?" And as usual, the answer will not come from any formal test—such as "direct bearing," "substantial effect," "essentially governmental," and so forth—although it may prove expedient to bottle some of our experience into containers with such or similar labels. The line will be drawn properly, if at all, only if our political instincts, our sense of proportion, our social wisdom, our institutional experience will dictate the answer and if legal skills will translate it into formulas that will give legislators, judges, and the people the sense of security that the law alone can provide.

The contribution to this "drawing the line properly" is one of the major tasks before us. Some controls have always been imposed upon private groups whether or not labeled *de facto* governments. Some will always have to be avoided. To argue today—in the name of philosophical pluralism—against the outlawing of discrimination in employment would seem to entertain doubts which even the Taft FEPC bill has already shed. On the other hand, Jews have no reason or right to demand equality in the Gotha Almanac or in fashionable golf clubs. Furthermore, to say that a law against discrimination can never educate people to tolerance is as wrong as to maintain that it can never increase prejudice. It seems safe to assume that everyone has the right to keep the company he prefers, that gentiles who happen to dislike Jews should retain ample opportunity to enjoy their exclusive summer resorts. Finally, none of us would like to penetrate a restricted fraternity with a sheriff's writ, any more than we would cherish the idea of winning a waltz by compelling a lady to keep her *carnet de bal* free from "discrimination on account of race, creed, or color."

To draw the line of demarcation is, however, more difficult than to cite these polar instances and requires an adequate knowledge of social data, both general and specifically Jewish. Not only considerations of political wisdom but the inevitable limitations on the resources of Jewish organizations, as well, dictate a policy of concentration on what is essential. The main fields of social or economic inequality with which we shall be called to deal are employment, education, housing, enjoyment of public facilities, and civil rights in general. The distinction between what is and what is not essential cuts across these fields. In each of them there are evils to be eradicated and imperfections to be tolerated. The latter will be only an inevitable concession to the basic nature of man, who cannot breathe pure oxygen and cannot live without a certain amount of arbitrariness and injustice. The thesis is certainly not destined to popularity, but the truth of the matter is that perfectionism is a dangerous ally in the struggle for freedom. The dispersion of forces may lead to a few more or less spectacular victories, such as the opening of a hotel or even of a college, and the overlooking of the more urgent needs of the Jewish community. Nor should it be forgotten that racial and religious discrimination are only two fibers of the complex fabric of human injustice and that these fibers themselves are sometimes intimately interwoven with discrimination based on wealth or with resentment due to poverty. Only an over-all vision of the complexity of the picture will permit the formulation of a plan centered on its truly strategic spots.

Specific Applications

Sec. 10. *Discrimination in employment*

The field of discrimination in employment is today an outstanding instance of the necessity of adopting and intelligently administering this principle of selectivity. It will have to be applied not only on the level of legislative action but, at least as much, on the level of law enforcement.

The historic importance of the enactment of fair employment practice statutes in the states of New York and New Jersey has been rightly compared with that of the adoption of Civil War amendments to the Federal Constitution. Just as the Thirteenth, Fourteenth, and Fifteenth Amendments aimed to abolish Negro slavery exploitation and assure federal control of state policies, the Ives-Quinn and Hill Acts aim to suppress exploitation of minorities by the state control of opposing industrial and union policies. Fifty-two per cent of all American Jews are subject to these two statutes, but their moral and political significance goes far beyond these figures. It is safe to assume that if the people of the state of New York will pronounce the Ives-Quinn Act a success, the adoption of similar laws throughout the nation,[3] and possibly on the federal level as well, will follow because of the logic of history. If the enforcement of the Act will cause more harmony than friction, more happiness than resentment, more understanding than hatred, then our cause is won—and not only in New York and not only in the field of employment. FEPC bills have been already introduced in other American key states in which the vast majority of Americans and 92 per cent of American Jews live. The possibility of their enactment and of their extension to the fields of education and housing will depend on the New York experiment more than any other single cause or factor. Conversely, a failure in New York would mean that no movement for the outlawry of discrimination in jobs comparable to the one originated during World War II could be mobilized for a decade or maybe for a generation.

Faced with this historic responsibility we should, in the first place, concentrate on an effort to make the New York and New Jersey laws a success, and then endeavor to spread their principles throughout the country.

Sec. 11. *The field of education*

The field of education, in itself of an obviously overwhelming long-range importance, must rank second only to that of employment in the present program of Jewish organizations. In this field we shall have to deal both with discrimination in the admission of students [4] and with discrimination in the appointment and treatment of teachers.

---

[3] As of early 1950 there were FEPC acts in effect in eight states.—Ed.

[4] As of early 1950 laws on this subject were in effect in three states—New York, New Jersey, and Massachusetts.—Ed.

As to the first item, we are confronted with the necessity of singling out the most important, strategic key spots of discrimination and devising adequate methods of legal and community pressure. The selection of the first objectives of an attack should be determined by one or more of the following considerations:

(1) The intensity of injury to the Jewish community. The general lack or the existence of comparable facilities in the same "educational market area" may be relevant.

(2) The impact exercised by the discriminatory practices of a given institution upon other institutions, upon student bodies, and upon the community at large.

(3) The weakness of the legal or social position of the institution guilty of discrimination, in the framework of the laws or social pressures to which it is subject.

In other words, the first organized action undertaken against an institution must be a good test case, clear on its facts, strong on its law, and appealing to public opinion. This selective approach may be disliked by fundamentalists who rightly believe that every discrimination is on principle equally bad. But realistic policies and the necessity to budget resources will require a careful choice of objectives.

Discrimination in the employment policies of private educational institutions does not generally come within the purview of laws against job discrimination. The New York and New Jersey laws and almost all the bills introduced in state legislatures exempt educational nonprofit organizations from the provisions of the law. This in itself indicates the need for caution. On the other hand, careful inquiry will disclose discriminatory practices by institutions directly controlled by states or cities. These practices would be a direct violation of constitutional provisions, state and federal, and could be attacked with great chance of success once the much more difficult problem of proving discrimination is solved.

Sec. 12. *Discrimination in housing, transportation, and so forth*

Discrimination in the fields of housing, use of public transportation, places of entertainment, hotels, and other public facilities presents, from the strictly Jewish viewpoint, a problem of relatively minor importance as compared with those of employment and of education.

Admission to, and equal use without segregation, of essential housing, transportation, and other facilities is not denied to Jews to any considerable extent. The exceptions are found in the field of restrictive luxury or summer resorts and hotels and in the existence of some exclusively gentile towns or villages. It need not be argued that such practices are, on principle, too reminiscent of a Nazi pattern to be admissible in a democratic country. Still, our policy of concentration on essentials would suggest that only limited attention be paid to the exclusion of Jews from luxury facilities, which does not impair the equality of their chances to decent jobs, decent living, decent education, or access to needed health and curative facilities.

Racial, especially anti-Negro, discrimination in housing and transportation has, however, a great indirect importance for our movement. This importance is dual. In the first place, restrictive covenants [5] are very promising fields for the successful testing of some of the theories aimed at the control of "private" arbitrary discrimination. Second, the alleviation of the Negro's housing misery and the abolition of segregation and other badges of slavery would be one of the greatest contributions to the cause of adjustment and harmony which in itself would strike at one of the causes of Negro anti-Semitism. It would be particularly fortunate if the results could be achieved through the doctrinal, legal, or political help of a Jewish organization.

Sec. 13. *Impairment of constitutional rights*

The problem of the protection of constitutional rights of the Jews is somewhat similar to the problem discussed in the preceding section. For the reasons heretofore stated, the problem of anti-Semitism in America involves defense of Jews from economic and social discrimination, not from the infringement of rights protected by the Constitution in its traditional interpretation.

---

[5] Cf. Shelley v. Kraemer, 334 U.S. 1 (1948).—Ed.

While occasional violations (and they sometimes occur in connection with governmental service, civilian and military, federal and state) should be competently dealt with, activity in this field should be conducted in close co-operation with general civil liberties groups and particularly with those which aim at the protection of the Negro, the wrongs against whom are still the main black spot on the American record of constitutional liberties.

B. PROTECTION OF CIVIL LIBERTIES

Sec. 14. *The freedom of the market of ideas*

The strategic importance of anti-Semitic propaganda in every fascist or neofascist bid for power or for public attention has been so much highlighted recently that there is no need of insisting on the dangers of this "secret weapon" of Hitler's regime. It may, however, be still worth emphasizing that Jewish concern with anti-Semitic propaganda is mainly indirect; it is the general breakdown of the democratic system, which is achieved through such propaganda and allied devices, that we fear rather than the immediate effects of Jew-baiting. Hence we believe that anti-Semitic manifestations and the remedies against them must be judged in the light of this general effect upon the democratic processes rather than with reference to specifically Jewish rights or interests.

A number of remedies have been suggested and sometimes applied in order to keep in check or lessen the evils of fascist propaganda. They range from the barring of literature from the mails to the barring of speakers from public buildings; from group libel statutes to prosecution for disorderly conduct; from boycott of newspapers to restraints on distribution of leaflets on the streets; from action by printers' unions to statutory requirement of identification of sources. Before deciding which, if any, of these legal and social measures shall be backed by democratic minority organizations, a basic ideological problem must be faced.

We should not forget, when *we* are the attacked, our devotion to the ideals of freedom of speech and freedom of the press. *Juif donc liberal* has long been the motto of the enlightened circles of world Jewry and progressive Jewish organizations must not be second to anyone in defending the rights of their opponents to utter their opinions. We should not try to qualify the truth that this country is predicated, to quote Holmes, on "free trade in ideas" or, to quote Justice Black, "on the fundamental constitutional principle that our people, adequately informed, may be trusted to distinguish between the true and the false."

It is in the light of these principles that we shall try to ascertain what are the rights of professional fascists, subversive Jew-baiters, or occasional attackers. Does the belief in "free trade *in ideas*" require the right of marketing worthless, mislabeled, adulterated, or poisonous goods, a right which has been denied to the free trade of commodities? Does the belief in the capacity of the people, be it the electorate or the jury, to "distinguish between the true and the false"—if "adequately informed"—require the absence or the presence of a trial judge with the power to exclude irrelevant, prejudicial, inflammatory, or just plainly incredible evidence? Does our confidence in the adequate results of a "trial by the consumer" require the absence or the presence of a Federal Trade Commission or of a Food and Drug Administrator? Does the trial by the electorate or by public opinion require the absence of every form of trial control while the trial by jury or that by the consumer requires, by common consent and as the very condition of genuine freedom, the presence of such controls? Does the difference between the subject matter of the trials justify this radical difference of treatment? We should not forget that these three forms of argument and persuasion—trade, judgment, and politics—were once carried out on the same spot: the agora or the forum. Today they are separated physically but their logical, psychological, and ideological structure remains closely kindred. We believe that the trade of ideas and the political forum can no more preserve their freedom when poisoned with unchecked licentiousness than could the trade in goods or the judicial forum.

The freedom of the market of ideas can be lost through control —or through its total absence. By advocating the proper, full, and truthful labeling of competing ideas we do not impair but serve the freedom of choice among them. The exclusion of politically lewd, clearly poisonous spiritual food, about whose contagious, hypnotic harmfulness reasonable men could not differ, would not prevent people from reaching a free decision. On the contrary, it would create the conditions under which they would be able to reach a decision worthy of being called *free*, and of being *theirs*.

Once more, the problem before us is where to draw the line. It will be our task—in close co-operation with liberal groups—to attempt the formulation of an approach which will promote rather than impair freedom of speech, freedom of the press, and a genuinely free functioning of political processes. In a great many fields the problem is not only one of exclusion but also of inclusion of ideas, the expression of which is barred by powerful combinations. Once again Holmes's "free trade" analogy proves correct. Freedom of the market can be impaired not only by the introduction of mislabeled or poisonous goods but by private combinations in restraint of trade or by undue governmental interference as well. The policies of newspapers or news agencies, that came only in part to the foreground in the Associated Press case, and the policies of the Federal Communications Commission, in the field of the radio stations at large and in that of the allocation of the FM stations in particular, are only some of the instances of these dangers.

Sec. 15. *Group libels and the individualistic fallacy*

Even the most fundamentalist defenders of civil liberties do not deny the constitutionality and the political wisdom of the existence of some law against defamatory publications. Unfortunately, however, the classical form of defense against defamation, the law of libel, can hardly be described, at least in its prevailing form, as an adequate weapon against fraudulent attacks upon the freedom of our market of ideas. This inadequacy may be due to several causes. But its main single reason—the absence of well-established and clearly defined sanctions against *group* libels—is in itself only a manifestation of that general individualistic fallacy to which we have already made several references and the overcoming of which is part of our general approach to the problem of Jewish action.

[238]

Denial of civil or criminal responsibility for group libel is consistent with the general character of modern law, which is a law of individual relations and has little feeling and even less skill for group relations. The idea of collective rights or of collective responsibility is by and large alien to a law which has accepted the general political individualistic ideology of the Renaissance.

The trouble with this attitude of our law is that, like the ideology on which it relies, it does not fit social reality. While the law centers on individuals, life evolves on the plane of group relationships. Whether or not the theory underlying the war criminals trial would have remained faithful to the notion of personal guilt —and it has not—it has always been obvious that the main forms of expiation to be imposed upon the Germans—loss of economic and political independence—could, by the very nature of things, be only collective. It is safe to say that the course of events of our individual lives depends at least as much on the fate of the groups to which we belong—our family or union, our tribe or race, our class or people—as it does on our individual characteristics or merits. A law which is blind to collective realities ignores the necessity of collective bargaining and the legitimacy of collective responsibilities on the various planes of social life or tries to deal with them through a series of more or less pernicious legal fictions, ranging from the rigidity of corporate personality to the one-employee–one-employer bargaining equality. When responsibilities are clearly collective—such as the responsibility of a lynching community—every attempt to break them down into individual guilts leads inevitably to the breakdown of justice. Germans have persecuted the Jews as a group. But legalistic convention maintains that neither the Jews as a group nor any individual Jew is entitled to ask that the defamers prove in open court the truth of their assertions or be branded as libelers.

Sec. 16. *Anti-Semitic propaganda: community sanctions*

We are confronted with a similar problem when fascist or racist attacks call for a concerted communal group reaction. The notion that secondary boycotts are illegal has taken the wind out of many an attempt of organizations to organize the defamed minorities for collective self-defense. A more aggressive treatment of the problem must be considered. The general maxim of illegality of boycotts must and can be overcome when an overwhelming public interest in the issue raised by the boycott demands that the citizenry at large be informed about it by all available means, and that the victim of a social injustice be permitted to appeal to the solidarity of public opinion. These principles have been recognized in the field of industrial relations and labor has received constitutional protection against attempts unreasonably to restrict its right to picket or otherwise to boycott in defense of its collective demands. American minorities should strive for the recognition of the truth that racial and religious tensions are of no lesser public concern than labor disputes and justify, with no lesser strength, the use of collective pressure.

What we advocate here, of course, is not concealed inducement of advertisers or subscribers to cancel their contracts. The method to be followed must be an open appeal to the conscience of advertisers, subscribers, and the public at large. Judges would be wise to repress concealed inducements as secondary boycott, while protecting open appeals as the exercise of freedom of speech. A public appeal states the issues, recites the accusation, and affords an opportunity to refute factual falsehoods and logical fallacies. It transforms a base conspiracy condemned by the law into what all forms of legitimate community pressure should be—a trial by public opinion, a manifestation of political vigilance, protected by the First Amendment.

Anti-Semitic virus often penetrates our midst through much subtler methods than outspoken propaganda, and not all of its bearers are conscious of the infection they are spreading. The use of prejudicial stereotypes or of more or less conventional images apt to stir racial, religious, or class prejudices is present in practically all popular arts—comics, films, radio, and so forth—and can be discovered with little effort in the lay and religious daily press and, unfortunately, in the lay and religious textbooks. The Latin world

[240]

has pointed to the fact that most unsympathetic characters in the Hollywood movies have Spanish, Italian, Mexican, or other Latin racial characteristics. This has not impaired the popularity of the films in Latin countries but has, at the same time, contributed to anti-American feelings.

Recently considerable efforts have been made to combat racial clichés. The Columbia University Bureau of Social Research, the Writers' Board, a Harvard group, and others have been active in this field. But what is needed is a systematic survey which would give us a fair picture of the policy followed, consciously or unconsciously, by the various publications. The results of this study should be brought to the attention of editors and publishers first, then of contributors, and, finally, of advertisers.

Sec. 17. *Anti-Semitic violence*

Violent anti-Semitic outbreaks often bear a clear causal relation to anti-Semitic propaganda, open or disguised. But even if they are only symptoms of underlying evils, they must be intelligently and courageously treated. It is a fallacy to import into the social sciences the metaphor of the distinction between "symptoms" and "causes." Even in medical science, symptoms are not a separate category of phenomena; they are distinguishable from other facts only because of their being perceived, not because of their lesser importance or lesser capacity of producing further harm. Vandalism in synagogues, breaking of store windows, and beating up of schoolboys often derive, it is conceded, from deep and complex causes. The way in which such incidents are handled can do much to limit the repercussions and possibly bring about some beneficial reaction. Legal assistance and social reaction in these cases must be focused not so much on punishment of individual violators as on the general deterrent effect. Jewish communities and Jewish youth must prove that Jews are not helpless, that Jew-baiting is not "a safe game," and that, like any other type of crime, anti-Semitic crime does not pay.

C. BUILDING OF A BETTER AMERICA

Sec. 18. *Reasons for Congress' intervention*

Our Commission must be instrumental in establishing an open, active, and stable alliance between liberal America and its oppressed minorities, on the one hand, and the American Jews, represented by Congress, on the other. The American Jewish Congress must be—with all other progressive American groups—in the vanguard of the battle for social progress, *whether or not the individual issues involved touch directly upon so-called Jewish interests.*

There is nothing new in the realization that the ideals, the tradition, and the fate of Jews are indissolubly bound to those of the forces of liberalism and progress, and opposed to those of social, political, or economic reaction. To state so publicly will not add to the forces of evil and hatred a single man or a single argument that they do not have or use already—well-meaning apprehensions to the contrary notwithstanding. But it will be the source of at least four major benefits:

1. American Jews will find more reasons for taking an affirmative attitude toward their being Jews if they are shown that *as Jews, as members of an organized Jewish movement,* they are part and parcel of a great American and human force working for a better world. By giving Jews a Jewish platform for general political action, we shall catalyze the Jewish interest in the Jewish community.

2. By offering our help to our real friends, by refusing to appease their—and our—enemies, by being at their side in every battle, in every difficulty, by putting our technical advice, our political resources, our intellectual faculties at their disposal, we shall achieve that type of solidarity and friendship of the liberal forces that can derive only from daily contacts in active work, and that occasional signatures on manifestoes can never bring about.

3. More especially, this policy will improve the relationship between Negroes and Jews. The Jewish community simply cannot afford to neglect any further the problem of Negro anti-Semitism and the great—indeed, physical—dangers with which the situation is fraught. Negroes and Negro organizations must learn as soon as

possible that in all the causes for which they struggle they can count upon finding the Jews and the American Jewish Congress on the side of justice. We must appear as witnesses before legislative committees, file briefs as friends of the court in judicial proceedings, and plead with our congressmen to support Negro demands for equality in political, educational, and economic opportunity. We may lose admission to a couple of fashionable Southern hotels, or the "friendship" of the white supremacy Bilbos, but we shall do what our religion, our belief in America, and even our selfish interests demand that we do: ally ourselves with those who are persecuted.

4. Last, but not least, by helping to destroy misery, oppression, hunger, and injustice, we are not only working for the realization of the ideals of Jewish morality but are also striking at the basic and ultimate causes of bias, prejudice, and persecution. Where the teachings of the Prophets are despised or ignored, their people can never be safe. Whenever injustice raises its ugly head, Israel is its first victim. In this inseparability of the triumph of ideals and of physical survival, in this historic impossibility of our compromising with the forces of evil, to appease them, or to purchase our safety through repudiation, lie the tragedy and the beauty of the Jewish fate, its physical misery and its spiritual nobility.

Sec. 19. *General topics of concern to Congress*

We hardly need to say that the necessity of husbanding the limited financial and human resources of Jewish organizations will put a considerable limitation upon the number of instances in which Congress will be able to take an active interest. We shall be compelled to select among the almost unlimited number of important general problems those which exercise the greatest impact on the general welfare or those which are particularly close to Jewish or other minority interests.

With respect to some questions—as, for instance, the question of full employment—there can be little hesitation. It is indeed strange that some Jewish organizations still hesitate to take an open stand in favor of legislation aimed at full employment. The example becomes dramatic when one thinks of the Jewish interest in the FEPC program. It illustrates the paradox of Jewish isolationism, of the attempt to confine the attention of Jewish organizations to so-called strictly Jewish problems. A simple reflection on social reality discloses that, while full employment does in no way guarantee fair employment practices, there is no chance to enforce *fair* employment unless *full* employment is guaranteed. In an atmosphere of unemployment and depression, the degree of resentment against legally enforced employment of minorities would be such as to make hesitant many an ardent supporter of the Ives-Quinn Act.

There are, of course, many other problems to which we may devote our attention. It is impossible and unnecessary to set up a complete catalogue of relevant problems. It is, however, safe to say that decent housing, adequate educational facilities, liberal medical care and social security, a fair deal for the veteran, and, of course, full protection of civil and political liberties of the Negro and other minorities are all topics. Nor can it be forgotten that a just and responsible international policy is part and parcel of a better and happier America.

Sec. 20. *Special remarks on immigration problems*

Among the general topics of special interest to Congress are those of immigration, naturalization, and deportation, and of the status of aliens and foreign-born citizens. Growing interest is being centered on this problem. Congressional hearings have revealed, however, that the Jewish and non-Jewish organizations which have been traditionally concerned with immigration problems did not have or were not prepared to present any comprehensive proposal dealing with this subject matter. We should devote the necessary attention to an inquiry into the facts and the law of immigration and present proposals which would make possible the abandonment of the system of racial or national discrimination on which the United States law is now based. Such proposals must be grounded in a knowledge of the present population, employment, and income trends in specific areas and trades. At the same time they ought to take into account political factors, such as the desire to avoid immigration of Nazis and of other enemies of democratic institutions.

The law concerning the exclusion and deportation of aliens also requires thorough revision. A number of well-grounded charges of rigidity, inhumanity, and antiquated medical criminological and psychological criteria have been brought against it. Many of the statutory provisions have been complicated and obscured by an impressive body of judicial and administrative decisions. A great number of provisions embodied in special laws directly apply to the same subject matter. Nothing short of a careful survey of the whole field will furnish an adequate basis for responsible recommendations.

D. WORLD JEWISH AFFAIRS

Sec. 21. *The international position of the Jewish people*

One of the cardinal traits of the Congress movement has always been its awareness of the interdependence of the various Jewish groups scattered over the world. It has not always been easy to see the connecting link among the various groups. The peaceful Italian Jews, for example, were much surprised when it was suggested that the introduction of the ghetto benches in Vilna—a city that seemed much farther from Rome than it does from Brooklyn—was a matter of direct concern to them. Recent history has made such connections more obvious and spread the recognition that what happens to some Jews in Poland has a direct impact upon the fate of Jews in Tripoli and Pittsburgh, Buenos Aires and Melbourne.

Still, even this recognition of a common destiny leaves the Jews with an alternative. *Fata nolestes trahunt volentes ducunt*: destiny will drag along the reluctant, but serves as a guide only to those who are willing. Jewishness must be more than the recognition of a bond imposed from without. It must be the assertion of a bond felt from within.

Nor should assertion be confused with mere emotions—even if

embodied in solemn manifestoes or lively press releases. The feeling of common destiny, the awareness of unity, and the faith in the future of the Jewish people as a whole are capable of being expressed through specific and affirmative action. Such action can be taken in, among other fields, the field of international politics and that of international law.

While analyzing the basic traits of our municipal, domestic law, we have repeatedly commented upon the little attention paid by it to the reality of social groups and the importance of the relations among them. A similar and not unrelated neglect prevails in the field of international law, which has little or no regard for the existence and the legitimate interests of nongovernmental groups. Consequently, if our national law can be characterized as essentially a law of interindividual relations, our international law is, almost exclusively, a law of intergovernmental relations.

Both characterizations, of course, are valid only as generalizations. We have already cited, in the sphere of municipal law, the growing number of cases in which the existence and the juristic personality, the rights and the duties, of collective groups have been recognized. Similarly, in the international field, individuals and groups have gained recognition, if not as juristic personalities, at least as subjects of international law. The Upper Silesian provisions, the other minority treaties, and the system of mandates have recognized international rights, respectively, of individuals and of ethnical or religious groups. As a matter of fact, the creation of the Jewish Agency for Palestine should be interpreted as the recognition, for certain purposes, of the legal existence of the Jewish people as a whole. Other international documents have granted recognition to other types of nongovernmental entities, such as employers' and employees' associations.

This incipient trend is capable of expansion—or of contraction. We should do whatever we can to convince the international public, political, and legal opinion that one does not need to be a "government" or a "sovereign nation" to participate in or appear before an official international assembly, court, or agency. Incidentally, quite a few Jews also need to be enlightened on this problem. To some extent we all are victims of an oversimplified political and legal picture of the world, according to which the international community is composed of nations only, and every nation only of individuals. The assertion of an international personality of the Jewish people, just as the assertion of the collective existence of the Jewish people within a national community, clashes with preconceived and orthodox notions prevailing among Jews and non-Jews. According to these notions, group libel cannot be punished and group sanctions against racism are, at best, unwise. Similarly, Jewish spokesmen may be permitted semiprivate contacts with international leaders, and Jewish experts may submit confidential memoranda to appropriate agencies, but the Jewish people as such should never attempt to appear officially on the international plane and act as a people.

Because this is an orthodox and prevailing notion, it is important that responsible Jewish organizations should do whatever is in their power to dispel it. The idea is growing that an international community is not merely a membership organization of sovereign nations, and that to act as a subject of international law one need not be either a nation or a government. To foster this idea—so important for the future of international law—the Jewish organizations must not only plead in its favor; they must act today in accordance with their belief in it. In the field of law, progress is always achieved through the assertion of rights made by the interested parties. Almost universally new claims are at first rejected. But there is no better means of political education than the official presentation of a claim and the public discussion which, when it does not precede, inevitably follows the adjudication of the claim.

By asserting the right of the Jews to speak as a group we shall serve the cause of international justice. It is just and equitable that the Jews who were murdered *as a group* should be afforded the right to complain about it *as a group*. To deny or recognize this simple claim is always a matter of conscience for those who sit in judgment. To present that claim is on some occasions—such as the war criminals trial—the inescapable duty of those who have taken it upon themselves to speak for the remnant of their people.

[247]

Judicial victory is not always the measure of a political success; a defeat in a court has more than once been the rallying point of popular sentiment. The feeling of "belonging" that an individual Jew proves with respect to his people depends on the extent to which that people appears a reality to him. And a people, as any other collective entity, be it a joint stock company or a congregation, is a reality only if there are those who assert its existence by speaking and acting in its behalf. It is vain to wait for leave to appear or for outside recognition. Recognition will never precede assertion.

Sec. 22. *Opportunities for action*

Fortunately or unfortunately, as it may be, opportunities for collective Jewish action are only too numerous. There are many unsolved international problems to which Jews, as Jews, are a party. They range from problems of major importance, such as the indemnification of war victims, to apparently minor incidents of protection of the assets of Jews of enemy nationality; from the universal question of international protection of human rights to the Anglo-American joint inquiry on Palestine, obviously of specifically Jewish concern.

With respect to none of these problems can the American Jewish Congress take the position that they are somebody else's business. Congress has taken it upon itself to offer to American Jews an integrated and harmonious philosophy of Jewish life in America. That philosophy and this life would not be complete without a stand on international affairs or without action on them. Nor can Congress shed the responsibility that derives from the facts themselves: from its being a spokesman for the majority of the largest surviving Jewish community in the world; from its being a spokesman for a group of Americans, citizens of the foremost international power of our times; from its being the principal member of the only existing world Jewish organization.

It is in co-operation with that organization, the World Jewish Congress, that we must approach the problems we have mentioned and those which may come up in the future. We believe that the keynote of our approach—the assertion of group existence and group rights of Jews—is susceptible of application to major and minor problems. Nor is the long-range value of that approach dependent on immediate success.

Thus, for instance, the main danger in the field of indemnification is that, if it will take place at all, it will be made on an individual basis. As in all cases of an exclusively individualistic approach, this would produce absurd and outrageous consequences. The murdering of a Jew will theoretically create a responsibility toward his children, but the wiping out of an entire family will extinguish the murderer's liability. The unlawful seizure of property will entitle the owner to ask for restitution, but if he was killed with his heirs, then the Fourth Reich will inherit the fortune the Third Reich had robbed. The cultural property that belonged to Jewish communities which had ceased to exist will be passed on to the cities and towns which had, at best, passively witnessed the annihilation of those communities.[6]

A basically more important instance of international action is that concerning the international protection of human rights. It is our belief that despite all their imperfections the human-rights clauses contained in the charter of the United Nations Organization represent important progress in the field of international law. Our task is not to decry their weakness but to strengthen them by developing their implementation and by underscoring the truth that essential human rights comprise both individual and group rights. A number of occasions offer themselves for a constructive Congress contribution: the peace treaties negotiations, the Bermuda conference on freedom of international communication, the recent Uruguay proposal concerning the intervention of the American republics for the protection of human rights in the Western Hemisphere—all these are occasions to prove that human rights can be more than a word. The American Jewish Congress has, in April 1945, gone on record as favoring the creation of an Interna-

---

[6] Cf. Joshua Starr, "Jewish Cultural Property under Nazi Control," 12 *Jewish Social Studies* 27 (1950).—Ed.

tional Human Rights Agency before an International Bill of Rights has been agreed on. Since that time other organizations and authorities have accepted this approach. Experience will show whether the other features of the agency scheme adopted by Congress should be preserved or modified. Among others, we must consider the problem of whether the idea of a universal, over-all Human Rights Agency should be promoted, or the notion of a piecemeal enforcement, that is to say, in specific territories and for specific rights, should be adopted.

There is, finally, one problem with respect to which the necessity for Jewish collective action is of paramount importance. There is no doubt that the Jewish people, as a people, should assert its interest in Palestine and repudiate the distinction advanced from so many quarters between Zionists and Jews, Hebrews and Jews, Palestinians and Jews, or Jews stateless and displaced and Jews well settled and well to do. The fatal slogan of separatism, "To your tents, O Israel; you have no part in David, nor any inheritance in Jesse's son," must not be heeded by our generation. Article 80 of the Charter of the United Nations pledges full respect for the rights "of any states *or any peoples*" upon territories now under mandate or which can otherwise come within the new trusteeship provisions. The rights of the Jewish people as a whole, with respect to Palestine, have been clearly contemplated by this clause. But they have not been defined, nor are they capable of automatic self-enforcement. They must be asserted. And since the unity of the Jewish people has been now officially challenged, it is not enough that the world Zionist organization or even the Jewish Agency alone make the assertion. This duty rests with the most articulate and advanced Jewish organization, with Congress. Someone must appear officially on behalf of the Jewish people. Someone must speak for the people which, as a whole, has made Palestine *ex nihilo* into what it is today; which, as a people, has acted in reliance upon the solemn charters of a community of nations; and which, as a group, advances today its collective claim. Congress must and can lead in the presentation of a brief on behalf of the people; Congress also must and can deliver the unequivocal proof of the endorsement of

its position by the overwhelming majority of the American and
world Jewry. A voting ballot for the election of a nonpartisan delegation that should present our demands to the Anglo-American
commission of inquiry must and can be distributed to, and collected
from, every Jew in America and in the world. The delegation elected
by this vote will approve and present the people's brief prepared by
Congress. Such an election and the presentation of the brief could
in themselves become historic manifestations of Jewish unity. The
situation, once again, calls for true leadership. Congress must accept the challenge.

E. ACTION WITHIN THE JEWISH COMMUNITY

Sec. 23. *Jewish action: communal self-knowledge and communal planning*

We come now to the last but, in a sense, the most important
aspect of Jewish action. This is action *within* the Jewish community. The vitality of any group can be measured by the energy
it devotes to the testing of its own strength and weakness rather
than to speculation about the power of its probable friends or the
infirmities of its inescapable opponents. He who defends the past
worries about friend and foe. The future belongs to him who centers on himself.

It is high time for us to plan our action from within in accordance
with our own needs rather than as a reaction to an external stimulus.
Thus, for example, the question "What kind of newssheet do metropolitan Jews read, anyway?" is a question that ought to have been
of interest to the Jewish leadership long before that sheet, in which
hundreds of thousands of Jews continue to take delight, became
isolationist, profascist, or Jew-baiting. The careful inquiry into the
kind of professional education Jewish youth genuinely want and
really need, rather than the disingenuous declarations of an outspoken president of a fashionable college, should be the starting
point of a positive Jewish educational or vocational policy. The
fairness or unfairness of the economic behavior of certain—no mat-

[251]

ter how thin, but nevertheless clearly recognizable—strata of the Jewish community should become the object of Jewish vigilance, and maybe of Jewish vigilantism, because of their inherent badness, and long before there is reason to fear outside reaction. What is needed, in other words, is communal self-criticism and planning, rooted in collective self-knowledge and aimed at the lifting of the general physical, intellectual, and spiritual standards of our people.

In fact, however, the American Jewish community is still by and large a dark continent for its inhabitants. So few, indeed, and on the whole so nonsystematic, have been the inquiries into the socio-economic structure of Jewish life that the net result is an almost total lack of factual material necessary for an intelligent over-all planning. We hardly know our own number, our age distribution, our birth rate, or our life expectancy. The situation is even worse with respect to the knowledge of our occupational stratification, our vocational needs, our economic resources, our cultural tendencies, our urban-rural distribution, and our criminality or morbidity. In the last five or ten years several voices were raised calling the attention of the Jewish organizations to the lack of knowledge needed for wise and intelligent planning.[7] Some undeniable progress has fortunately been made in the meanwhile. But the general picture is still that of a great community which lives without a budget or a plan, without a balance sheet of the past or a vision of the future.

Let there be no misunderstanding on this score. We do not believe in the magic value of "scientific planning." To take, in the desert, the count of the children of Israel may be the surest means "that they suffer no defeat in battle" or that at least "there be no plague among them." At other times, however, for a king to number Israel and Judah leads to "a pestilence upon Israel from the morning even to the time appointed." There are, this seems to be the lesson of the Scriptures, times in which popular instincts and traditional folkways can provide a wiser guidance than statistical graphs and demographic charts ever will. And there are times when custom and grass-root intuition will not suffice and when an over-

---

[7] Cf. "Jewish Social Research in America," IV *Yivo Annual of Jewish Social Studies* (1950), 147 ff.—Ed.

all picture, enlightened by national purposiveness, is called for. The conflict between planning and intuition is not peculiarly Jewish and appears in all fields of human endeavor. Neither is a disaster-proof recipe, and each has a proper season. There is a time to count and to plan, and there is a time to forget figures and act on the spur of an impulse. Our conviction that more knowledge and more planning are needed today in Jewish life does not mean that "sociology will provide all the answers." It simply means that Jewish communal laissez-faire policy of haphazard interventions has not stood the test of our times. It took the depression of 1929 to convince the American people that plague would not necessarily follow the counting and planning of national resources. The recent Jewish disaster should convince the Jews that the time—a time of desert rather than of kinghood—has come for us to take stock of all our resources.

A better knowledge of our over-all population trends, of the vocational and intellectual interests and tendencies of the new generation, of our chances for biological and ethnical survival, and of the socioeconomic facts of Jewish life and their consistency with the Jewish moral ideals will permit a profound change in the choice of our objectives and in the selection of our weapons. An over-all picture of the Jewish situation will permit us to evolve a genuine *Jewish action,* carried out as an action *of* the community, led *by* the community, and for the sake of the values inherent *in* the community itself.

Sec. 24. *Communal action and self-control*

Our statements about the necessity of Jewish collective self-improvement are apt to be criticized or looked upon with suspicion by those of our friends who have rightly grown tired of the attempts to tone down the Jews and their Jewishness, to "improve their manners" or to hush-hush their distinctiveness. Among the better-informed and more courageous students of Jewish life the well-considered opinion has gained acceptance that, as a recent writer has put it, "since anti-Semitism is not created by the behavior of Jews, Jews would do well to stop blaming themselves and one

[253]

another for it." Nor should—it is added—Jews assume a responsibility for the misbehavior of a few members of their community. As another writer put it some forty years ago, "like everybody else, the Jews are entitled to their own crooks."

We can and do accept these theories only with three important qualifications, which—it should be added—have been often implicit in the thought of those who have advanced those theories.

To begin with, we do not have in mind "manners" but ethical standards. Hence, strictly speaking, anti-Semitism is not an issue. Even if, in other words, it were proved that the ethical improvement of the Jewish community—the creation of a healthier, more dignified, and better life for its members—not only would not cause a decline but would be sure to provoke an increase of anti-Semitism, Jewish leaders would still have the duty of striving toward these ideals. *After all, we are Jews and not just anti-anti-Semites.* The furtherance of cultural, ethical, and spiritual values within the community and the creation of a favorable social and economic background for them are self-justified aims, the validity of which cannot be tested by their effect on anti-Semitic behavior.

In the second place, it is of course unfair to impose upon the Jews a form of moral tithing, the medieval responsibility of a group of ten for the misdeeds of every one of its members. But, on the other hand, we are not permitted to embrace an ultraindividualistic conception when, instead of group rights, we are faced with group duties. It will not do, on the one hand, to assert our right to speak on behalf of the people and to claim for it an opportunity of collective self-expression, and to avoid, on the other, all responsibility for individual mischiefs when they are frequent enough to become "typical." Of course, there must be no attempt to institute Jewish kangaroo courts to deal with Jewish offenders; they must bear their individual responsibility before the general community. But when a type of behavior or of misbehavior becomes too frequent or disproportionately frequent among the members of a given group—be it an ethnical, vocational, or territorial community —the group's leadership, to be worthy of its function, must examine the social, psychological, or economic conditions in which their group lives, investigate the necessary and possible changes, and act to promote them.

Finally, it would be a new thing, indeed, for the Jews to enter so flat a denial of a relation between their behavior and anti-Semitism. The best tradition in Israel, that of its Prophets, has never ceased to point to the faults of the people for the disasters that have befallen it. While every heathen leader tells his people that it is righteous but "encircled," the grandeur of Jewish history is that our leaders have never tired of calling for Jewish self-improvement. It is true that popularity was rarely the Prophets' reward. Nor has our generation the great inspiration that is needed to preach its faults to a martyred people. But we would betray our inalienable "sixtieth of prophethood" if we were so "arrogant and stiff-necked that we should say, we are righteous and we have not sinned."

This approach can inspire specific Jewish action in a contemporary political setting. Should, for example, the house ownership in any given slum area inhabited by non-Jews become overwhelmingly Jewish, anti-Semitism in that area would be inevitable. Human nature being what it is, resentment against exploitation by landlords who, as a type, happen to be Jewish is bound to become a resentment against "Jewish exploitation." In such a situation the Jewish cause can be helped, we feel, only by the clearance of the slums. Pamphlets showing how in history Christians forced the Jews to take on certain professions will hardly do. Nor can great benefit be expected from educational pictures showing that "many Jews are poor," that "Jews are not a race," or that to "tell a Jew" is more difficult than you think. Even less could be obtained by an attempt to outlaw human nature by passing a group libel statute. To be true to itself, the Jewish community must help in the only constructive direction: the clearance of the slums.

Situations similar to the one we have envisaged here may be few in reality, but their strategic importance cannot be measured by their number or even by their magnitude. The Harlem situation yields profits to a microscopic minority of Jews, but it throws a dark shadow upon the vast network of Negro-Jewish relations. Something should be done about this and other strategic key spots of racial tensions. Something must also be done about the slums inhabited by Jews. This something must be along the lines of a reform of the economic situation in those areas. They must be adequately studied, and public, possibly legislative, action promoted. Jewish organizations should take the leadership in advocating a housing program for the suppression of the slums in strategic key spots of interest to Jews. Jewish investors could be interested in the project; conceivably, through the threat of impending action, even the present owners could be awakened to their group responsibility; the power of eminent domain and city or state financial support should be asked for this and similar projects. To repeat a brilliant dictum—let us stop swatting mosquitoes and start draining swamps.

III. THE COMMISSION'S TECHNIQUES

Sec. 25. *Law, knowledge, and action*

If, at the end of a lengthy discussion of our major tasks, readers were not, by and large, aware of the techniques in which we believe and which we intend to employ, we should have failed in our purpose. We should have pictured ends severed from means and discussed aims and tasks disconnected from the techniques and methods of their achievement. That would be fatal, indeed, to the presentation of any program for political action.

We trust, however, that our previous discussion has made it reasonably clear that we intend to pursue our tasks through the means of social research, community pressure, and legal action. Rather than a recapitulation of the application of these three devices in the different situations with which we have dealt, a few general remarks will be appropriate at this point.

To begin with, the creation—through a merger of the Commissions on Economic Discrimination and on Law and Legislation—of a Commission on Law and Social Action is the result of the acceptance of the modern technique of integrating legal and non-legal skills. Contemporary experience has shown that no political, social, administrative, or legal action can be conducted efficiently unless means are found to narrow the gap between those who devote themselves to the study of social reality and those who, in legislative committees and courts, shape the law of the community. On the one hand, law is, indeed, too serious a business to be left to lawyers. On the other hand, social studies and social action can hardly live up to their mission unless institutional reality and the peculiarities of the legal structure are taken into account and skillfully utilized. Law without a knowledge of society is blind; sociology without a knowledge of law, powerless.

This is why investigation into the facts of Jewish life can be fruitful only when it is entrusted to the same functional unit which is in charge of legal research, and when research activities of both kinds are carried out through a daily exchange of data, a close-knit integration of projects, and an informal intraoffice co-operation. The same type of integration must be achieved between social and legal action and between research and operational activities. Modern methods of action necessarily range from a publication of sociological findings to the throwing of a picket line, from friendly negotiation to a law suit, from an educational campaign to the introduction of a legislative measure. Ultimately, success or failure will depend on the skill with which these various techniques are combined into one well-integrated strategy.

Sec. 26. *Law and legislation*

In the second place, it is important to note that we do intend to place only a limited reliance upon legislative action. A great many public-spirited groups and individuals have treated legislation as if it were the only conceivable vehicle of social reform. The truth of the matter is that it is neither the only nor the best. Great strides toward general welfare have been achieved through changes in judicial or administrative attitudes, changes which were often due to intense educational influences. We intend to follow and adopt the latter technique. A great many of our proposals—from the creation of a Human Rights Agency in advance of a bill of substantive rights to that of protection against discrimination in education through the challenge of a tax exemption of the dis-

[257]

criminating institution—are inspired by our belief that a new statute, or at least a new substantive law, is not always either necessary or sufficient.

The formulation of new and sometimes controversial claims, based on propositions which are on the very frontier of legal thinking, is a difficult task and may require frontier imagination and frontier ingenuity. Thus, for example, to refer to our remarks about the typical features of the American brand of anti-Semitism, there is no settled, ready-made, classroom law about "private governments and equal protection" which can be looked up in a digest, safely canned, and neatly labeled by a West Publishing Company key number. The very formulation of the trend, the choice of scattered decisions, holdings, and dicta, and the selection of proper occasions present a more difficult task than the drafting and endorsing of a legislative measure. We believe that it is also a more fruitful one.

Sec. 27. *Action and survival*

Finally, the special place of community action in our general work should again be emphasized. Important as the other two techniques—social research and legal action—are, community action has for us a meaning all its own. In fact, it is not simply a method or a technique for getting results. It has more than an instrumental value. When a community is aroused in righteous indignation, when it acts as a whole, it represents more than a means to an end. It represents a great collective reality in itself, bearer of a value of its own. What will happen afterward has sometimes little importance. The successes—a given practice is dropped, a tax is repealed, an innocent individual is acquitted—become only incidents of a historical movement. And historians are often surprised by the modesty of the protagonists or the incidents that were the occasion for a great popular wave.

The truth of the matter is that at times any action *by the community* serves its survival better than any "successful step" taken *in its behalf*. We believe that it is high time for the Jews to regain —through trial and error, if necessary—the habit of collective ac-

Postscript

THE TRAGIC DEATH of Alexander H. Pekelis in the plane crash on the Shannon highlights the fate of honest European intellectuals through the last thirty years. Launched into the world in 1902, in what was then the peaceful city of Odessa, Pekelis exhibited from his early youth an unconquerable ambition for scholarly achievement. The rise of Bolshevism and the wrecking of the Russian universities drove him out of Russia in 1920, to study in the universities of Leipzig and Vienna. Having been deprived of his Russian citizenship in 1922, he became a man without a country, a situation very unfavorable to advancement in the German university world. He traveled to Italy on a Nansen passport, studied law at the University of Florence, became an Italian citizen, and set out on what promised to be a brilliant career as professor of law. The rise of Fascism drove him from his chair at the Royal University of Rome and compelled him to emigrate to America, where he joined the Graduate Faculty of the New School for Social Research in September 1941, offering courses in public and international law.

He was impressed with the wide gap between the European and the American legal systems, and registered in the Columbia Law School, carrying the heavy load of legal study along with his full-time teaching program. As everywhere, Pekelis distinguished himself in the Columbia Law School and became the first foreign-born editor of the *Columbia Law Review*, an office he filled with such extraordinary competence that the new office of graduate editor was tion. Thus and only thus will Jews be able to end a state of affairs in which things keep happening *to them*. Thus and only thus will the Jewish people cease being an object and become once again, and in our lifetime, the *subject* of its own history.

To achieve this result, no amount of legal skills, sociological inquiry, or psychological devices will suffice by itself. Nothing will do, short of an indomitable people's will to survive, manifesting itself in a wide, strong, articulate, selfless, popular movement. To serve such a movement is our paramount aim and our highest ambition.

created for him by the Board of the *Review* for the year 1943–1944.

He was a frequent contributor of articles to legal and other journals, articles dealing in a masterly way with the differences in the procedures of American and European law in relation to concrete legal problems. He was a devoted student of the Supreme Court, and planned to set up a monumental publication, year by year, of the proceedings of the Court. While he had qualified himself for private practice, he was mainly interested in matters of public policy. He held an important post as consultant to the American Jewish Congress, and served as chairman of the committee of lawyers who drafted the New York statute against discrimination in education.

In the trip to Europe that proved fatal to him, he served as Labor Delegate to the World Zionist Congress at Basle.

The bare outline of his career indicates that Alexander H. Pekelis was a man of mark. It can give no idea of the gallantry and the intellectual enterprise of the man. Repeatedly forced to readjust himself to a new career, he faced the necessity blithely, determined to profit by it.

When first he began to publish articles on American legal problems, colleagues who had never wholly overcome the superstition of nativism feared that with his European preconceptions he would distort the fundamental American legalisms. We were wrong. Pekelis had, not a European mind, but a true mind, catholic and universal. Few American lawyers could handle an American legal problem with equally inerrant judgment.

He appeared destined for a significant career. A man of great intellectual power, of great force of character, possessed of a commanding physique and a magnificent voice, he remained modest under his triumphs—but never let his modesty wrong him.

Those who knew him loved him, and they were many. We have all become inured to crushing losses in the late bitter years, but we feel the loss of Alexander H. Pekelis as irremediable.

ALVIN JOHNSON

Index

INDEX

Babylonia, Jewish autonomy in, 222
Bacon, Francis, 4, 71
Bagdad, Jewish autonomy in, 222
Barthélemy, Joseph, 60
Baxter, Richard, 139
Beard, Charles A., 112, 113
Beccaria, 17, 18
Belgium, awarding of damages in, 54
Benham, F. C., 33
Bentham, 18, 28, 34, 40, 104
Bias, racial, used by New York *Daily News*, 157
Bill of Rights, 91, 94-95, 106-113; *see also* Amendments to the Constitution
Bill of Rights, international, 181-183, 186, 250
Bills of attainder, 93
Black, Justice, 107, 197-198, 237
Blackstone, 110
Bodin, 104
Boycott, right denied to minorities, 188-190, 240
Brandeis, Justice, 163
Brissac, de, 55
Bureau of Corporations, 84
Business: social responsibility of, 129-130; as a private government, 130-135; prices and profits of, 135-138
Butler, Justice, 198
Butler, Nicholas Murray, 102

Calhoun, John C., 104, 112, 127
California, compulsory racial segregation in public schools of, 159-174
Case law, development of, 89
Cases "rejected" by Supreme Court, importance of, 207
Censorship of radio, 144, 149
Chapelier Law, 221-222
Chavez, Senator, 119
Chicago, increase of Negro population in, 178
Children, effects of segregation on, 167-168
Chinese, segregation of, 169
Circuit Court of Appeals (San Francisco), review of "separate but equal facilities" doctrine by, 159

Cities, American: power to remedy defaults of federal or state legislatures, 175-177; reinterpretation of existing laws by, 178; racial conflicts a specific concern of, 178; increase of minority populations in, 178-179; dominated by rural counties in state legislatures, 179; importance of using dormant power of, 179-180
Civil law, *see* Common law
Civil liberties: international enforcement of, 181-185; protection of, 236
Civil Rights cases (1883), 106-107, 119
Civil Rights statutes, 164
Civil War, 95, 97, 114, 126, 227
Classic v. *United States*, 107, 111, 113-114, 229
Clear and present danger standard, 116
Cohen, Morris R., 104
Cohn, Oscar, 61
Coke, Sir Edward, 59, 71, 110, 120
Collective bargaining as a defense against conspiracy charges, 189
Collective Jewish action, opportunities for, 248
Collective responsibility, 239
Columbia Law Review, Supreme Court survey in, 207
Columbia University Bureau of Social Research, 241
Commission on Law and Social Action, American Jewish Congress, 218-259; aim of, 218-224; tasks of, 224-256; techniques of, 256-258
Common law compared with civil law, 43-74; contempt of court, 45-53; damages, 53-55; religious influence, 56-58; oath-taking, 58-60; investigation and disclosure, 59-61; trial by jury, 61-66; individualism and decentralization, 67-71; conflicting jurisdictions, 71-73; dissenting opinions, 73; and administrative control, 75-90; importance of judicial lawmaking in, 200
Communal action, need for, 253
Communications Act of 1934, 148, 149
Community, necessity of laws for, 211
Community action, importance of, 256, 258-259

INDEX